What's wrong

With You

What's Wrong With You

Seven Logical Steps to
Understanding Emotional Illusions

Benjamin Fry

First publication in Great Britain

PRINTING HISTORY
Workshop Edition published 2004

WHAT'S WRONG WITH YOU
MARAKI BOOKS : 0-9761214-0-9

Set in ITC Garamond

In Memoriam

My Mother

25th July 1945—30th July 1970

Myself

21st August 1969—30th July 1970

The "What's Wrong With You?" Forum

I have included in this book extracts from the forum at my website, which I call wwwyou?forum for short. These illustrative passages would not be possible without the brave contributions from the members of this forum. I have tried to answer questions helpfully, but inevitably will fail to provide a complete solution. I offer this failure here as an example of the challenges of finding an answer to what's wrong with you.

All the members of the forum have kindly agreed to donate the copyright of their written material to this book, and I am enduringly grateful to them for their participation. There is inevitably something voyeuristic about illustrating ideas through the examples of other people's suffering. I apologise for this. It is the reason that I have used my own life as the main thrust of this book's case studies. However, I am a narrow cross-section of society and issues. I hope that these real life examples will put some flesh on the theoretical bone. They are in any case already in the public domain on the internet.

The forum will continue and particularly be available to serve the needs of those who have read this book and need help applying it to their individual circumstances. All questions, feedback and comments are most welcome.

Please visit us at www.whatswrongwithyou.com if you would like to discover more.

Acknowledgements

I'm grateful to all the individuals who have helped me to learn about myself and the world around me. Many of these were kind and dedicated professionals who did so on purpose. Some of them were not so benign and did so by accident. Most of them were just other human beings doing their best to get through their own lives while trying to avoid what was wrong with them!

Specially I'm grateful to my therapists and teachers along the way. Theirs is a difficult job, little understood and rarely done perfectly. However, without someone being prepared to try to do it the world would be a great deal bleaker for us all.

Mostly I'm grateful to my wife and children for their extraordinary love and support; wisdom and insight; energy and forgiveness. Without my wife Dorothea's guidance I would be but a furious engine with no rudder, going nowhere and looking pretty stupid while doing so; she is my mentor, editor and muse. And without my children I would have learnt nothing about the innate wisdom of the soul; they are my true teachers and unconditional critics.

Finally I'm forever indebted to my parents, my father Charles and my step-mother Jane for always doing the best they could, and for continuing to do so.

August 2004

The Seven Steps

Man

Consciousness

Unconsciousness

Projection

Relationships

Society

God

Table of Contents

Foreword

What's Wrong With Me?

It was like a bomb had gone off in my head. Nothing made sense any more. I was aware of was the noise of the lunchtime crowd braying in every corner of the basement bar where I was having a business meeting.

I fled to the toilet. I steadied myself with some cold water to the face. I looked in the mirror. I saw a ghost. I knew about panic attacks because an ex-girlfriend had suffered from them. But she was just highly strung, or so I thought. I wasn't like that. I was a strong, successful, intelligent and capable young man, hatched from the crème of London society, groomed at Eton and Oxford. I was all alpha-male. I wasn't having a panic attack. I took a long hard look in the mirror, steeled myself to return to the bar and then suddenly all my courage deserted me. I knew for the first time in my privileged life the bottom-less terror of real vulnerability. I was falling apart and I had no idea why. Something was seriously wrong with my perfect self. I just stared at my reflection, terrified, lost, and thought for the first time in my unerringly confident life, "what's wrong with me?"

I could not have known at that instant that I was about to embark on a journey that was to save my life. A journey that was to reclaim the lost memory of my own mother, reclaim myself and lead me back to a place of real happiness with a family of my own. But back then, all I knew was fear. It wasn't the fear of a man looking up at a great mountain that he must scale, but the fear of a man who thought he lived at the top of that mountain and who suddenly realised that he was falling; further and faster than was supposed to have been possible for someone of my class, education and abilities.

I was the perfect little rich kid. I had everything anyone could ever desire. Money, looks, brains, women, connections, talent and the best education money can buy. But I was about to lose the one great ally that I had always depended on to keep me safe and to defend me from all my long forgotten demons: my mind.

A decade later, I'm writing my travelogue from that journey which I began on that day. But it is not a guide to any foreign land. It's a guide to our most familiar territory: our own hearts and minds. That's where I made this journey, and ironically that's where we find ourselves most lost; in the privacy of our own psyches we discover the hardest road of all to travel.

I circled around many, many methods and techniques for healing. I studied some and practiced others. I became frustrated with their fragmented approaches and the lack of unity in the theory of the mind. From all of these encounters, lessons and experiences, I began to distil my own understanding of the processes that had led me to my own watershed. From this I formed an understanding of what lies beneath the techniques that had brought me back from the brink.

I was able to answer my original question, "what's wrong with me?", and the solution was remarkably elegant and simple. Seeing through the fog of contemporary healing to find this logical and powerful understanding was a real step for me along the path to a better life. And now I apply this learning daily in my life, which has improved remarkably as a result.

Introduction

*Why don't things work out more easily for you? Why
is everything so frustrating? Why can't you seem to get
what you deserve? What's wrong with you?*

What's Wrong With You?

Do you ever wonder what is wrong with you? Why life
seems so difficult no matter what you do? Do all the things you
hope for seem to be just out of your reach? This may be even
though you have done everything that was supposed to help
you to realise your dreams. Do career, relationships, marriages,
children, money, friends and family all have fuzzy edges round
the perfect mental pictures that you once painted? Perhaps it
just doesn't all quite add up and you don't know why? After
you've blamed everyone else, at some point did you ever wake
up, catch your reflection in the mirror and just wonder what's
wrong with you?

It is actually quite simple to explain what's wrong with us.
The difficult part is believing it. The reason that so many of us
are struggling through our lives, finding so little satisfaction
despite our enormous effort and desire to do so, is that we
really don't know what we are doing. Imagine the frustrations,
for example, of excavating for antiquities without any idea how
to survey the land for clues about where to find then. All the

hard work in the world wouldn't be enough without a large slice of luck to go with it.

Compare that with the experience of modern archaeologists armed with high-tech equipment to tell them where the relics are. They stroll easily to their goals, dispensing the minimum of energy and getting more than those who lack their advanced equipment. Do you know people like this, who just seem to float on through life and effortlessly get what we wished we had? They are either lucky or they know something we don't. Luck runs out, so if you want to change your life, it's the knowledge that you need.

Scientific advances leave most of us cold. Psychology can seem like another language. In fact, most of the time it is another language. Often it is necessary to engage with a new vocabulary in order to understand a new idea. The modern movement of "self-help" has spawned a whole raft of new terms which sound vaguely scientific and are meant to help us understand how we approach our goals of improving our lives in some way. However, these are just variants on a theme. If you are familiar with any of this literature, it can sometimes seem like much of it is repetitive, sounds great in short punchy sentences, gets you excited for a day or two, and then you find yourself fairly soon looking in the mirror still wondering what's wrong with you.

The reality is that all the output of all the world's wisdom factories is the same. It just goes round and round and manifests itself in different ways. At the core of it are universal truths that underlie the basic structure of each human being on this planet. It is the understanding of these truths, and particularly the way that they interact to bring real consequences in our lives, that is the new wisdom that could lift your own life's struggle out of the mire of unrewarded effort.

There are no quick and easy solutions to what is wrong with us. However, if at least we are able to understand what's wrong with us, then we can begin to make some decisions for ourselves about what we would like to do about it, instead of just forging ahead with the masses, all chasing the same elusive goals of the standard formula for success.

That understanding is what is offered in this book. It is relatively simple. None of it is particularly original. All of the ideas exist elsewhere, and many have done for centuries. However, it can be hard for us ordinary people to put these lofty ideas together in a simple way which applies to our everyday lives. Frankly, most people just want to know how to get on better with their jobs; have less stressful relationships with lovers and families; feel less worried; scared; angry; depressed; have more fun; and, more often than anything, make more money, more easily, more of the time.

This book can't give you specific ways to make that happen in your life, but it can explain to you why it isn't happening already and what you can do to change that. Once you understand that, you can begin to realise that you already have the power to make everything run more smoothly. All you need to start working on this goal is an understanding of what's wrong with you.

This book explains systematically and logically what's wrong with you. It sets out this explanation based on a series of hypotheses about the state of your reality here as a human being on this planet in this universe. The trick with acquiring this knowledge is to suspend your judgement about these assumptions.

One of the main reasons why most of us are so frustrated already is that we never moved on very far from believing all of the things that the highly frustrated generation before us believed. Opening up to new ideas is very challenging, because it momentarily creates a terrifying world where we don't know anything. That is hard to bear and is the reason why we generally change so slowly.

However, you don't need to believe anything you read in this book. You don't have to reject any deeply held views that this book might contradict. It doesn't even particularly help if you already agree with all of it. You just need to follow the logic of its argument. If an assumption says that the sky is yellow and you don't like it, don't worry about it. Just see where it takes you. If it takes you to a place of clarity where before there had been only confusion, then maybe you might be inclined to look again at the colour of the sky.

Even then, it really doesn't matter what colour the sky is or what colour you want to think it is. What matters is that you acquire the understanding that can help to live happier lives on your own terms: terms that you now understand.

That's what this book is for.

It's been written to help you learn how to be happier by understanding what's wrong with you.

ONE

Man

I am a homo sapiens. I am an evolved piece of meat.
That is the basis of my existence.

Theory: Darwin's Theory of Evolution

In one respect, all of us individuals are exactly the same. We are the result of a process of evolution that has been going on for millions of years. We are aware of Darwin and his work and theories. We have some notion of primordial swamps and slime turning into amoebae, and then something inexplicable happening before monkeys started coming down from the trees. It is pretty hard to get your head around. Any process that has been going on for literally billions of years just isn't something any of us can imagine. Indeed some people don't think it even happened at all. Creationists believe it all came about just as described in the opening chapters of the Bible, which is a shame because, if you think about it, evolution is just as much of a miracle as anything else.

Single-celled animals apparently started the whole process of life on this planet. Imagine there's nothing on the whole planet but the earth, the sea and a few amoebae: no plants, no trees, no animals, no insects. No life at all but the simplest of organisms. These organisms split into two to reproduce, sometimes causing random changes in their genetic structure.

These changes allow some new amoebae to survive better than the old ones. This is the process of evolution, or of natural selection. The theory goes that stuff randomly changes over time, via some kind of genetic mutation, and that these changes are selected for continuation by survival.

There's no real consensus on why things randomly change, just a consensus that it is observed that they do. In the end, one of these random changes actually produces something that works better in that environment than its predecessor. The effect is to make it look like the species changed on purpose to help its chances of surviving: survival of the fittest. But really it's just random. It's like typing randomly on a typewriter and every now and then pulling out the perfect poem which supersedes all previous poems. You have to concede that it is possible if you wait long enough for a random event to generate something that is so perfect that it looks like it could only have been designed. And the thing that we always have to remember with evolution is that it has been going on for a long, long, long, long, long time. The universe is older than we could possibly conceive of or imagine.

Now what would it have been like to have been one of those amoebae? Can we imagine the experience of an amoeba? It just blobs about absorbing food from the water, and then splits into two. Every now and then, one of the new amoeba that it splits into changes a bit. Most of the time this changed amoeba malfunctions and dies. Very rarely, however, this new amoeba actually survives better than its predecessor. One amoeba has to watch the other go out into the world healthier, stronger, more robust than it is. Remind you of anything?

Isn't that one of our fundamental experiences as human beings, that we are constantly evaluating ourselves in comparison with others? Go on, be honest, isn't there always some sort of instant equation formed between ourselves and any other human being? Of course, not being single-celled amoebae, we have a vast variety of possible comparisons to make, and we usually look to compete in areas that favour our strengths. But it's always there, ticking over in the background, a survival pecking order based on the way that we choose to live and to view the world with its concomitant particular priorities or threats.

It's not our fault. We can see that it is the nature of things. Ever since the dawn of time, circumstances have been sifting out who is going to survive from who is not going to. It's not even a question of being better or worse. It's just a matter of circumstances.

There's no easier way to see this than to look at the dinosaurs. They ruled the planet when it was important to be bigger, stronger and faster than the other species to survive. Their circumstances were such that these attributes helped them to gather plenty of food and to defend themselves from other animals that were a threat to them. As a consequence, their children survived without being eaten or starving to death. As each generation went by and more and more children survived, so they became more and more dominant compared with the other species, whose children were being eaten or starving.

It's a game that needs no referee. Those species that were not well adapted to their circumstances did not survive and reproduce as well as those that were. Dramatically, the dinosaurs' circumstances suddenly changed. Following some environmental cataclysm, size became a burden in a scorched earth without adequate food. As a result, the dinosaurs died out. Their children died out. And their children didn't have any children. The whole process of reproduction was halted because they couldn't get enough food to fuel themselves to protect their young until they in turn had bred. They didn't suddenly go from being good to bad (they were the same dinosaurs) but their circumstances changed, and as a result they quickly became extinct. The dinosaurs lacked the attributes to survive the change in their circumstances.

Instead we now have a new dominant species on this planet: our own. We have managed to negotiate many changes in our circumstances. We were not all killed off by the ice ages, volcanoes, floods or any other natural catastrophe. Some people survived at every stage of the planet's development, and the population that you see on the planet today is the by-product of all those human beings who survived. They were able to cope with many different circumstances, to feed themselves and to protect their young. That is what survival is; quite simply being able to eat enough not to die, and being strong enough to stop anything killing you and your children. That's what we as a species do, and we do it better than any other.

Case Study: Mama

They say I ran over the gravestones at her funeral. I'm not sure if that is true. I perhaps would have been too young to walk, but I don't know when I took my first steps because no-one has ever told me. That's the kind of detail that a mother usually remembers. I don't know if my mother ever even saw me walk. What I do know is that she fell into a coma in Newport, Rhode Island the day after her twenty-fifth birthday and that my father and her family turned off her life support system four days later in a hospital in Boston. She was American, my father English. They had been married for five years. She had finally died twenty-three days before my first birthday.

There used to be an antibiotic, subsequently withdrawn for safety reasons, which was capable of triggering Aplastic Anaemia in something like one in a million people. It is a bone marrow and blood problem similar to leukaemia. My mother had a severe flu during a Christmas skiing trip. Italian doctors prescribed this antibiotic. She was the one in a million. There was no cure at the time. She was twenty-four years old. My father was thirty. She was dead within six months of her diagnosis. Apparently, she died without ever really believing that she would. There was no memento left for me: no parting words or gesture. There was no note.

She left me nothing but a gang of grieving relatives, deeply in shock and mostly lacking in the emotional apparatus to cope. My father was a decent middle-class English gentleman brought up by parents who had lived through the war and struggled to educate their sons in boarding schools. My mother's own family just fell apart and scattered to the wind. Her father announced two days after her death that he wanted a divorce. Her brother, my uncle, left his own wife and home soon after. None of them knew how to deal with this overwhelming blow.

My father returned to London to work. He met a woman on the plane and had a relationship with her for a few months. I was left in the care of my American family. At the end of the summer I went back to England to live with my mother's best friend and her family, which included a little girl about my age. Apparently when I arrived I was so thin that I was nearly hospitalised. I refused to eat. In the end I was force fed until I gave up my protests.

My father visited at weekends. They say that he had a few girlfriends and eventually, less than five months after my mother's death, met my step-mother, eight years his junior and a receptionist at a firm that he did business with. They established a home in London and after I had been with my new surrogate family for just over a year, I too moved in with them. I had a new mummy. Again.

Then an odd thing happened. I don't remember why or how. I don't have any real memories before I was about four or five years old and by then my step-mother had become my mother. Not just in role but in reality. She is the only mother that I can remember. She was referred to by my father as "mum". She described herself as my mother. I called her mummy. My real mother, Alice, was lost. Her memory had been replaced by the reality of the second woman who had married my father. There were no photos of my mother in the home. There was no reference to her in conversation. There was no place for her in our new family. And I never, ever, thought about it. She was just never mentioned.

I internalised their own presentation of our family as whole. I grew up with no other mother in my mind than my step-mother and no notion of my family other than the one that was now physically around me. When I thought about relatives from my original mother, I never placed them in connection with myself through relation to my mother. They were just grandmothers, uncles or cousins: not my mother's mother, my mother's brother or my mothers relatives. It seems perhaps absurd, but that was the reality of my own mind. But why?

Understanding Why

My father's solution to the nurturing of his infant was to place me in the care of women whom he believed would approximate to the mothering I lacked. First, I was placed in the family of my mother's best friend. Then I was settled back into my father's family, but this time in the care of my step-mother. This is where my own evolutionarily necessary adaptation began.

Like all children I instinctively perceived what was required of me in order to benefit from the aids to survival provided by the adults who cared for me. At the fore of this team was my step-mother who herself had been adopted. And so I internalised what she most wanted me to become; I took on the role of her child. Perhaps there are also intra-psychic reasons too for this internal deception. I would have wanted to forget the pain and difficulty of my past too.

This wasn't an elective choice on my part. We are all the product of years of refinement in the survival instinct and genetic programming. There is no more vulnerable homo sapiens than an infant. Unable to walk or talk, death is a certainty in a matter of hours if abandoned by its adult keepers. I had experienced one abandonment by my familiar keepers. Once finally resettled in my father's home, I wasn't going to risk another one. I clung to my only source of food, shelter and security. I was more than happy to adapt to whatever was necessary to create the converse side of this bargain. My stepmother wanted a family. I wanted a mother. The deal was done.

Trait: We are Survivors

Now that we have thought a bit about the process of evolution and what it might mean, we can begin to think about it in reverse. We want to find out what's wrong with us, and to do this we first need to know what we are. What is the basic constituent element of these malfunctioning human beings? It is completely exhausting to try to sum up the constituents of human beings simply by attempting to observe them and to describe them. Those are the sciences of psychology and anthropology, and these fields of study are vast, complex and contested.

Instead what we want to do is to try to find a simple starting point. This will give us a basic platform on which to build our understanding of ourselves. If we can make a logical deduction from some uncontested facts, then so much the better. Observation and speculation definitely have their place in the growing understanding of humans' lives, but if we want to keep it simple, we can start from the simple truth that we are alive.

That may seem banal and of no consequence, but at least it is something that you can be sure of. You are reading this book because you exist and are able to read. You exist and are able to read because you are alive. You are alive because your parents survived until adulthood and then had a child whom they kept alive. They survived until adulthood because someone had been alive to look after them. And so on and so on and so on. In the end you can be sure of one certain deduction from the simple fact that you are reading these words: that you survived, your parents survived, their parents survived and all of their parents survived. In fact, every single one of your ancestors, since forever, survived long enough to have a child, and then that child survived long enough to have a child, and so on and so on, until your parents had you.

We might think that our families are totally screwed up and have nothing in common, but we'd be wrong. We all have the basic fact of our existence in common: the fact that all of our parents lived long enough to have us. It's actually a family trait, something that unites everyone in your family, everyone in your town, everyone in your state, everyone in your country and everyone on this planet. Despite all our multiple differences, we all have one fundamental thing in common. We are the children of people who survived.

We often try to understand ourselves by looking at our parents. It gives us clues about what we might be like. It is easier to get a somewhat objective view of our parents than it is of ourselves, and they are often the people who are most like us, or a great indication of what we might become if we're not careful! Try looking at your parents a different way. Try looking at them simply as people who survived long enough to give birth to you and then long enough and well enough to keep you alive until you were old enough to do that for yourself. Do you think that you inherited this ability from them? Where do you think that they got that ability from themselves? Are you glad about this? Are these aspects of your parents that you wish to emulate? Do you want to stay alive? Do you want to have kids and keep them alive?

We are the children of a million generations of survivors, millions of years of not dying in a hostile and threatening environment, millions of years of keeping the young alive long enough to reach adulthood. The simple fact that we are alive is proof that we are the outcome of a breeding process that breeds only survivors. At our very core we represent millions of years of refinement in the genetic code of a species that has come to be known as mankind.

For all of the generations that precede us (and remember that they do all exist, and they do all go all the way back to the dawn of life) each generation has produced its own mutations, and most of these will not have been helpful to the species in its particular circumstances. But we can be certain, simply from our very existence, that all of the mutations that existed on the way down our own family trees from the very first amoebae were helpful in making us better adapted to survive. That has always been the determining factor in assessing how the human being would develop. The criterion for the survival of any species has been its ability to survive and to adapt to many different, changing circumstances.

We are the children of these survivors. That is our essence. That is the core of our activity on this planet. Before anything else that is who we are. Survival, not happiness, is our goal. If you don't like it, do what the rest of us do when things go wrong. Blame it on your parents. It's their fault for not dying young.

Look at it another way. Long ago, back in the bronze age, a new tribe of people developed on earth. Somehow they had mutated into a subtle shade of our species with one different, outstanding quality. They were always extremely happy. Their happiness was remarkable and they lived a tranquil, easy existence, never plagued by doubt or disappointment. Whether they were rich or poor, well or sick, fortunate or plagued by bad luck, they found a way to rise above it all and to remain eternally happy. What do you think happened to them? What happens to people who are happy about being poor, happy about being sick, happy about being unlucky? I suspect that they would have made poor contestants in the real-world business of surviving.

There's not much motivation to make things better if you are already content. There's not much reason to struggle through difficult times if accepting them is just fine with you. There's not much motivation to fight to stay alive when times get tough.

It has not been until very, very recently in mankind's history that times have not been very tough, very often, everywhere. All kinds of other types of human beings may have developed over the millions of years that we were evolving, and many of them may have been much happier than we are today, but unfortunately they would not necessarily have been very well adapted to deal with their circumstances.

They were not like our ancestors. They may have been people that we'd like to be or not like to be. They may have been better or worse. They may have been happy or sad. But it doesn't matter because they are all dead, extinct. They have no descendants among us. We are what we are today not because we were better or worse than the others, but simply because we were more durable. We are the children of the people who lived the longest. Our prevailing quality is our ability to stay alive. And unfortunately that has nothing to do with staying alive happily.

Case Study: Step-Mama

The arrangement whereby my step-mother had become my

"mum" was supportable for many years because no-one had any wish to challenge it. I simply never thought about it and if the subject of my mother was raised by a third party, I just blanked it from my mind. Even when I began to recover my connection with my feelings about her death and to delve into the consequences that abandoning those feelings was having for me in my adult life, it was much easier to retain the status quo with my family. My father and step-mother had had twins, a boy and a girl, just before I was six years old. We were to all intents and purposes a nuclear family of mum, dad, two boys and a girl: perfect. No-one wanted to rock the boat.

However, this charade began to fall apart when I got married. By then I was more reconciled to my past even if my parents still struggled with a full acceptance of it. My Greek wife and her family came to this situation as mere observers. Greek culture is an exquisite blend of Middle Eastern and European sensibilities. Death is accepted as part of life and the dead live alongside those who miss them in life. The separation remains solely physical. Emotionally and spiritually they stay connected to those they love long after they have literally left them. Furthermore in the Greek Orthodox Church (as in its close cousin the Roman Catholic Church) the Virgin Mary is a paramount symbol of life's sanctity. Therefore the relationship between mother and child borders on a holy reverence. For these people, the early loss of my mother presented no conundrum. Their sympathies were genuine and always freely offered. At times when it would be obvious that my mother would be missed, such as at my wedding, they would kindly offer me their condolences and comfort on her absence. This had never happened in my English family.

Matters were complicated by the birth of my first child. As she grew up it became clear that there was going to be a tension between my new family and my family of origin about exactly what our relationship was. The objective truth was easy to understand. Our child had a mother and a father, and they each had a mother and a father. One of them was dead. We weren't going to lie to our own child about where she came from and to whom she was related. However, my step-mother loathed to be referred to as a step-mother. Both she and my father quickly adopted the title of "granny" for her in relation to our first born child.

I had grown up with three grandmothers and eventually didn't understand why. My mother's legacy could not be eradicated from my grandmother, who had moved to London soon after my mother's death. The amazing thing was that I never connected the existence of my grandmother with the absence of my mother. The fact that I had three grandmothers didn't occur to me as unusual until I was about five. I asked my step-mother about it and that was the first time that I remember being told my mother's life and death. I didn't bring it up again.

My grandmother didn't discuss my mother with me. She told me years later that after my father had remarried it had become increasingly impossible to mention my mother around my family. In the end she feared that if she did, she would have less access to me. My step-mother has subsequently told me that my grandmother said to her early on in their relationship that I would never forget my mother. Possibly it was a mistake for her to lay down the gauntlet like this to a determined young woman, but to be fair to her, she was right.

But this isn't a story about bad people. This is a story about normal people, people like you, me and everybody you know. Like so many English people, my father never been given permission to experience his emotions, and had never been given any support in doing so. No-one had ever even thought to help my step-mother to discover her own feelings about her family history. And before she had had the chance to develop psychologically herself, she was creating another family history.

My father and step-mother are two of the most decent, caring, helpful and kind people you could ever hope to meet. That I am not in a gutter somewhere stubbing out my repressed trauma with a syringe of heroin is a testament to the care that they provided for me. But like all parents they weren't perfect. They had their own crosses to bear and inevitably they couldn't help but pass some of that burden onto me. My problem was that I'd already had more to deal with in my short life than most people would wish to attempt to cope with as adults. I just didn't have much room left for other people's problems.

Understanding Why

Successful evolution requires two things: your own survival and the nurturing of your young. Things can get difficult when these are in opposition. My father faced this dilemma; firstly he needed to secure the transmission of his genes by ensuring my (his only child's) survival, but secondly he would also have been concerned with his own survival.

The threat in his case was not the same as for an abandoned infant, but can seem just as real and pressing. His survival mechanism would have been pricked by the difficulty of coming to terms with the emotions unleashed by bereavement. This may have had very deep resonances with his own infancy when his eldest brother died. If so, then this new death in the family would have triggered very real life and death concerns from that time.

The very same survival game that I was now playing may have been playing through his mind by proxy from his infancy. Although the events were long in the past, the impression of the threat can be just as real in the present. The solution to this threat was to undo the circumstances that created it; he found himself a new wife and a new mother for me. This may explain the speed with which he was able to re-establish the dynamics of family life.

My step-mother also suffered greatly at a very young age due to being put up for adoption. It is inevitable that the presence in her adult life of a very young child who had lost his mother would have triggered threatening resonances from her own infancy. The real child standing before her would have been an uncomfortable representation of her own motherless self, a self that had faced real concerns about her ability to survive and to succeed evolutionarily. The solution to this threat was to extinguish its trigger by recasting the real motherless child standing before her into an integral part of a whole, intact family system. Thus airbrushed into a state that would not impact on her own echoes of survivalist concern, I was bearable as long as the fantasy held up.

Both dynamics return each parent in this scenario back to a time in their own infancy when survival would have been of urgent and paramount importance. They, like me after them, would have relied upon the adaptive mechanism to massage their circumstances into those that were most likely to lead to successful competition for resources and nourishment. These adaptations stayed with them (like my own) into adulthood. Therefore as adults, confronted by a problem that pressed sorely on the apparatus of these adaptations, they pushed back firmly to restore the status quo. My mother's life and death suited neither of them. They came together in a concerted effort to remove that event from their reality. It was a matter of survival.

Step 1: The 1st Hypothesis

You prioritise Survival over Happiness

You are a survivor. That is the building block of your experience as a person on this planet. You will prevail through all circumstances. You have been selected by evolution to be able to stay alive regardless of what life throws at you. It is your top priority along with preserving the life of your children (if or when you have any).

There's no exciting reason for this. It's no reflection on you as a person. It is simply an unavoidable logical conclusion from the simple fact that you are alive today. The fact of your existence reveals that you belong to a long line of distinguished family members who survived and kept their young alive too. That is your heritage. That is where you come from. That is who you are today.

Try to remember this. It is not as simple as it might seem. You are not a survivor because you are determined to be. You are determined to be because you are a survivor. You are simply the result of some members of your species being randomly more determined to live than others.

There is no act of will on your part to be determined to survive. It is part of your genetic code; part of your ancestral inheritance; part of the necessary conditions that you are alive, here, and able to read these words. You don't have any choice. You are only here to think about it because you are the off-spring of those who wanted more than anyone else for you to be alive and here to think about it. It is not just in your nature. It is the logical conclusion of the simple fact of your existence.

This is the first step to understanding what's wrong with

you. Understand that you don't have any choice over what are your most instinctive and basic desires. You want to stay alive. You want to protect yourself. You want to be healthy and to protect your children.

You want, no matter what, no matter what it costs, and no matter what else is compromised, to stay alive and to keep your children alive.

You want this not because you want to want it but simply because you are the biological product of people who survived because they were like that. You know this because you are alive. You know you are alive because you are reading this book, and in reading this book you are learning what you need to know to begin to understand what's wrong with you.

Exercise 1

What did you survive?

Write a timeline of your journey so far through life. Put your age on the left and next to it what happened to you: what you remember, or what you think might have happened to you. Like this:

11 months	*Mother died.*
1 year old	*Moved in with mother's friend.*
2 years old	*Father married again. Moved in with father and step-mother.*

and so on up until the present day. Don't leave anything out and don't think anything is too small to be relevant. It's your list. The longer it is the better it will be for you.

Next you are going to make a table from this list. You can add another column to your list or write down your age again on the left, the same ages as in the previous list. This time you will speculate how you adapted yourself to cope with each of the events that you have identified at that age. Like this:

11 months	*Refused food, perhaps to attract attention to emotional distress.*
1 year old	*Became member of new "family". Befriended adopted family's daughter to try to fit in.*
2 years old	*Delighted to be back with father. Tried to please step-mother so that I could stay there.*

Now read through your speculative answers about how you

may have adapted yourself in response to the various events of your life. As you read each one individually, ask yourself, "did this adaptation help me to become happier or help me to survive?" If you think you prioritised survival over happiness in response to that event, put an S in the margin and work your way through each line one by one. If you can't come up with an answer one way or the other then just leave it and go on to the next one.

Finally, count the number of S's in the margin and express them relative to the total number of events. This is a measure of how much you have given up of your original perfect self in order to pander to the deepest instinct of all: survival.

The higher the percentage, the more likely you are to have relationship difficulties, mental health issues, suffer from addictions, just be generally dissatisfied and wonder what's wrong with you? Those other people who you think find life so easy have a lower number than you.

If you are too far on the wrong side of this equation then you really need to finish this book!

Q&A

From the wwwyou?forum. You can see the original text and ask questions at whatswrongwithyou.com.

So what's the answer Ben?

Posted by: Jo Jun 13 2004, 05:04 PM

I so identified with your article (the urban buddha one) and was hanging on its every word – and then I got to the crux of the matter, you say you "found it" – what is it???

I'm intelligent, attractive, apart from not being a normal size 12 (more like 18) have a good job and family and friends. I'm normal enough from the outside but inside I feel completely neurotic and fearful, not in a mental health sense, there's nothing wrong with me in that regard apart from depression for which I'm on Prozac at the moment. And scared to come off it. I'm single and 32. Fearful I'll never meet anyone before this biological clock stops ticking...

I'm in a 12 step group – Overeaters Anonymous – for compulsive overeating – have been on a path of self development as a result of this for 10 years. Have lost 5 stones but still 3 or 4 to go – I still use food compulsively. Can't seem to surrender to God as they tell me to in OA.

I've done the Hoffman Process too, the workshop to end all

workshops that one – you walk round for 4 days with a label like 'needy and stupid' or 'not good enough' and beat cushions pretending they're your mum and dad, I've had therapy, read the books, got the t shirt. I think the one by M Scott Peck, where the opening line is "Life is difficult" is probably the one that speaks the most sense. Is it all about accepting the moment as exactly how it's meant to be?

So, go on, give it me in a nutshell, what's the secret to it all, or am I destined to be a self help, workshop junkie for the rest of my life?

Posted by: benjaminfry Jun 14 2004, 05:29 PM

I can see that you have been there, done everything and got the T-shirt. Congratulations on maintaining a sense of humour about it!

Actually the answer is not "to pull yourself together" but instead to let yourself fall apart. I perceive from what you say that you may exhibit a degree of emotional self-control (who told you to "pull yourself together"?) which would dovetail with a history of eating disorders. It also fits with the trouble you are having "surrendering to God" in OA. The food is likely to be a physical manifestation of a need to form a barrier between yourself and the emotional reality that you would be experiencing were it not to be treated with the food. It is that emotional reality that you need to find a safe way to reach.

For me, the answer to this was to be able to understand the process that was going on inside my own mind. That is why I likened it to the difference between watching an illusionist with and without an understanding how it does this trick. With a little knowledge what can seem baffling and frightening to observe becomes ordinary and commonplace.

It is this knowledge which is the subject of my book and a structured rational explanation of what's wrong with me.

Here it is as requested in a nutshell:

1) You are the product of millions of years of evolution. The very fact that you are alive reveals that you are above all an organism that is programmed to survive. Happiness is a very much secondary consideration. Safety comes first.

2) Uniquely among species (so it seems) you have a conscious mind. This allows you to observe your own self, your environment, and your universe. Understanding your environment can be a big help with your survival. However, being able to observe yourself can be a big obstacle to happiness if you don't like (or don't feel safe with) what you see.

3) There is a great deal of activity in your own mind of which you are unaware. This is your unconscious mind. This part of your brain is very capable and very active but we tend to dismiss it because we're so pleased with our conscious mind.

4) Your unconscious mind contains your greater wisdom and is seeking to bring you to a place of great happiness. In order to direct you towards an emotional resolution to allow you to move on in life, it creates within your own mind projections which alter your perception of reality. These projections provoke an emotional response and are designed to be helpful for you to process the trauma which you store in your body. We resist the flowing out of the feelings from the thawing of this trauma (emotions) because our conscious mind doesn't understand them and is therefore scared of them.

5) Projections cause all manner of complications in relationships, specifically when it appears that two people can have very different views about this same reality. This is because they are having different projections

placed over their mutual reality by their differing unconscious minds.

6) The same idea extends into society. We create the
bogeyman in other tribes and nations to represent what
we most fear within ourselves or what is closest to us.
The recent global schism between the American admini-
stration and the Muslim world is a typical example.

7) The way we relate to the idea of God is in a sense our
ultimate projection. We may not be able to test the
reality of God's existence but it would seem that we are
very capable of using the idea of God to carry many of
the more highly functioning processes of our own
minds, bodies and souls. (This notion may particularly be
useful to you if you are struggling to accept the traditional notion of "God" as part of your 12-step work.)

Thus the secret to it all is to stop the conscious mind im-
peding the important work of the unconscious mind. This
means that whatever your life is, wherever you are, whatever
you are experiencing and whoever you are with, these people,
events and the projections that you place over them are there
by your own design – simply to help you experience certain
difficult and troubling emotions.

If you react like the ignorant audience to an illusionist trick
and run away in fear from these emotions, then they will repeat, and repeat, and repeat until you accept them. If however
you view this illusion from a position of knowledge and wisdom, you can just accept your emotions and let the whole
process flow.

In a way your whole life is a self-help workshop. The more
fully and fearlessly you participate in it the more quickly you
will be rewarded and move on to different tests.

I know it's a large nut that fits in this nutshell, but I hope it's
of some help.

Posted by: Jo 1 Jun 15 2004, 07:32 PM

Thank you Ben, I have printed out your reply and stuck it on my fridge along with my "healing words" fridge magnets! Lol.

You can tell how co-dependent I am because I am worried that you will be inundated with so many queries on this site that you'll not have time to do anything let alone answer any of them. I'll let that one go just for now.

You talk a lot about the unconscious mind and it containing your greater wisdom — I think I'd agree with this — do you suggest hypnotherapy or anything else as a helpful way of accessing this? Are there any other ways for a very practical, down to earth, non-flaky person to develop these skills other than opting out of life and meditating under a tree forever?

Also, when does your book come out? I am now dying to read it. You've spoken the most sense I've heard for a long time.

Thanks for taking the time to respond.

Jo

TWO

Consciousness

I think. Therefore I am conscious of myself. The ultimate evolutionary tool. The connection of past to future. Will and have. It's all about resources.

Theory: The Conscious Mind

As you read this book, you are doing something no other species on this planet does. You are reading a book. It seems so commonplace, but it is extraordinary if you think about it. This planet has been evolving for millions of years. Think about millions of years, if you can. Think about your one millionth ancestor, and realise that this person, or animal, wasn't even around early enough to see the dinosaurs. A million generations is hardly the blink of an eye in the history of our evolution.

An extraordinary passage of time has shaped this world and the multiplicity of living organisms on it. In all of that time, all over the planet, among all of those species, only man, a relative newcomer to the evolutionary race, has exhibited the capacities to read a book. We are the only animal on the planet to behave like this, and it is perhaps reasonable to assume, therefore, that we are the only one ever to have developed an advanced conscious mind.

And so, we think. But what does that mean? Let's try to

think about what it means to think. It's actually quite hard to do. It seems to be a phenomenon equivalent to having a dialogue with ourselves, inside our own heads. However, this dialogue itself is dependent on the capacity to use a language. It is unlikely that we would have a language to use if we couldn't think in the first place. Thinking gives us ideas to express and the capacity to learn a language. So even without language, is it possible to identify and understand the process of thought? It is obviously a complex issue and we need to start from somewhere, so let's accept one of the many ideas about what thought is.

We can define thinking as the process that begins with our awareness of the decisions that our mind-body system is making. It then evolves from there, with the tool of language, into ever more complex sophistication, but the initial impulse, the mechanism that leads to us having a consciousness, is the awareness of the normal flow and process of the mind and body. Consider this; as you read this book you are breathing in an out, moving your eyes across the page, and organising your heart to beat to meet your body's current demands. You are not aware of these processes. Indeed, if you are now becoming more aware of these processes because you have been invited to think about them, they may become more difficult. That is the genesis of thought, as we colloquially describe it. It is the awareness of something going on in our mind or body. As we become conscious of something, so we are able to think about it.

The consciousness is the part of our mind-body system that we are aware of, or conscious of. Hence the term "the conscious mind". Everything else that goes on in our minds and bodies is not apparent to the consciousness, and therefore not included in the conscious part of our mind-body system. That is why it is called the un-conscious, or "the unconscious mind" (sometimes also referred to as the subconscious).

Both the conscious mind and the unconscious mind are still within the scope of our whole mind. They don't live side by side. They are simply different views of one integral entity. It is like looking at the moon. There is a part we can see, and a part that we can't. But the moon itself is one perfect integrated sphere. Just because we have one view and not another doesn't change what we are looking at. It is still just one perfect moon. And so it is with our minds. There is no physical distinction to be made between our conscious minds and our unconscious minds. There is just the mind, the processes that go on in it as we live, and a certain awareness of that.

That awareness is an extra process: a process that stands above and apart from the ordinary processes of life. This is the process that lets us become conscious of some of the activity of our minds. That is what the root of thought is. It is an awareness of ourselves: an observation of the mechanistic processes of our mind-body system.

From there we have developed ideas about these thoughts, commentary on these ideas, argument to this commentary and language to communicate our observations of this. So for you right now, thinking is not just the awareness of your mind. It is not only the conscious observation of your own automatic processes. It is a highly evolved dialogue, commenting on every aspect of your thoughts, from thoughts, from thoughts, from thoughts, and so on a million-fold until you reach your earliest thoughts, which may have been simply to notice that whenever you get hungry, you cry, you get fed, and then you are no longer hungry.

This ability to develop conscious thought is the evolutionary masterstroke of our species. It is the one single aspect of ourselves that separates us from the so-called animals. We are almost completely the master of any threat from any other species. We are the top of the food chain. Think for a moment how different that is from the experiences of any other species on this planet. Even a lion, the king of the jungle, has to be careful not to get ambushed at a kill by a bold pack of hyenas. Think how much worse it is for a humble gazelle.

We very rarely have that problem. We usually are that problem to other species. We kill animals in their millions, daily, to feed ourselves. The animal kingdom is lucky if it gets back at us a handful of times a year. We have gained this evolutionary mastery though one, simple mechanism. Whereas the dinosaurs ruled the earth because they were bigger, faster and stronger than the other animals, we are now the top species because of one, simple and more elegant feature. We have a conscious mind.

This allows us to do two very simple but powerful things. First, we can observe. We can observe ourselves, and hence begin the process of bringing our mind-body system into consciousness. Second, we can make connections between observations: the genesis of reason. This capacity to observe and to reason is a double whammy that generates our most powerful skill of all, the ability to use observation and reason to connect the past to the future. This is the mother of all evolutionary skills.

It greatly surpasses the learning that, say, a dog exhibits when it gradually connects good behaviour to treats, or poor behaviour to punishment. The ability to use observation and reason to connect the past to the future actually allows us humans to make predictions: to hypothesise the future based on the past. That is the basis of all science, which is the basis of all technology, which is the real basis of our supremacy on this planet. In much the same way that the army with the best weapons seems to have an unassailable advantage in modern-day warfare, the species with the best technology prospers as no other species can hope to do.

We are no longer necessarily defeated by freak weather, famine, floods or drought. We are able to organise our communities to forecast and to take account of most possibilities. We are able to put into place all sorts of safeguards and contingencies, and to take some preventative measures to increase our chances of survival when otherwise the normal ecological system of the planet might defeat us. And so we have multiplied and multiplied, triumphing over the odds that keep the animal populations in check. In the process we have taken over and dominated our planet.

Science, logic and reason have really only one idea at their core. The idea that our universe, and that includes our own mind-body system, is causal. That is to say that one thing causes another, and that this creates a relatively predictable system to observe and to begin to try to understand. Science is really just the endless work of guessing and testing hypotheses about what causes what.

Think about an apple hitting you on the head as it falls out of a tree. Sir Isaac Newton did. He discovered gravity as a result. He was apparently sitting there minding his own business reading a book, just like you, and out of the blue an apple hit him on the head. Perhaps because it was an event that he was not expecting, he observed it in a different way to the way that falling objects had always been observed throughout time by all other human beings.

He had been struck on the head by an apple, and he wondered why. What had caused this apple to hit him on the head? He realised that there must be something that had made the apple move from one place to another. There was an effect, so there must be a cause, just like balls on a billiard table. He had no idea what the cause of the falling apple was, so he made one up, and called it gravity. To this day there is really very little further understanding of what gravity is, but it is routinely observed. It has been successfully described in a way that makes it useful to predict its effects (the attractive force that is exerted between two objects, equal to the product of their masses and the gravitational constant, divided by the square of their distance), and thus it has helped us to understand and to control our environment by accurately forecasting the future.

We do this ourselves all the time in our own lives and quite often with much less concrete examples than Newton's apple. It is this connection between past and future that really tips the scales in our advantage as a species. This is a skill that has survived the evolutionary process of natural selection. The species that has become more aware, more conscious of its own mind-body system, has survived better than the species that has not.

There is no magic or mystery to it. At some point homo sapiens made a leap into an active conscious mind. At this point it started to pull ahead of its rivals for domination of the planet's resources. Just as the dinosaurs had prospered through their size so mankind prospered through its capacity to connect the past with the future, the ability to notice what causes what, and the ability to use this information to reach desired outcomes and to avoid undesirable ones. There really isn't anything that remarkable about it. It is as basic a survival skill as size and strength was for the dinosaurs. The existence of our conscious mind is the reason that we win our competition with other species to sustain our own lives and the lives of our children.

Case Study: Dorothea

I knew the moment I saw her. "That's the kind of woman I need in my life," were the exact words that ran through my mind the first time I saw my wife. She had walked into a room of strangers and smiled. It was a smile of such warmth. It contrasted so markedly with my own frigid nervousness. I couldn't believe it when she came and sat down next to me.

We were attending the first day of a five-week summer

foundation course in psychotherapy. I was at the time the managing director of a successful London nightclub company, and was enjoying all the pleasures and status that came with owning a trendy West End club. Dorothea was on the path to continue a life-long quest to train and qualify as a licensed psychotherapist. Then she would return to her homeland Greece. I was quite stuck-up, pleased with myself, English and lived a glamorous life in Notting Hill. She was warm, open, Greek and lived with students in Peckham. We really had nothing in common.

In fact I really should not have been there in the room in the first place. And yet I was. Something nagging inside me had drawn me to explore a longing that went beyond material and superficial satisfaction. I had been having psychotherapy for a while now following my initial panic attack a year or two previously, and I had become fascinated by its insights and learning. But more than that, I was amazed that so much useful knowledge was so acutely absent from most people's education. I had been to Eton and Oxford. I thought I was educated. But in the most important lessons of all, I'd never even attended class. I came to this summer school to see what I had been missing and with half an eye on changing my future. I could never have guessed how fundamentally and completely that would happen when Dorothea walked into the room.

Meeting Dorothea was perhaps the greatest challenge that I have faced as an adult. The issues that this relationship threw up for me were not in themselves new. I'd had long relationships, but they were marked by physical absence, or infidelity, or both. And besides, I'd never before had this feeling that I had now: that I'd met someone I wanted to keep. That meant moving on to a whole new dynamic.

We saw each other every week day for five weeks. We lived in a bubble. The world was not much wider than our class and we were happy there. The sun was shining and we would take our breaks in Regent's Park, basking in each other's company. Thoughts of the future were put on hold as we simply relished the moment. As the course drew to a close, it was clear that we would need to address the real world and our strong mutual bond. Nothing had been done or said that indicated a romantic relationship, but we were by then inseparable. I was due to go on holiday to Italy with some friends for two weeks and although five weeks earlier had been longing for this break, now faced it with the apprehension of wondering how I could get through so much time without her. Something had to be done, and I would have to be the doer. So I presented her with an aeroplane ticket; a romantic gesture that I'd always wanted to make, but never had someone to make it to. We consummated our relationship in Italy, on my birthday.

The initial scenario of romance is somewhat competitive. There is a game played that by definition requires two opponents. If the game is won, in the deepest sense, then the game ends with the two opponents on the same side. I don't think that I'd ever made this progression. I was always engaged in a tug-of-war. I swung from needy to needless and in that sense was always suffocating or denying love. I was used to being a nightmare to women in relationships. My problem now was that Dorothea and I were already on the same side. We were firm friends. I didn't know how to be with her as a man and not destroy that. I certainly did my best.

I didn't want to be in a relationship. At least that was how I was thinking. I was happy to have lightweight affairs with a number of women. What I didn't realise though was that I was already in a relationship defined by the bond that had grown up between us. I was adamant that I didn't want to be her boyfriend but just that I wanted to continue an unspecified casual liaison. I was in denial.

Not long after we returned from Italy I was invited to Tatler's "Little Black Book" party allegedly featuring the most eligible men and women in town. I was a shoe-in for their list that year. I was by most accounts very eligible and very single. News of my new life with Dorothea had not yet filtered out, even to myself as it turned out. By midnight I was in one of my nightclubs in Chelsea, drunk, in the privacy of a secluded booth with a pretty blonde Tatler employee I had met at the party. By the early morning we were in bed together. Sober, in daylight, it was a hard reality to take on.

My only thoughts were of Dorothea and I surprised myself by finding a shred of elation in my regrets. I'd never before experienced such a desire not to lose someone. I realised that I'd never valued a relationship like I now did with this one. I knew then that there was no future in my pretence that I didn't want a committed relationship with her. I was already committed, utterly, in my heart. Clearly it was the head that was having the problem. I was now face to face with the necessity of learning to treat a woman properly in a relationship, or else I would lose the only woman I'd ever wanted to keep.

Frankly I didn't rate my chances. Commitment was something that I had shunned in all areas of my life. I didn't mind it in name, but I'd never really tried it in deed. I was already aware that this deep bond and union with Dorothea was bringing up something that I couldn't handle. I knew that I would have to take urgent action to change. Something drastic was needed. My therapist had told me about a clinic in Arizona where people could go for concentrated, residential therapy. She was keen that I should try it in order to attempt to contact and shift some of the trauma surrounding my mother's death. I had resisted it. It terrified me. The thought of sitting around in the desert with a bunch of strangers for a few weeks was far too intimidating for someone used to the Tatler lifestyle. However, I now had an incentive. As far as I was concerned the stakes could not have been higher. I knew that if I didn't bottom out my dysfunctional behaviour around relationships, I would lose the love of my life. By then I knew plenty about loss. I'd already lost the first woman of my life, and I really didn't want to do it again. So I resolved to go into the desert.

Understanding Why?

The conscious mind is a marvellous tool for approximating to desired outcomes. This allows us to make predictive forecasts and therefore to tailor our actions in the present towards a desired outcome in the future. We spend most of our active mental time trying to learn what leads to what in order to improve the likelihood of our lives taking the course that we think we want them to.

I had had relationships before and had slowly begun to recognise my patterns in them. I understood that I was exhibiting the behaviour of someone who would ultimately sabotage these relationships. This was inevitably very painful and I now had a conscious desire to avoid this. One morning I woke up to find the wrong woman in my bed and I was faced with the reality of my own behaviour. I was returning to a pattern of behaviour that had in the past been very detrimental to my chances of maintaining a happy and intimate relationship. Therefore I used my conscious mind to put 2 and 2 together to make 4.

I had other information to hand too. I had leaned about people and their patterns of behaviour from experiencing and studying psychotherapy. I knew that there were certain predictable causes and effects here too. Generally, negative behavioural traits were very hard to eradicate from one's actions simply by deciding that it should be so. These traits represented an "acting out" of an emotional articulation that had not (or could not) be made in words. The deeds represented an emotional release that was being frustrated by a lack of conscious awareness of the underlying problem.

I knew enough to know that I was prone to a pattern of

behaviour that would change only if I changed myself in some fundamental way related to my own inner emotional architecture. Again I used my conscious mind to speculate on how this might be done. It doesn't take a genius to come up with the conjecture that my difficulty coping with intimacy with women was related to the early death and loss of my mother. There were outstanding emotional issues here that I knew were yet to be resolved. Therefore, it seemed that the way to attack the problem of dealing with the behaviour that threatened this relationship was to urgently address the probable emotional causes.

Trait: Control through the Correlation of Cause and Effect

If you think about who you are, and how you got to the point where you are sitting here, alive, today, reading this book, and if you take seriously the ideas in Step One that explain how you are the survivor of millions of generations of survivors, then hopefully you will begin to understand that there is a reason why our minds have evolved to be conscious of what they are conscious of. It is no accident that we think the way we do, form the concepts we do, and have the ideas that we do. It is exactly the way that a species would need to think in order to increase its chances of survival and therefore of evolutionary success.

Basic thoughts are based on past and future, cause and effect, reason and logic. Areas such as beauty, truth, love, creativity and compassion are a more luxurious elaboration. When it comes down to life and death situations, the conscious mind is focused on results. It assesses where we are and how to get us to where we need to be, based on what it knows about cause and effect in our current situation.

This is a very important point to remember because we will

see in Step Three that it is the life and death situations that we have already experienced that are the root of our present suffering. And therefore it is the way that our conscious minds react to life and death situations that underlies what's wrong with us.

We may not think that we have ever experienced a life and death situation, but we would be quite wrong. Birth was a life and death situation. The first time we were ever hungry, probably right after birth, was a life and death situation. We had to get fed or we would have died. We would have known that instinctively. It is the legacy of a million generations of survival. In fact it would have been just about all that we would have known. That is why babies that are held close to their mother's skin as much as possible for the first few months of life are more relaxed. They know where the food is and they know it is available when they are hungry. In many primitive cultures the mother literally wears the baby for the first few months, and the babies are rarely observed to cry.

When it comes down to the difficult and threatening experiences of life, we revert to our greatest survival skill, our evolutionary triumph, the use of our conscious mind to help us to avoid them. It is constantly at work keeping us alive. Its focus is on understanding the past, and using this to try to connect with the future so that this future can be better controlled to facilitate survival.

We have evolved and survived to be conscious of past and future and of cause and effect. The very concepts of past and future might be just a fraction of the temporal spaces we could think about. There may be far, far more to know (and our mind may indeed know it all unconsciously) but past and future, cause and effect, are all that we are conscious of simply because that is what it is most useful for us to be conscious of as evolutionary competitors.

These concepts are the ones that are successful at keeping

us alive. We are here today to think about it because the mind we have is the one that survived most successfully on a planet full of life and death situations and with limited resources.

The whole structure of the way that language has developed bears out this mental evolution. Our language is essentially made up of subjects, verbs and objects; past, present and future. Something does something to something else. It is a very practical structure describing cause and effect in a very useful way. There was something, there is something, there will be something: past, present, future and how they are related. Again, it all helps us to better understand cause and effect. It is all about practical actions and learning which actions get you where you want to go. The very words that we use to describe the past and the future give away the language (at least in English) as being about the connection of resources from what you have to what you want.

The past tense is literally constructed by saying, I "have" something-ed, and the future tense by saying, 1 "will" something. "Have" is the word that describes ownership (what we have) and "will" is the word that describes desire (what we want, as in it is my will that such and such should happen, he has a strong will, last will and testament etc.). This construction of our language shows how the past is associated with what we already have, and the future is associated with what we want to get.

It is all about the acquisition of resources. We have learned that resources result in more favourable outcomes during difficult times. The more resources we have, the more likely we are to survive a life and death situation. It is all about survival. Consciousness is about survival. Language is the currency of the conscious mind concerned with survival.

That is not just a nice theory. It is a logical necessity. It is a necessary condition for you being able to be here to read this book. Had you been part of a developmental branch of any other tree of homo sapiens, a branch that had been less able to develop and communicate survival skills, you would not be here because your ancestors would have been too dead to breed you.

Don't get too overexcited about the ability to think. It is just something that happened. And it happened in such a way as to make it easier for us to survive in the particular circumstances that have faced us and our ancestors on this planet. That is all. It may seem the most amazing thing in the world to us but then Tyrannosaurus Rex was probably pretty impressed with his size and strength too.

Case Study: Dorothea plus one

I booked my trip to the psychotherapy clinic in Arizona for three weeks, leaving on Boxing Day. The day before Christmas, Dorothea told me that she was pregnant. I'd only just got used to the idea of maybe having a girlfriend again. I was about to go into the desert to learn to cope just with that. We'd only known each other for five months. A baby was not what I needed at that point. She wasn't that pleased either. She had finally started her MA in psychotherapy, four years after leaving Greece to pursue that goal. She had sweated through studies in Birmingham, Swansea and South London to get this far, living sometimes on nothing but the fruit she found hanging on the trees. A baby was not part of the plan. A baby! It was a nice idea but a terrifying reality. What were we going to do? In my teens a girlfriend of mine had had an abortion and with hindsight it was one of my greatest regrets. I knew that I couldn't live with myself if I was involved in another abortion, and I had been very careful never to be so again, until I met Dorothea. I suppose I just knew that I had to find some way or other of keeping her, and as it turned out fertilising her did the job quite nicely. She was also against an abortion for herself in theory, but now we were really putting theory to the test, for both of us.

We decided that I would go to Arizona and think it over in the desert while she went back to Greece to see her family. We'd make a decision before I came back and then deal with the problem together one way or another.

The clinic in Arizona was an amazing experience. However, I was slightly surprised to be practically strip searched on admission. It turned out that it was mainly an addiction clinic that treated its patients with therapy. I suddenly found myself in the middle of a twelve step frenzy, but with little claim to any obvious addictions. Frankly, I felt a little bit of a fraud and wondered how exactly I'd ended up there. Little by little however, I began to see how it really didn't matter whether or not the problems were clear or opaque; easily bore a label or were more difficult to articulate; were fully blown or waiting to sabotage you in latter life. All of us shared the same essential difficulty; we were human beings struggling to live our lives in a "normal" way.

I recognised that although I wasn't an alcoholic, I did use alcohol to change the way I experienced my feelings and my emotions. A little latter on I realised that I used relationships the same way. I was in some sense addicted to the highs and lows of the romantic roller-coaster. It helped me to keep down the darker, more permanent feelings that were yet to surface and to resolve themselves from my childhood. I realised that I was using women in the same way that others there had been using their drugs. The twelve-step meetings that I attended began to make sense to me. They had a much broader vision than just the suspension of the intake of drugs or alcohol. They really spoke to a vision of a life that did not rely on substance or behaviour to alter our pre-existing state of mind. They showed me how far and fast I ran to avoid what I could never be rid of: myself.

I had a decision to make amongst all this. It was terrific to be in that place at that time. I was surrounded by compassionate, interested and helpful people with whom I could discuss my predicament. Many of them were older than I and had a perspective on children that I couldn't yet understand. I well remember one alcoholic from Las Vegas telling me that children were heaven and they were hell. I thought that was rather extreme. Now I understand. They are heaven but they reintroduce you to the hell of your past, and that was something that I'd spent a lifetime up until then avoiding. In the end I remember just feeling overwhelmed by the idea of actually having a child. I was sure that I couldn't cope with an abortion but equally I was sure that I couldn't cope with a child. I could see the convenience of the status quo and the choice to remain childless but it seemed so blank and nihilistic. And yet I couldn't find the courage to accept the huge change that a child would bring. I despaired of my dilemma to a fellow inmate. She told me that whenever she had a difficult problem she would go to bed at night and pray for an answer the next day. I wasn't big on prayer, or even God for that matter, but sitting in the desert in Arizona clueless, lost and confused, it seemed that I really had nothing to lose. So I tried it. I prayed that night as I slept that God (with the unusual caveat of "if you actually exist") would provide me with an answer the next day.

The next morning my uncle called to say that my grandmother had died in the night. She was eighty-five and had been very frail. She was my mother's mother and I had always dreaded her passing. I was afraid that I would be losing my one and only direct connection to my mother and that it would reignite the grief and shock of that original loss. I had dreaded it for many years as she became older and sicker. Now it had happened. However, there were two things that were absolutely wonderful about her timing. First, I was in the equivalent of an emotional intensive care unit. Second, in my shock and in my grief I suddenly knew the blessing of life. I knew of love and life and the urgent priority of grabbing it wherever it could be found. I knew my baby was more precious than the stars and the moon. And I knew the greatest mistake I could ever have made would have been not to accept this ultimate gift of fate.

My granny chose her moment well. In the shadow of her death was the dawn of a new life. She and my daughter passed in opposite directions through the revolving doors of life. I've never known a more poignant moment or felt so cared for by the great inexplicable circle of life. For that brief moment in the still of the desert through the veil of my tears I knew the magic of the universe, its tricks and its secrets. And it was all so blissfully simple. A new life was there to be cherished. The universe was bringing me love. I laid down my objections, my arguments, my reason and my fear. I accepted then the wisdom of my destiny and above all accepted some measure of humility in the playing out of the drama of my life. I felt for the first time subservient to fate and my God was it finally a relief.

I returned to England and to the reality of a new chapter in my life. I had seen myself in a new light. My girlfriend was going to have my baby. I was on my way out of the nightclub business. I had always known that I could not let Dorothea go and now that we were going to start a family together it was time to formalise that with a proposal. I was surprised by how nerve-wracking it was. In the end I blurted it out in the bath in Paris. It was surreal to hear the words coming from my own lips. Dorothea and I began to look for a home to prepare for our baby. Then I just fell apart.

I began to experience the panic again but this time in a more raw and frightening way than before. It was not just a moment or an attack of panic but more like a reliving of a state of intense life-threatening fear. At first it was so bad that I thought I would have to go to hospital. I was literally shaking under the duvet. Dorothea helped me through it but it wasn't an easy time for her either. She was carrying the child of an unemployed nervous wreck whom she'd not yet known for even a year. I had become convinced that Dorothea wouldn't survive giving birth. It was as if death was a certainty. In fact the only certainty was that I had experienced my own mother's death shortly after my own birth. This fear remained with me right up to her trouble-free labour.

I found eating difficult. I just couldn't ingest anything in that state of fear. It reminded me of the stories of me not eating when I came back from America after my mother's death. I realised that I was feeling the emotional residue from my childhood but today in the present as an adult. I was absolutely shattered by anxiety, fear and panic in alternate states. I was a baby who had lost his mother. Except that as far as my family were concerned I had a mother. And as far as the rest of the world was concerned I was a successful businessman. And so, I was alone with my pregnant bride-to-be, devastated by a fear that others didn't even want to acknowledge.

In retrospect I can see how important a time that was for me, but back then I would have done anything to escape it. I would have even traded in Dorothea for a nightclubbing blonde or two. I was desperate to escape my state of mind. I didn't realise that I was getting what I had asked for. I had money. I had someone to care for me. I wasn't working. I had the time, the love, the care and the space to finally process some of those traumatic feelings from my childhood; the same traumatic feelings that were undermining my previous relationships with women; the same traumas that I went to the desert in Arizona to try to unlock and to dispel.

I had invited into my life the healing that I needed in order to be able to have a life with Dorothea, and then I hated it when it happened. I didn't understand it. My rational mind could not make sense of it back then. All I knew was that I was broken, imperfect and I hated myself for being so incapacitated. I was terrified of losing my mind, my one great weapon historically against the tides of fate. I was failing evolutionarily. I was very far from my desired alpha-male status. At the time it felt like the end of the world. In fact it was just the beginning.

Understanding Why?

Here we see the limitations of the conscious mind and its careful plans. My knowledge of both myself and psychotherapy were limited to, well, exactly what I had learned so far. My ability to forecast the future from my understanding of the past and its concomitant laws of cause and effect were limited absolutely by how much I knew, how much I had leaned, and how much I was prepared to understand. When considering the self, this last factor can be a severely constricting component.

I was unwilling to see myself as emotionally vulnerable. I wanted to have the self-image of confidence and power. I approached my own inner journey with the same swagger that I approached the velvet ropes of my own nightclub. I had determined that I had a problem and set about solving it. But this wasn't a building site or a balance sheet. The substance of the affair was perhaps my very soul itself. I had deluded myself into believing that I knew what I was doing. I didn't.

First of all I had got Dorothea pregnant. I was fully aware of the causes and effects relating to impregnation. Therefore if my conscious agenda was to try to carefully nurture this relationship to good health, I wasn't making it any easier by ignoring my understanding of the reproductive cycle. Secondly I had bitten off perhaps more than I could chew. There was a reason why I had not yet dealt with the serious emotional consequences of my mother's death. I wasn't ready. My system couldn't take the shock. That was exactly why these experiences remained repressed. However, I had determined in my conscious mind that now was the time that these stains on my ability to relate successfully must be swept away. I had a narrow conscious focus on the outcome that I desired. Its lack of context left me heading towards that outcome, but in a much different way than I had had in mind.

By not having at my disposal a complete understanding of myself or the mechanism of the mind, I was only able to approximate towards a result without the ability to fully control the outcome. This is a familiar problem for our species. In my case, I had successfully excavated some of the issues and emotions that were being played out in my behaviour in relationships. This took the pressure off the automatic response to behave in those ways, but it had other unforeseen consequences. Had I been aware of those consequences in advance, I doubt that I would have chosen this course of action. The limits of my conscious awareness, my conscious understanding and my conscious connections between causes and effects led me to take action that both delivered me to my stated consciously desired outcome and to a new level of complexity in my emotional difficulties.

This is often the result of using our conscious minds to manage present problems. We fail to see how the solutions that we come up with create new problems of their own. This is simply because we don't know everything – at least not consciously!

Step 2: The 2nd Hypothesis

Consciousness is the Tool of Survival

There is nothing that remarkable about the conscious mind. Consciousness is a tool that the human being has developed, through evolution to assist with its survival. That in itself does not make it so special. After all, it was the dinosaurs' size that killed them off. The one thing that kept them so dominant for so long actually destroyed them when their circumstances changed. They are now extinct. Look at how mankind's conscious mind has created similar threats for itself. Weapons of mass destruction, global warming and the general depletion of the world's resources create the possibility of human extinction. Thus your own great evolutionary success may ultimately be the root of your own extinction too.

You have a mind. It is the process that runs everything that you actually do. It keeps your heart ticking over; it moves your lungs in and out; it makes you jump when you see a mouse. Your mind is what happens in-between your body taking on the fuel to keep you alive and the actions that your body takes with that fuel. If you are healthy and able to walk, there must always be a decision taken where to walk, or not to walk. That decision could be taken for a million different reasons, but in the end something within you makes you move or not move. That process is run by your mind. You are aware of some of those processes.

You dominate your planet's resources and other species. You eat whatever you want, and nothing eats you, all because of one some simple evolutionary development. You began to be aware of your mind-body system. You observed yourself.

You became conscious of yourself and how you were operating as a mechanism. You noticed a pattern of cause and effect. You learned to connect these observations, and to reason about them. You extrapolated. You began to make predictions. You continued to observe. You continued to reason. You continued to match cause and effect. You became master of your environment: master of your world which until then had been the master of all of its inhabitants.

But that's only half the story. Things don't always go according to plan. Survival you can pretty much take for granted these days. It is not just being alive that challenges you now, but how to really live. Happiness is remarkably elusive even though resources are plentiful. The conscious mind has done its job well enough to keep you alive, but is limited in what it can offer you to help you to find a way to use that life most effectively. You are aware of that and you are wondering why. That is why you are reading this book.

If you can continue through this book, and learn to understand why you are only aware of, or conscious of, so little of the vast ocean of your mind, then you have a chance of learning what has prevented you from being able to live a rich, satisfying and automatically happy life.

If you can understand that then you can actually begin to use the conscious mind itself and its capacity for understanding to gain a chance of being able to change the limits of your own conscious mind. And thus your whole life will become open to change, if first you can just grasp, understand, retain and work with a real conscious understanding of what's wrong with you.

Exercise 2

What did you decide?

Construct a list of conscious decisions that you have taken in your life. Put your age or a date down the left and next to it the plan that you made. Like this:

29 years old   *Decided to try to solve my relationship issues by concentrated therapy*
29 years old   *Decided to keep the baby with Dorothea*

and so on. Try to include anything that you can remember being a significant decision in your life. These would be decisions that reflected your choices, ambitions and hopes for the future, like perhaps going to graduate school, moving in with a boyfriend or starting a business.

Next you are going to make a corresponding list of your intended outcomes for these choices versus the actual consequences of these decisions. Like this:

29 years old   *Wanted to make myself more comfortable and less dysfunctional in relationships. Actually led to a minor nervous breakdown.*
29 years old   *Wanted to embrace life and avoid negative emotional consequences of abortion. Actually ended up confronted by very difficult feelings from my own infancy.*

This way you can see that what seems like a simple idea designed to orientate your life towards a desirable goal can often lead you off in a different direction. There is nothing wrong with this, other than that you may not be very comfortable with the notion that you really don't know what you are doing.

However, if you review your list, then it is likely that you can learn from it the limitations of the conscious mind to forecast cause and effect completely. You may move forward to a stated goal, but all sorts of other effects will also come into play. These are often where the true opportunities in life lie.

Complete this exercise by listing next to your stated goals what new or unexpected challenges were thrown up by your decisions. Can you list what you learned from these unwanted obstacles? If so, then you can begin to understand the difference between getting what you need and getting what you want. That is the skill of your unconscious mind which you will learn more about in Step Three.

Q&A

From the wwwyou?forum. You can see the original text and ask questions at whatswrongwithyou.com.

Why do I feel like this?

Posted by: Ian Jul 20 2004, 01:00 PM

Hi Benjamin, perhaps you can help me understand. I am 35 years old, a professional, have my own house, have great friends and are reasonably intelligent. But that did not stop me becoming an alcoholic! Correction, a recovering alcoholic, I have been in recovery for 3 months now and it is going reasonably well. I realised that I cannot have the life that I want if I drink, but I can if I don't, and I am determined to have that life. However, the problem is that I can't get away from is my underlying self loathing. I think of my self and very unattractive guy and a failure. I feel that everyone else is normal and that it is I who is abnormal because not only of my drinking but because I am unable to attract women and have the marriage and children that I so desperately want. I understand that there is someone for everyone and that you will not find the perfect person straight away, but I suffer terrible depression from rejection and I seem to suffer rejection all the time. It seems that all my dreams are broken and that I will ultimately live a

lonely and worthless life. Why can I not accept that if a relationship does not flourish it is because it is not right and not
because I am an ugly, worthless, recovering alcoholic
(obviously I do not tell dates that I am an recovering alcoholic!). This is not a recent problem, I have always struggled to
get girlfriends. All my friends seem to go from one girl to the
next and now are all married with children...I am still on my
own with very few experiences with relationships. My friends
say I'm a good looking guy with a great personality, but inevitably I just think they are saying that because they are my friends.

This all seems very sad, even as I write it, and that just adds
to my anxiety and gives me more ammunition to hate myself
with. I have had a failed suicide attempt recently and I do not
want to go through that again. The only thing worse than
suicide is a failed attempt from my experience. Facing friends
and family!!

Any advice Benjamin that I might take away and work
with...I want to feel happy with myself...If I can accomplish this
I'm sure my life will click into place. Many thanks.

Posted by: benjaminfry Jul 21 2004, 09:56 PM

Congratulations on three months' sobriety. You've turned a
corner in your life and made a very brave decision. It is a
victory won every minute of every hour of every day. Obviously you have a tough time ahead but I hope that you can
make it and find that it is worthwhile.

My first observation would be about the suicide attempt.
There was a theory that drugs like Prozac were triggering
suicide because they were lifting people up just enough to have
a bit of enthusiasm to do something to end their persisting
depression. Perhaps giving up the drinking can have the same
effect. The absence of the alcohol in your system would pick
you up in some respects but the psychological battle that you

face to stay sober is a severe one. It can therefore be an alarming cocktail and I sincerely hope that you are getting the support you need in order to stay safe.

At some point in your life, probably very early on, you were made to think, feel and understand that you were ugly and worthless. You were rejected when you should have been nurtured. (Tell me if I'm wrong). This is a deep and mortally painful wound. It is the reason why you drink. It is the reason why you suffer so from rejection (that you logically understand is commonplace). It is the reason why you have such a low opinion of yourself.

The only way forward from here is through these feelings. You were overwhelmed by them when you were young and have therefore stored them up in your system as an overload of trauma. They try to escape, but you don't understand them and they freak you out. So you drink. Or they do escape and you think that they are about you in the here and now; so you project them onto others and think that everyone has this opinion of you.

It is very sad. And if you have any conscious connection with the source of these issues you might also be very angry. However, these are your crosses to bear. This is the grist in your mill. If you dedicate yourself to working with it, understanding it, feeling it, processing it and letting it go then you will recover in more ways than you ever thought possible.

Check with your AA group how you might best go about connecting with these lost feelings from the past. Psychotherapy is a great adjunct to twelve step work. You probably already know about journal writing and other inner disciplines such as meditation. Whatever your path, you have to go back into the feelings that you have run away from for so long. You already know unconsciously that you would rather do this than continue to drink to avoid it. Now you just have to bring the conscious mind along too (it can be a bit dim I'm afraid).

Remind yourself constantly that all the worst feelings in the world can never kill you, but repressing them can stop you living.

Incidentally, don't be afraid to be honest about who you are with dates. A recovering alcoholic is a much better catch than an alcoholic and if you are prepared to be ruthlessly honest about who you are, you stand a much better chance of finding someone right for you in the long term.

Finally, make friends with rejection. This is where you will find the fuel to move on past your trauma. Each time you feel the dreadful agony of rejection, redirect your focus away from thinking about the person who rejected you and instead concentrate on your own inner state of mind. Amplify the feelings instead of medicating them. These are exactly the feelings that you are trying to process and be rid of. If you let your wise unconscious mind do its work properly, it will trigger these feelings and then you'll be rid of them. If you stick stubbornly to the superficial wishes of your conscious ambitions, then it will be a much longer haul.

If you want to feel happy with yourself, then stop minding feeling awful. Relish terrible emotions and make friends with them. They are your passport to inner peace

.

Posted by: Ian Jul 23 2004, 12:19 PM

Thanks for the support and advice Benjamin. Your words were very helpful and I will try to out in action what you have suggested. The recovery is going well and sometimes I don't give myself enough credit for trying to change my life around. But the most important thing I have taken from you response it the need to accept, deal with and even embrace some of the emotions I feel now I'm not drinking. Drinking drowned these emotions for so many years that they do freak me out a bit now, but I will try to accept the rejection feeling for what they are and every time I come out the other side I will be a stronger and better person for it.

I am journal keeping and trying CBT too. I regularly attend AA meeting and try to contribute as much as possible. With you kind words too and the support of friends and family I really feel I can win...slowly.

Thanks again.

Ian

THREE

Unconsciousness

I think. Therefore I am completely ignorant. The conflict between the blunt instrument of the conscious mind and the brilliant unconscious mind-body system.

Theory: Trauma and its Effects

The conscious mind is very good at forecasting cause and effect on a practical level and using this ability to avoid adverse circumstances. But it is also the cause of our greatest problem outside of immediate life and death challenges: our unhappiness.

Unhappiness is rife these days. It doesn't matter how many ticks we place against the boxes which magazines tell us will contribute to a satisfied life; unhappiness will persist. Even when we experience a sense of real happiness from a change in circumstance, or luck, or fortune, or mood, it eventually fades away. But we stay alive. We were not bred for being happy. We were bred for staying alive and for doing some breeding of our own.

Happiness is not required for survival. Our conscious mind is a slave to survival. It is hardwired to protect us and to promote our health and resources. It didn't develop and survive the natural selection of evolution to help make us happy. It might think that we want to be happy, but that is not its skill.

Its skill is to help us to orientate ourselves successfully towards desirable, practical goals.

We are well past the point of needing our conscious minds to help us to stay alive, so we have given it other tasks: a promotion perhaps, or a bigger apartment, a nicer girlfriend, a larger chest, a better wardrobe, more interesting friends, a hobby, a new education, a luxurious holiday or some time spent helping others. It doesn't matter what the goal is, our conscious mind will help us to try to achieve it. That is what it is good at.

However, what it is not so good at is choosing what to aim for in the first place. Nebulous concepts like happiness are not its speciality. Concrete objectives like warm shelter, stored food for the winter, avoidance of dangerous animals and finding water are its real forte. These factors affecting our survival are largely under control in the modern industrialised world. So what is an evolutionary superstar to do? The next task on the rung of survivalism seems to be not just to survive, but to survive more happily.

Modern life has become not just the daily pursuit of avoiding extinction, but instead the daily pursuit of searching for a happier life. Life itself is now largely taken for granted. Quality of life however is a real challenge that we all face in confusing and uncharted territory. What can we do when life just doesn't seem to make us as excited and happy as it should: given all we have done, all the efforts we make, and all the successes we've achieved? At this point the conscious mind is no longer our ally.

In fact the conscious mind is our enemy in our search for happiness.

It's not its fault. It doesn't do it on purpose. It is not part of its survivalist agenda to keep us miserable. It is an accident: a side effect, if you like, of the development of its exceptional survival skills.

Remember that we are the progeny of the most excellent survivors on the planet. And remember that our trump card in this process is our ability to use the tool that we call our conscious mind. This ability has allowed us to connect cause and effect and to control our circumstances to enhance our chances of survival. It is the ability to connect the past to the future that our conscious mind relies on. We are driven to survive and to understand phenomena, through the logical deduction of cause and effect. It is what has kept us alive.

If this understanding were to break down, we would be highly alarmed. If we were no longer able to make a rational connection between two phenomena, the whole basis for our confidence in our survival prospects and abilities would be undermined. It would literally freak us out. For example, have you ever observed the audience at a magic show? Stuff happens that should not happen. People react to this with amazement and even a sense of shock. Sometimes, if the magic is particularly convincing, people can't handle what they are seeing. It freaks them out. They don't want to believe that it could be real, but they can't escape the evidence of their own eyes.

Imagine your own reaction if you were to look at someone and they were to rise up, hovering above the ground, levitating. Imagine how that would affect you. Wouldn't it alarm you? The moment you catch sight of the thin wire suspending that person from the ground and realise that you have just been tricked, you recover immediately and have no fear at all. Your emotional reaction to observing the same phenomenon is wildly different simply because of the understanding that your conscious mind has of it. When it can not adequately connect a phenomenon with a cause, it is terrified. Once that cause is made clear, it is calm.

Anything that we don't understand really freaks us out. In order to not understand something, we obviously have to have a conscious mind that is in the business of understanding stuff in the first place. If we didn't spend our whole lives observing, reasoning, and connecting phenomena into accepted cause and effect patterns, then we wouldn't be afraid of experiencing something that we didn't understand. Therefore this fear is a problem caused by the conscious mind.

The tool that has let us dominate our planet has an Achilles heel. It makes us terribly threatened by things that don't yet make sense to us. Both our circumstances and our belief in our ability to control our circumstances are threatened by unexplained phenomena. This leads to a profound fear (literally founded on the fear of death) and like any organism that has survived the natural selection of evolution we take extreme action when faced with the fear of death. We fight, flee or freeze.

This abhorrence of the conscious mind to stuff that it doesn't understand, or more seriously to stuff that seems to directly contradict what it thinks it does understand, is the arch-enemy of happiness. To understand why, you have to learn about trauma. Once you understand both the conscious mind's fear of the unexplained and the mechanism of trauma, you will have learned just about all that you need to know to begin to understand what's wrong with you.

Trauma is what happens when the mind-body system is overwhelmed by negative emotions. Everyone has their own threshold for dealing with a stimulus in their mind-body system. Some people can weather the cold better than others. Some people don't mind being hungry. Some people can cry for days. Some people can't. Everyone is different and everyone's threshold for what is emotionally overwhelming is different.

There is no clear reason why an abundance of a strong emotion should be overwhelming, but it is clear that being overwhelmed is an experience most people can relate to. It happens when something becomes too difficult to bear and we just can't take it any more. Somehow, whatever it is, it is too much. This is the genesis of trauma.

We know of trauma as applying to extreme situations, but it is much more widespread than we might think, or remember. Trauma prevents overload. It is the mind-body system's safety-valve. It has evolved in such a way that the priority is survival (safety), not truth. When the truth experienced all at once might seriously harm a person's mental state and affect their ability to survive, the mechanism of trauma keeps that person going. It edits. It filters. It conceals. It deceives. It moves the boundaries of the conscious mind so that what is known is not known. What is felt is not felt. What is experienced is not experienced. It changes the viewfinder of the conscious mind so that an overwhelming experience is no longer in the part of the mind that we are conscious of. It goes over to the dark side of the moon. It recedes into the unconscious mind, and there it stays.

You may remember having been so upset about something that you just went blank. The emotions had disappeared. This is the process of trauma and it happens when we believe that our survival is threatened. So we fight, flee or freeze. Of the three, freezing is the most associated with creating trauma in the mind-body system. It doesn't have to be a literal freezing of the body (although that is observed in many species). It can just be a freezing of the emotions. It is this freezing that creates trauma. It is when an experience is absorbed back into the mind-body system. Often people who have suffered a great deal of trauma can be seen to exhibit it in their bodies. Tension, stiffness, poor posture and frequent illness can be signs that the body is carrying what the mind couldn't bear. Addictions are other signs of the body literally trying to stuff something back inside.

The mind and the body are a united system. We are the whole of ourselves. The conscious mind is just a part of our whole unified mind and body working as one. When we suffer trauma our whole system is affected and often the result is the storing of that trauma in our bodies. Most people don't think that they really carry any trauma. They look back on their lives and don't remember any axe murdering or otherwise newsworthy incidents in their past. People associate trauma with the extreme and the justifiably unbearable. However, the truth is that we will all have experienced a great deal of trauma in our lives.

Trauma is simply what happens when we are overwhelmed by a threat, either physical or emotional, be it a paedophile or an insult, real or imagined. Everyone has their own threshold for what is overwhelming and so there can be no presumed correlation between events and trauma. Some people are more sensitive that others. These people have lower thresholds to being emotionally overwhelmed. You may be one of these people and not even know it. That's how pernicious trauma is. By definition it's something that we are not aware of.

Case Study: Hot Rod

It turned out that there were four paedophiles teaching at my prep school. That's quiet a lot among the staff for only one hundred and fifty boys. The school was a top quality boarding school for young boys. I went there a few days after my eighth birthday. I was there for five years before going on to Eton. It was known as a prep-school because originally these kind of schools were used to prep-are boys for their grown up boarding schools. Its main duty to the parents was to groom the boy for entrance to the school of their parents' choice. Unfortunately while doing so, some of the staff had it in mind to groom the children for an entirely different sort of graduation.

We were there for eight months of the year. Each term

there was a long weekend allowed at home for half-term. Otherwise you could go out for the day on Sunday (after chapel) three times each term. I have no idea why it was restricted to three times per term. I can only imagine that the school didn't want to create an inequity among those boys whose parents could make it more often and those whose parents were not so keen. In any case it wasn't much relief: eight hours at home, three times in three months. For the rest of the time we were living with our schoolmasters, the paedophiles in loco parentis.

I only became aware of this furtive undercurrent to our education during my final term. The deputy headmaster of the school, known as Hot Rod, was becoming a larger and larger figure in my life. He was an urbane, charming and educated classics scholar. He had been at Oxford with my father. I had always felt comfortable with him because of the family connection. He had suggested that I learn a musical instrument and pointed me to the French Horn. He conducted the school orchestra. He was the head of the house where I slept. He taught Latin to the top form. And crucially now, he was the master in charge of cricket. It being the summer term there was a new cricket team to be found and a new captain to be appointed. It was clear from the opening games of the season that I was first choice for this post.

And so we fell into a cosy relationship. He would be the one to turn out our lights at night and to wish me goodnight. He would wake us up in the morning. He would supervise our washing. He would take morning assembly. He would teach me Latin. He would conduct the orchestra. He would coach the cricket and increasingly annex me into the management of this term's cricket team. There would be conversations snatched during the morning rush to prepare for the day. There would be conferences in the hall before bedtime. I felt quite grown up, quite a part of his world.

There was always something a little unbalanced about Hot Rod. He had a temper, that much was abundantly clear. He was middle-aged and yet single. He was rumoured to drink, although we had little idea what that really meant. But to a prepubescent boy, the strangest thing about him was undoubtedly his habit of wearing his shirts tucked into his Y-fronts. These Y-fronts would protrude above the waistline of his trousers and had the moniker Y-jockey repeated around their elastic waists. Seeing the deputy headmaster's pants was hysterical for us small boys.

However, it is hard now not to reflect differently on Hot Rod's pants. Was it an unconscious leak of where the man's real thoughts lay? Was it a warning to the boys? Or to the staff? Or a coded message advertising the existence of the demons that perhaps he used the drink to keep at bay? I can not in retrospect see it as a coincidence that every boy in the entire school was able to see the pants of the most senior paedophile on the staff. After all you'd have to presume that pants was what he wanted to get into. Perhaps this was his way of playing 'I'll show you mine if you'll show me yours'; something that the boys themselves were innocently pursuing as they stumbled into the earliest stages of adolescence.

I wasn't the easiest pupil. Despite intellectual and sporting talents, I was quite frequently in trouble. I never fitted easily into an organisation. I didn't cooperate naturally with rules. I liked to understand them and appreciated their structure, but more than that I liked to break them and to get away with it. I was a compulsive rebel, but I managed it with charm rather than confrontation. It created quite a conundrum for my teachers. On the one hand I was engaging and talented, just what the school looked for to promote its qualities, and on the other hand I undermined the institution with my behaviour.

It was still early in the term and I had found myself in serial trouble. I can't remember the details. It was always something trivial, a missed music lesson here, a bad prep there. The incidents themselves never provoked too much outrage but the pattern had the teachers flummoxed. This flouting of authority challenged them all the more because I should have been a shining example of the school's successes. Finally, I was summoned to a crunch talk with Hot Rod. There had been dark muttering about my behaviour rendering me unsuitable to be appointed captain of cricket. Such an important member of the school should not be transgressing its rules so regularly. The issue needed a resolution and, unusually, I was invited to see Hot Rod in the private side of the school in the headmaster's house.

I went after lunch. There was always a strange feeling to these rooms. They had a musty smell and a lack of proprietary care that comes from staff accommodation. There was no-one there on that day but Hot Rod. He invited me into the study to talk. He seemed a little distracted. He began by cataloguing my failures that term and outlined the concerns of the staff about my suitability for any kind of senior responsibility. I was used to this. I'd had it on and off for the last five years. I would tend to argue a bit, justify a bit, apologise a bit, charm a bit and get through it. But there was something different going on today. I was hesitant in this intimidating atmosphere and Hot Rod was almost conspiratorial rather than didactic in his recital of the staff's concerns.

He presented little admonishment, more the proposition of a problem that we needed to solve, so I had little to say in return. He paused, presumably wrestling with himself, and then handed down his sentence. He had decided that I was to be beaten. This would then be sufficient to absolve me of all my sins so far that term and we could start from a clean sheet. I would be free to become the cricket captain in my pristine state of virginal discipline.

This was a shock. Corporal punishment was whispered

about but even in those days rarely encountered. When it was so it was usually for quite severe and dangerous transgressions such as the wilful destruction of property or malicious harming of a pupil or teacher. It seemed to me to be such a harsh word: beaten. I was to be beaten. And for what? Missing a few music lessons? Cheeking a few teachers? And what was this artifice for? To purge me so that I could be appointed the cricket captain? Even then I was aware that something didn't quite add up although I could not have guessed yet the real motives at work.

I half expected that he was joking, that he would relent and send me on my way. Indeed it seemed that he was himself struggling with that same possibility. There was a pause, his opportunity to reverse the course of events that he may had plotted for some time, but in the end there was no mercy. He left the room and returned a little while later with an object that shocked me anew. He was holding what was euphemistically referred to as a hairbrush, but I believe that the only hair that it was meant for was on horses.

Now, what was a stable grooming instrument doing secreted in the headmaster's quarters? Hot Rod was well known for carrying a butter pat in his briefcase; a small wooden paddle that he threatened as an instrument of discipline. (A butter pat in a briefcase! How could that not alarm adults who encountered him?) I'm not sure that I had had any idea what to expect, but I suppose the butter pat had seemed likely. Instead I was facing a much more fearsome weapon. The hairbrush was about three feet long with a heavy wide head where the bristles were mounted. It looked dangerous. Hot Rod had a strange excited air about him as he asked me to bend over. Thankfully my clothes stayed on. I was grateful at least for that dignity as I grabbed my knees, unable to imagine what was about to happen.

He struck me damn hard with the first blow. I couldn't

believe the violence of it. The pain was bad enough but what was worse was to be assaulted like this, in cold blood, by this otherwise avuncular figure in whose pastoral care I found myself more often than any other teacher. He was, on purpose, attacking me, literally beating me, and all the while on the most flimsy of pretexts. There were other blows that followed, but by then I was in shock.

When he had had his fill, he invited me to stand. All I could do was to choke back the tears. I couldn't speak. He let me go. I walked out of the room, down the hall back to the school, and when the door closed behind me only then did I let the sobs overwhelm me. I couldn't believe the pain and the violence that I had just experienced in the tranquil setting of the headmaster's study. All I could remember was the gentle ticking of the mantelpiece carriage clock suddenly being interrupted by the explosive force of the hairbrush on my arse. Tick tock, tick tock, beat my arse, jolly good, well done fella.

Half an hour later Hot Rod was taking our fielding practice on the cricket pitch. I was late. He smiled at me in welcome as if nothing had happened. My whole bottom was black and blue for days. But I was appointed captain of the cricket team the next day, and from then on was able to spend even more time cloistered with my assailant.

Understanding Why?

As a child of twelve, the relative physical differential between me and Hot Rod was considerable. So when he said that he was going to beat me, there was very little that I could have done to prevent it. This was further complicated by the pretence that this was an important process of following the school rules. My response was automatic. I had no chance of winning a fight should I chose to start one. As a member of a residential school, I certainly could not flee (others had tried only to be hauled back by the police). Therefore my only option was freezing.

I remember very well my utter surprise at the sheer force of its violence. But after that, once the reality of the threat became overwhelming, the physical assault and the concomitant pain were impossible to bear. That was when I shut down; I froze. I don't remember the rest of the beating. I only remember afterwards standing up, shaking, trying not to cry. I was numbed with the shock and still partly frozen being in the proximity of my assailant. It was only later when I was return-ing to the boys' side of the school, that I began to be able to cry. The freeze started to thaw.

What has happened to those few seconds during which Hot Rod was repeatedly beating me? What emotions were stirred within me during that physical assault that I had to repress? Had my opponent been another twelve year old boy, I can imagine that I may have become very angry and reacted with great force and intensity. That anger and indignation were instead held at bay by the mechanism of trauma. It would not have been safe for me to have responded to a grown man in a physically aggressive or angry way.

Trauma kept me on hold, safe until I could re-experience the lost emotions later in a physically safe environment. However, that wasn't going to be at my school. Half an hour later we were running the cricket team side by side and in fact I was rarely far from Hot Rod's gaze for the rest of my time at the school.

Trait: the Consciousness is Shrunk by Fear

To understand how much we may have been affected by trauma, we need to review our lives and think about where and when we might have faced overwhelming situations. We do this from the start. If we were able to do this honestly (and most people can't – it's too traumatic) then we would realise that life for a long time was little else than a series of seriously traumatic experiences.

It begins with birth. We were stirred from our amniotic slumbers, and expelled out of the warm bath of our mothers' wombs into the harsh world outside. This could have been a serious threat to our lives. We may not have known if we were going to survive. Indeed the adults around us may not have known if we were going to survive. However, we did survive. We may have been lucky enough to survive and be placed next to our mothers' skin and thus finally felt safe. Or we may have been taken away, examined, kept apart from our mothers, operated on, isolated for observation or just left in a basket to sleep.

Throughout all of this, only one process would have been active in our new infant minds: the business of survival. If at any point the threat to our survival became overwhelmingly strong, we would have suffered trauma. Remember that we couldn't see, speak or understand anything. All we knew were our mothers. If we couldn't get sufficient access to this safe haven we would have been terrified, and if we were too terrified for too long we would have been traumatised. This process then continues through childhood.

And so it goes on throughout life. Always the underlying fear is of death. We have evolved to avoid death at all costs. Sometimes the fear of death itself becomes the most present threat to us, and sometimes that itself is overwhelming. That is when we are traumatised. At other times, we are overwhelmed by feelings of great sadness, loss, anger, horror, despair, pain, grief, regret, guilt, shame, rage, hopelessness, hate, even love. Perhaps the worst aspect of this process is that it is cumulative. People who have been traumatised will find situations that echo the circumstances of their original trauma even more threatening.

For example, if we were left alone a lot as a child by our parents, then we may be more demanding of the company of other people. Being on our own is more frightening than for someone who was constantly surrounded by trusted family members as a child. Or if we were constantly threatened as a small child by a very angry, shouting adult, such as an unhappy or alcoholic parent, then we will find it very difficult to cope with angry people as we grow up.

Each time we face such behaviour it will add to the trauma that we already carry. Each fresh confrontation with situations that we have internalised will most likely add to the burden of emotional backlog. And so we will begin to avoid those situations or not be able to deal with them. The emotions that surround them will become repressed and thus no longer exist in the conscious mind. E-motion implies moving out (as in the Latin prefix ex- or e-, motion). If we don't let these feelings move out, then they disappear back in, stuffed down into the unconscious mind. But trauma's momentary victory over what is overwhelming exacts a terrible compensatory price in the longer term.

Before the age of five or six, we probably experienced traumatic reactions to events thousands and thousands of times. We would be unlikely to remember much of it, but we may have a memory or two of something that really affected us and was not entirely repressed. The majority of our experiences would have been not so significant: fleeting, largely unimpressive if related to an outsider. The trauma may have been slight. It may even have been partially released almost instantly. But patterns would have developed, like water stains on the outside of a house. The first few drops would have found some common ground and formed a drip, then a dribble and then a rivulet, always following the path forged by their predecessors. Before long, an established route would have been worn, damaging the property and eroding its structure: all from a random smattering of tiny, individual rain drops. A wooden building can collapse entirely if it is left to the mercy of damage from the rain; if it is untreated. We are not much different.

The rain can come thick and fast when we are young, particularly when we are very young and can't actually register a complaint or explain clearly what we need to feel safe. Children are the most vulnerable members of society and even those with the most enlightened and attentive parents will suffer from the vividness of their own imaginations. It is all potentially traumatic. If the child is particularly sensitive, then the smallest thing, a thing no adult could ever predict or notice, might freak it out so much it would never talk about it. However, a more emotionally robust child might not even notice the same event. It is hard to know. Unfortunately, the early trauma is the most damaging because the rest of our lives are built on the foundation of this experience.

Think about the example of the wooden house. Imagine that it rained a lot when its foundations were being built. It was unprotected from the rain and untreated after being in the rain. The lowest layers of the construction were beginning to rot even before the rest of it was built. Even if it never rained again and a magnificent house was built on these foundations, a day would come where the wind would blow and the storm would rage outside and the house would begin to give, because beneath that marvellous exterior lay a damaged, rotting core.

We are that house. We were from time to time unprotected as we laid down our own foundations in life. We were also untreated after being soaked when it rained during these times. We may have built impressive stories on top of this early beginning, but we will not be able to stay stable through the worst of storms if we don't go back into our basements to treat the damage that lies there, rotting our foundations, undermining our whole structure.

Fortunately this is relatively easy to do. In fact it is really quite hard to avoid. Our entire mind-body system is actively engaged in the business of sorting out this problem for us. It doesn't like to carry trauma around. Remember that trauma is only an emergency measure. It's not supposed to be a permanent remedy but merely a pause; a chance for you to gather some more resources until you are ready to feel again.

Here's how it works in the natural world. It is well observed that when a gazelle is faced with attack by a lion, it will fight, flee or freeze. Usually it runs. When it is caught, it fights. When it loses this fight, it sometimes freezes. It can literally go into an all-over bodily freeze. Sometimes this even confuses the lion enough to save the gazelle's life, since a lion will not eat a dead animal. If the lion leaves the gazelle for dead, the gazelle will remain frozen on the ground until some time after the lion has gone.

When the gazelle un-freezes, it returns to life, as it were, but it doesn't just get up, look around, thank its lucky stars and walk away. It gets up and starts to behave exactly as it was behaving the moment that it froze. It is still freaking out, trying to get away from the lion to avoid being killed and eaten. But the lion's not there any more.

Now just imagine for a moment what that is like for the gazelle. Its nervous system and body is behaving as if there is a lion about to eat it, but there is no lion in sight. Its mind-body system is acting as if it is at that moment under great threat from a predator. But there is no-one there. It is freaking out, but for no reason. Sound familiar?

Now imagine that the gazelle had the capacity to observe both its environment and itself. It would see no lion but it would observe itself to be freaking out as if there was a lion's jaw poised behind its haunches. What would it make of that? What would we make of that? How would we feel if we suddenly felt an emotion that did not seem to correlate with our circumstances? We don't get hunted by lions much any more but nonetheless we have many times experienced an emotion that was somewhat at odds with our observed circumstances.

The gazelle's behaviour is the normal and natural process of resolving trauma. When the circumstances permit it, the trauma comes out on its own. It's dying to come out. It needs to come out. The mind-body system can't wait to expel it (to experience the e-motion) and get on with something else.

However, in our highly developed human self there is a big problem: ourselves. We have this blunt instrument of a conscious mind that observes our world and connects the past with the future, rationalising through cause and effect. It is the skill that has led us to dominate our planet: our great survivalist triumph. It is the intelligence that lets us know when something is not right, when phenomena are out of the ordinary. It tells us to run like mad from things we can't understand. It connects cause and effect. It is only comfortable with events that make sense: events that can be explained. Freaking out about a lion when there's no lion to be seen is very bad news for the conscious mind. There is one very serious drawback to this wonderful conscious mind that we have developed to dominate our planet. It doesn't yet understand what the hell is going on when our body tries to release its trauma.

The one important point to take away from this book is that **when the body tries to release its trauma, the conscious mind can't understand what's going on; and when the conscious mind can't understand what's going on, it freaks out and gets traumatised again**.

The conscious mind finds the release of trauma literally traumatically disturbing in itself, and as a result instantly re-freezes the emerging e-motions. Thus the trauma is resealed inside. The experiences in life that trigger another attempt to resolve this trauma freak us out again, and again, and again, and create more trauma that is also sealed, and resealed, inside. And so the reservoir of trauma grows from humble beginnings to a vast lake of unexpressed pain and suffering; fear and rage; shame and abuse.

Our psychic house is never rescued from the trauma that rained down on it. It really wouldn't matter that it got so wet if we dried it out and treated it, but the conscious mind won't let us treat it because it doesn't understand what is going on. The conscious mind can't find a causal connection between the event that stimulated the emotions and the emotions when they are finally experienced. Trauma has hidden the causes of this effect from the conscious mind. That link has been frozen by the mechanism of trauma in the mind-body system and thus the causal connection has been lost. It is not broken but disguised by the passage of time. The conscious mind does not understand the connection between the original event and the present emotion because the conscious mind is not aware of the initial trauma. The whole point of the trauma mechanism is to spare the conscious mind the awareness of it in the first place.

For example, soldiers with post-traumatic stress from battle in the Falkland Islands returned to the islands to try to get over their trauma. Returning to the site of the original incident in some cases triggered a release of the emotions of that moment many years ago. They would have been prepared for this and guided though it by psychologists to prepare their conscious minds for the shock of this time-lag in cause and effect. Their minds were ready for this otherwise inexplicable phenomenon.

Our minds can also be similarly trained. We might wonder what we can do to help our conscious minds to be less alarmed by the resolution of trauma in our mind-body system. But the wonderful thing about the conscious mind is that it can learn. It is already doing so. Just reading this book is a good enough start. We can retrain our conscious minds to understand that there isn't anything to be freaked out about when experiencing emotions. Then it won't freak out when we are experiencing them. The way to stop our conscious minds becoming freaked out is learn the connection between cause and effect. We have to teach our conscious minds the cause and effect between seemingly unrelated events.

We have to educate ourselves. And then we must do it again, and again, and again, and again. Then our conscious minds won't get so freaked out by the resolution of trauma. We will understand the delayed cause and effect mechanism. We will begin to allow it to happen because we will have learned to understand the truth behind the predictable, logical, causal process that underlies what's wrong with us.

Case Study: Hot Rod, at home

Nothing wrong with a sound beating, I hear you say. Sounds like the snotty little nerd got what was coming to him. A horse's hair-brush a paedophile does not make. Possibly. But you wouldn't say that if you were in the cricket team. That wasn't the end of Hot Rod's special relationship with instruments of flagellation and it wasn't the end of Hot Rod's interesting ideas for new ways to interact with me.

Hot Rod was a favourite with the boys. He played up to his popular appeal. He was suave and charming, urbane and intelligent. The other teachers mostly faded in his shadow. He carried with him a particularly fine confection called "Black Bullets". These were no ordinary sweets. Sweets to us were consumer products that we smuggled back to school, snatched hastily from a newsagent as our parents bribed us to go willingly. Hot Rod's sweets were luxury goods. They were as impressive and seductive to us boys as the gleamingly new white BMW that he parked in his drive. And these sweets gave him great power, a unique hold over his inner circle.

The routine after a match against another school was to repair to Hot Rod's boarding house, the one where I was now the senior dormitory captain, and to post-mortem the game in Hot Rod's sitting room. Inevitably there were complaints to be made against players and issues raised. This was a great opportunity for Hot Rod. He cajoled us on the one hand, entertaining us in his rooms, pouring out the ginger beer, raising team morale and solidarity, but then he would turn his critical eye and his fragile temper on the stragglers who were failing to follow his directives. There developed a formula for dealing with such failures, a formula that I was already familiar with. During our cosy debriefings, among the fizzy drinks and the black bullets, Hot Rod effortlessly introduced the butter pat into our sporting lexicon. The solution to our weak squad was to punish our transgressions in play with a mild spanking. He would identify a player who had underperformed and then there would be a reckoning. A few mercifully light taps with the butter pat would have them restored to team status, and of course it was all presented as a bit of a gag, a bracing piece of boarding school life: manly stuff.

It had become inevitable that certain individuals were always going to be targets for his post-mortem spankings. He reverted to his technique that he had applied with me of offering a salvation from the beating. He made his victim a hero with a consolation supply of black bullets. We were all getting a black bullet here and there but unreliably and they were heart-stoppingly delicious to small boys eating filth day in and day out. Now Hot Rod introduced the idea of a reliable supply. Those who took the butter pat would get the bullet. Carefully he manipulated the presentation so that the boys began to realise that this relationship could be inverted. Remarkably quickly, he had established his private salon of young boys of sporting excellence, secreted in his boarding house, a thousand yards from the main school, and there, in the cosy seclusion of his sitting room, he dispensed voluntary beatings in return for a gratefully received reliable supply of sugar.

Picture the scene of eleven twelve-year-olds, after a long afternoon doing battle on the field with local rivals, gathered in the warm well furnished rooms of the deputy headmaster. The rest of the school was ploughing through its Victorian routine, stuck in their shorts, sat on stiff wooden benches in cold inhospitable classrooms. But we were regaled, entertained, cajoled and provided for by Hot Rod. Mainly it was a very pleasant diversion and a just reward for our elite status as school representatives. We weren't looking to find anything wrong with it. Okay, perhaps it was a bit weird that Hot Rod would inevitably open up his briefcase as some point and produce the butter pat. Perhaps it was a bit unfair that one or two boys were always the ones to find themselves on the wrong end of the butter pat. But it wasn't going to ruin our fun. We were being spoilt. We didn't want to see that we were being spoiled. Boarding school life is exceedingly grim, especially in terms of creature comforts. We took our pleasures where we could find them. Hot Rod knew exactly how to seduce us.

Not surprisingly, I never asked for a black bullet via the butter pat. By this point I wasn't entirely comfortable with Hot Rod, his weapons, or his schemes to raise a spanking, fair or foul. Three other very odd things happened that summer. The first was shortly after my initial beating and subsequent appointment as cricket captain. One of the rituals of our mornings was to take it in turns, dormitory by dormitory, to go to the washrooms. This was a process sometimes supervised by Hot Rod himself. Then we would return to our dormitories to dress and tidy our beds. This morning, Hot Rod asked me to come to his room when I was dressed to discuss the cricket team. His room did not mean his study but his bedroom, which was about ten yards down the hall from my bedroom. I duly ventured in after getting myself ready. He called out to me to enter, but he was not there. He was in his en-suite bathroom and emerged naked from the waist up, brushing his teeth. His signature Y-fronts were most firmly in evidence. He finished his brushing and we made some small talk about the cricket team. Again he seemed somewhat distracted and again I was aware of the incongruity of discussing these ordinary school details but in the extraordinary setting of his bedroom with him half naked. Then without provocation he suddenly clasped me to his chest and exclaimed, "my dear boy, how could I have done such a thing?"

Of course I knew what he was talking about. I had known that there was something weird about the beating he had given me and now I had the evidence. His remorse clearly signalled to me that what he had done was wrong. However, this latest chapter was another weird and confusing incident. I had not spoken much about the beating partly due to the shame of it, but also because there had been something creepy about it, something that was easier to forget. So I wasn't going to broadcast this new incident. It was just too weird for me. Adult passions, rage, violence, grief, shame and remorse were beyond me. I was just a small boy in a dangerous place trying to stay safe. I hoped that would be the end of it.

No such luck. Some time later Hot Rod took me aside towards the end of the day as we prepared for bedtime. He invited me again into his bedroom. He said he had an idea for a game and seemed very excited. That was odd enough in itself. He explained to me in detail his cunning plan. In the morning, he would summon me to his bedroom as he invited my dormitory to go for washing. Then we would play a trick on the other boys. He would shout something at me and then smack two slippers together to make a loud beating noise. This would fool the other boys into believing that he had been beating me. I would then go down to wash. What a brilliant game!

It didn't really involve me doing anything but I had a very weird feeling that this was not normal. How was this amusing?

It what way was it a game? What was the point in trying to pretend that he was beating me? After all, he'd shown that he had the inclination and authority to do so for real whenever he pleased. So just what was the point? Morning came and Hot Rod duly carried out his plans. I was somewhat dumbfounded, hoping I suppose that he would have just forgotten about his silly idea. I stood in his bedroom as he shouted something and then he beat two slippers, very loudly, against one another, after which I went down to the washrooms with the others. No-one said a word. No-one wanted to get involved in what was going on.

There were small boys everywhere in pyjamas and dressing gowns, washing, dressing and undressing. For supervision they had Hot Rod, the Y-front toting grown-up who played spanking games with slippers behind his bedroom door. Was he masturbating in that bathroom, the echo of fresh blows ringing in this ears, young boys in various states of undress so close to him all around the house? Maybe not. Would you rather think not? If you'd paid most of your disposable income to have your son be there, in that house at that moment, would you really rather not even consider it? Perhaps I'm being unkind. Perhaps Hot Rod was just a reluctant and clumsy disciplinarian who had a bad sense of humour. There surely must be an explanation? Was he avuncular and lonely, or really perverted and dangerous? I was going to be given one final opportunity to find out.

I never found it that easy to get off to sleep. I think that I must have mentioned this to Hot Rod once because one night, as he was putting us to bed as usual, he casually let it be known, fully audible to the whole dormitory, that if I didn't get off to sleep I was welcome to join him downstairs for a drink in his study. I mumbled some reply.

Now I knew what happened in movies when people asked other people to have a drink with them, especially late at night.

Even in my innocence and chastity I couldn't see this as anything other than an overture of some kind. Sexual? Romantic? Familiar? I didn't know. I didn't even know what those words meant. But I did know that down there, in the room below my bed, separated from me by a few joists and floorboards, waited for me a world that I was not advised to intrude upon. Hot Rod was rumoured to drink whisky. A lot of whisky. What was the plan? Were we to share a tumbler late into the night? The housemaster and the twelve year-old boy?

In the morning I saw him again in the washroom. He hadn't forgotten. He perhaps seemed relieved that I had not come. I wonder how long he waited; how he wrestled with himself over what he might do if I did arrive. He joked with me that I was bound to have fallen asleep straight away after such an invitation. I don't remember answering. The truth was that I had hardly slept at all.

The following year I heard news of Hot Rod from my old school friends who had gone with me to Eton. He had been asked to give some extra lessons during the Easter holidays to a pupil who lived near the school. Hot Rod attempted to sexually molest the boy while giving him some remedial Latin. Hot Rod made a mistake here. He had acted outside of term-time. The boy went straight home and told his mother. Hot Rod "left". The rumour was that he went to America. Not jail. That would never do, after all he was the deputy headmaster. Did the police ever investigate? Certainly no-one ever asked me any questions. How many other boys had been interfered with, threatened, toyed with, groomed? Was he acting alone, or was he being encouraged? Did they ever try to find out? Had they done so, they might have spared the student population of my school yet more suffering.

Before I had left Eton I heard of three more paedophiles unmasked among the teaching staff of my prep-school. I was told that one had gone to jail and the two others, one of them an old-Etonian, took their own lives when caught. They were all on the staff when I was there. How many boys had suffered and in how many ways before that tally was reached? How many suffer still today, having never breathed out loud a word of their experiences? How many other children are being freshly damaged every day and every night, while their schools employ perverts to watch over the future leaders of our companies, councils, schools and assets?

Understanding Why?

One of the key symptoms of trauma is that the usual responsive apparatus of the mind and body is short-circuited. This is exactly how it provides a safety valve for the system. However, there is a rather disturbing side effect of this: especially in the experience of children who live in unsafe domestic conditions.

It would seem clear that at some point someone should have said something to somebody about Hot Rod's behaviour. For my part, I can honestly say that it never crossed my mind to do so. I never even got to the stage of wondering who to say what to. I just never held the experiences in my mind for long enough to want to take any action on them. My response to the strange and threatening behaviour of this adult was to very studiously ignore it. My mentality was that I was trapped with him and therefore the way to survive was to pretend that it was not happening.

Each incident seemed to me to be the last and I allowed it to stand somewhat in isolation as a freak. I could not put the sum of my experiences together and make from there the obvious judgements. I was just unable to collate all of this information in my brain because of my instinctive response to this threat. I should have immediately sought out a senior member of staff and had them use their adult resources to place me at a very safe distance from Hot Rod. But instead I just shut down around this behaviour and the result was that I stayed right at the epicentre of where it was most dangerous for me, like a dumb animal caught in the glare of the headlights.

This is sadly the experience of many children who are unable to find a safe space in which to be nurtured and to develop. It also shows the importance of finding a way to release trauma so that we do not wander blindly and repeatedly into situations which repeat the original trauma.

It is not until later that I was able to discuss these experiences with others. The emotions that would have been repressed at the time would begin to come up in me as I read articles or watched television shows about the abuse of young boys. I found myself enraged and wanting to take action. Over twenty years after the event I was releasing my state of mind which froze at that very moment when I was most afraid of Hot Rod. The feelings were intense. It was as if it had just happened. And yet it was a long time in the past.

Step 3: The 3rd Hypothesis

Trauma is the Enemy of Happiness

Your trauma mechanism and its constant cycle of freezing and refreezing leads you to a shrunken consciousness. This in turn makes life more threatening, which in turn lowers your threshold to what you find traumatic. If you are already on edge because life itself seems so full of threats, then the smallest thing can become traumatising. And so starts a downward spiral. The trauma that began in the earliest part of your childhood starts a chain reaction that builds on your stored experiences of trauma, while your conscious mind defeats the efforts of your mind-body system to resolve that trauma.

The effect of this trauma is to shrink your conscious mind away from the original state of intuitive awareness that you would have had as an infant. The further away from this state that you get, the more and more frightening the world seems to be. There becomes no counterbalance to the threats of life, no deeper connection to set against the constant vigilance of the evolved survivalist mind. There is no trust in the wisdom of creation, just a terror of surviving its manifestation. There is no faith in anything beyond your present comprehension. And without this, without any of the higher functions of the mind to set against the difficult business of mundane survival, life becomes constantly terrifying and beyond comprehension: routinely traumatising until you no longer notice it at all. Your fear of death becomes so commonplace it recedes into the background. You develop into a permanently traumatised state of existence and constantly live as if in a dream.

Your traumatised state is so thorough that life is filtered constantly through it, and you don't really see anything clearly any more. You just concentrate on the world in front of your face. You become a beast moving joylessly from task to task, hoping at the very worst just to survive and at the very best just to get on a little further with your nearsighted ambitions. You've lost the whole point of life: the wider vision of the vast complexities and unimaginable beauty of living.

You become the rat in the rat race, scurrying along hoping to come out a little bit ahead of the rat next to you. Trauma has reduced your conscious mind to the smallest component of your reality. You've lost touch with all that is magical in yourself, consigning it to nothing but fable and myth. The rest of your mind remains hidden in the vast field of what is left unconscious.

This makes it harder and harder for you to experience life without trauma, and so you end up in a rut, living without any true authentic connection to yourself while your conscious mind is working overtime to preserve your trauma. You don't allow the emotions that resolve it to emerge because they don't make sense, and what doesn't make sense scares you.

That's why you are so frustrated. That's why things don't work out. That's why you can't find meaning in your life. That's why relationships are so difficult. That's why you don't know what to do any more. That's what's wrong with you.

Exercise 3

What did you repress?

Write a list of events in your life that you may be able to recognise as having had a traumatising effect on you. There may be many similarities with the exercise in Step One but things that traumatise us are not always the same as things that we survive. They tend to be more specific, almost microscopic in tone and quality. It is a moment rather than a general situation. You might survive a hurricane, but be traumatised when the roof blew off your house.

Again use a timeline and just put down anything that may or may not be relevant. Beware though! Traumatic events are things we try to forget or deny. If you are in any doubt about including something, do so. Like this:

12 years old	*Beaten by Hot Rod*
12 years old	*Stalked by Hot Rod in my dormitory house*

and so on until you feel that you have it all down on paper. Now you are going to try to associate some emotions with these events. It won't be easy since these feelings were repressed at the time (that's what trauma is). But nonetheless just write down anything that comes to mind. Like this:

12 years old	*Repressed angry violent defence from this assault*
12 years old	*Repressed fear of sexual predator and shut down my recognition of what was happening*

Now look through the list of what you have repressed in order to try to cope emotionally at those moments. Take it slowly and get as familiar as you can with this list. The next step is to try to see if you can associate these feelings with anything else. They will inevitably re-emerge and this is your opportunity to try to see where: perhaps in relationships, or the workplace, or on your own.

We usually repress these feelings time and time again. As a result the incidents that led to them often re-occur in different shades of reality. See if you can find any patterns in your list of recurring events, emotions or themes. Get to know these off by heart.

Finally, just think about where these patterns find a place to be expressed in the here and now. You should find that, having identified them correctly from the past, the present doesn't feel so loaded. Remember this when you next encounter them. Also remember this for Step Four where you will learn to give this process a name: projection.

Revision

Steps One, Two and Three

These first three chapters and their hypotheses introduce the fundamental dynamic of the cyclical process of the conscious mind's relationship with the unconscious mind. These two opposite mental attributes are stuck in a vicious cycle unable to move on from life's events in the simple linear way that the gazelle's nervous system would.

The Vicious Circle of Life, Trauma, the Conscious and Unconscious Minds

From birth onwards, you are faced with the external reality of life and death situations. You respond to them in the only way that would be consistent with your evolutionary survival.

You prioritise Survival over Happiness

You use the mechanism of trauma to remain functional and to survive a threat. When the crisis is over, trauma will begin to thaw and the frozen emotions will be re-experienced. Your conscious mind observes these emotions. The conscious mind can see no cause for these emotions. Therefore, the conscious mind cannot explain them. The unexplained is perceived as a threat to survival. The conscious mind must respond because:

Consciousness is the Tool of Survival

The possible responses are to fight, flee or freeze. The conscious mind does all three. It represses the emotion. It blocks it with logic, with chemicals or with trauma. The e-motion can not move out. Some time later another new attempt to release the trauma is instigated by your unconscious mind which knows that:

Trauma is the Enemy of Happiness

Your wise unconscious mind tries to increase happiness by releasing trauma. The frozen emotions will be re-experienced. Your conscious mind observes these emotions. The conscious mind can see no cause for these emotions. Therefore, the conscious mind cannot explain them. The unexplained is perceived as a possible threat to survival. The conscious mind must respond because:

Consciousness is the Tool of Survival

The possible responses are to fight, flee or freeze. The conscious mind does all three. It represses the emotion. It blocks it with logic, with chemicals or with trauma. The e-motion cannot move out. Trauma is not released. Happiness does not increase. The conscious mind has reminded you that:

You prioritise Survival over Happiness

This cycle happens to you all the time. It's the reason why you are so rarely happy. You shut the door firmly on the direct efforts of your unconscious mind to resolve your trauma and to increase your happiness.

As a result, the unconscious mind has had to adapt and become more cunning; and it has developed a strategy to overcome these strong conscious defences. It is called projection and it is the subject of Step Four.

Q&A

From the wwwyou?forum. You can see the original text and ask questions at whatswrongwithyou.com.

Drifting

Posted by: bluesky Jul 31 2004, 06:46 AM

I don't know where to start with this one. I have no sense of enjoyment in my life and frequent periods where I wonder about the point of it all. I do have problems with my sense of self and frequently feel "incomplete" and without a foundation.

I'm 39, never had a relationship and am still a virgin. I have something called vaginismus, which means that sex is painful. I've had a variety of counselling and therapies, but the real issue is trust ultimately. I had shamanic healing last year and healer stated that I'd been raped in a previous life. This made perfect sense to me, even as a young child (7-8), I was scared of sex and being sexually assaulted.

I lived in London for a number of years and then went travelling. On my return I continued letting my flat, until it became a burden (problems with tenants) and decided to sell it, moved back to the family home to start a business.

This is all surface stuff really. The core of it is that I've been at home for a number of years now with my mother (my father lived abroad for a long time – they were only geographically separated, not legally – it's a bit complex). For the past 10 months, my mother joined him and now he's coming back because he has been ill.

I have three elder brothers, the youngest of whom was mentally ill for a long time. My other two brothers are married and thriving. I'm the youngest and the only daughter.

When I moved back home initially, it was with some relief. I no longer enjoyed living in London and began to feel disconnected. What I didn't realise is how this disconnection has been so much a part of my life. When I first moved to London, I had lots of friends, active social life – even if relationships were difficult. But as time moved on, friends paired off, I became increasingly isolated. This wasn't helped by buying a flat in an area I didn't really like.

But actually, I've felt disconnected all my life. I was always overprotected as a child, very sensitive (my two elder brothers were outgoing) and often felt like an only child. I never felt listened to or understood and there was some sex play between myself and my second brother (I don't know if it is abuse). I've often found it hard to be myself with others. My family was judgemental and because I was sensitive I often withdrew into myself. Even at the age of 10/11 I used to cry myself to sleep for reasons even now it's hard to articulate.

But more than ever I feel as though I've lost my identity. I didn't like the area I grew up in, have no good memories of it, but feel like I've returned to my jailor! Even though it was my choice, I have no home of my own, no boyfriend, children, few friends (and most of the ones I have are married with children). There are times when, in a strange way, this feels like a liberation.

But now, I'm now terrified of becoming carer to my parents and any chance of me being anything more than a poor spinster is lost. There are times when I feel lost in the firmament, wondering around like a lonely star. I don't feel emotionally robust or able to connect with others the way I used or don't even feel interested. I always feel disappointed and let down by people – sometimes with good reason, other times not.

As a child I felt that my problems didn't matter and as an adult, feel that the same is true. Although I can articulate the sense of hopelessness and despair – it isn't really understood, not within the family setting anyway. I'm happiest away from my home environment, where I'm not just a sister, a daughter – the "nice Girl" (yuk!) – but now hardly have the motivation to travel or meet new people, which I used to love doing.

Financially, I've made some big errors and I'm also aware of how my options are becoming increasingly limited. Because of fear and desperation, I've spent more money in the business without getting a return. I also know that unless I get more emotional stability, I don't really have a business. I feel as though my life is going downhill, and everything I do just drives me into a bigger, deeper hole.

I do exercise, have just stopped smoking, eat quite healthily, meditate. But I haven't been sleeping recently, which has a big effect on me, as I become more prone to depression. I've always had a sense that I could be better than where I am. I know that I'm attractive, that I could make a success of the business and have fulfilling relationships, but I'm scared to. I read a post where Ben said that it's hard to express yourself fully, if you feel that you don't have an emotional safety net and that's so true.

I often feel myself going into "nice girl" mode and not expressing myself fully – I guess because my sensitivities were often ignored or dismissed. Anger (for a woman) was not encouraged – "you mustn't be angry" I was told. Now I'm trying to be more emotionally honest with myself and other people, but it's hard not to revert back to my default position. Ultimately, I've always felt alone and unsupported, even though on the surface, this doesn't seem to be the case. I guess what I mean is that I want understanding. I seem to be able to give it – but not receive it. I've become less giving in lots of ways, because I feel as though I'm running on empty.

This post feels all over the place, a bit like me. In the past week (due to not sleeping well, stopping smoking, hormonal stuff) have felt quite crazy emotionally, continually crying, whacking cushions against the wall, all the rage and anger from my past resurfacing. I did consider suicide. In fact occasional thoughts of suicide have been recurring for the past 15 – 20 years. The only good thing was that I was honest about my feelings at the Stop Smoking clinic – before I would have kept this in. And it was reassuring to know that I wouldn't be judged for having these emotions.

I guess that I wanted to vent and put my anxieties down – not sure where to go from here. I've seen counsellors, therapists – have tried practically everything going – but in the end I just feel lonelier, more disconnected and unable to escape from the family claws.

Posted by: benjaminfry Jul 31 2004, 05:37 PM

Your post isn't actually all over the place. It is a very good and complete summary of what you need to look at to understand what's wrong with you. I'm going to explain this to you from a very objective point of view (from which we can notice what is happening unconsciously).

Your life has moved forward and then backwards. You grew up, became an adult and then at a point where other adults continued to move forwards, you selected a reverse gear, starting probably when you went travelling (a bit like slipping into neutral before reverse). You don't identify your age at this point, but I suspect that it coincided with the development of deeper longer-lasting relationships among your peer group. It seems that this may be where you begun to get stuck and to wonder why.

From there you life has moved backwards. You have sold your property and returned to where you came from, both physically and emotionally by going back to your parents' home. You have retreated away from the territory of forming an adult relationship of your own and returned to your position as a child. There must be a reason for this – at least unconsciously. And I think your post gives enough material to speculate on that reason.

You mention that there was sex play between you and your brother but question whether or not is was "abuse". I'd encourage you not to think of labels or blame, but instead to try to recall the effect that this had on you. Sexual abuse in childhood is deeply traumatic. It is often linked with serious dissociation since this is the only way that a child can escape the invasion of their body. You give many details in your post, but are vague about this one vital central element. That is a clear sign that you really don't want to think about it. However, your retreat from adult relationships with men and the return back to the family home suggests that your unconscious really does need you to return to it.

An unconscious trauma can often give a clue of its repression through the body. In your case, you identify vaginismus as a persistent disease in your life. There is a clear connection here between childhood sexual abuse and the manifestation of a symptom that makes having sex "painful". I'm not saying that it isn't real or actually painful, but I think there is a deeper pain here around the issue of sex and your vagina. I'd be prepared to gamble a speculation that the sex play with your brother involved vaginal penetration which you had very mixed feelings about. How might this also have affected your brother? Is this the same brother that has been mentally ill?

We can also take this a layer further. It may well be that you were raped in a previous life (I don't pretend to know either way). If so, then you have moved through your incarnations in exactly the way that reincarnation philosophies describe. You chose a new life in which you would be able to replay the psychological (or karmic) issues that remained unsolved from your previous one. This illustrates how according to one school of thought, it is not just this life in which we repeat situations to try to find some healing, but we could also be playing out this drama over and over again in sequential incarnated lives.

I note that you have tried many ways to help yourself and already practice a healthy lifestyle. Putting all of this together leads me to one conclusion: that the healing that you need will be found in your family. I think that you and your brother need to talk about what happened in your childhood. If you can do this with an awareness of your combined innocence at the time and do so without "blame", it could be hugely healing for both of you. You may also need to talk to your parents about this too so that they can better understand their whole family.

I think you may have been longing to do this emotional housekeeping ever since the prospect of needing a serious relationship came onto the horizon. The opposite of doing so is to be the "nice girl", but that just leaves you empty and absent. When we don't do what we must, we really can't do anything. I'm not surprised therefore that your business is in trouble. Until you engage with what you need to in order to properly separate from your family, you will probably just become more and more lost within it.

I have seen siblings bringing up very difficult issues such as this from the past. The years of distance can be rolled back in a few seconds and the mutual relief can be extraordinary. You may however wish to have some help with this. Sexual issues are very powerful and families unfortunately have a habit of rejecting both the truth and anyone who wants to say it; sometimes. There are other families though where these things can be done very well. You might think about getting a family counsellor to help you to air this issue. This would make it safer for you and probably easier for your family.

If you would like to make a start by explaining more clearly what actually happened with your brother here, then please do.

Posted by: bluesky Jul 31 2004, 06:34 PM

Dear Ben

Thank you for your response. I had realised that my life went downhill after I went travelling, but didn't realise so graphically. I was 34 when I went. I had actually wanted to go for about 10 years, but this was the time I summoned up the courage to do so (after several mini meltdowns). I have always been a late developer – I think that I wait for things to get too bad before I can make changes. I blossom when I intuitively make changes.

As for the sexual abuse. I don't remember vaginal penetration – I guess you'd call it heavy petting – I was about 9, he was 13. I do remember feeling very highly sexed as a child and at the time, felt that I enjoyed it – but it is a family secret and one which is highly charged.

As for the brother – well, it's the brother who is thriving. Married, now living in New York with a high powered job. I often feel that he's "stolen" my light away. As for discussing it.................it seems damn near impossible, our family would shun away from anything like this, I'd be the scapegoat (only last year when I had a disagreement with my mother, she said that "I wasn't right (mentally), something was wrong with me") and life would become damn well near impossible.

I can't imagine the havoc it would wreak – but I feel I would be vilified – and have no support net. I used to get the most awful depressions and suicidal compulsions in London – which no one knew about and when I did mention it to my mother, she said: "well, I never saw it" – therefore, it means nothing. I know that you're right about talking within the family – but being within this, I just can't see it happening without me falling apart completely – which may be what I need...........

It may sound strange, but I've often wanted to have a nervous breakdown – to clear the air, to fragment, so that I can build my true identity – I've come close, but never enough. But then I've always been afraid that I'd be overprotected or shunned, or dismissed and never recover.

I've just had a thought. I plan to visit my brother in New York in Sept/Oct and maybe this would be an opportunity to discuss it – but I do wonder – it'd be on semi neutral territory – but...........I still think I'd be dismissed and rejected – he'd probably go into denial.

The thought terrifies me but I know I need to move on. As for my parents....well bearing in mind what my mother said over a relatively minor disagreement, I dread to think what her response would be. They understand my brother's mental illness, because it wasn't "his fault". But they think that any emotional pain I feel is "my fault", which only causes me more emotional pain. As a family, we're completely emotionally illiterate and barbaric at times.

At times, I feel that I want to annihilate my whole family – everyone of them, the anger is so intense. Not in a physical way, but emotionally, psychically. I think that I need a safe space, maybe I can ask a friend if I can stay with her for a while. I definitely feel the need to leave – because I can't bear being with them – it's driving me insane.

I once had a dream several years ago, all of us were going into the family home, and I was being stabbed in the throat by an unknown assailant. My family just walked by and went into the house, I felt that I was screaming and no one heard me. That seems to say it all to me.

Maybe my father coming back is the impetus I need to confront him (there was some physicality here too, which is hard to explain and define). My relationship with my dad is difficult. As far as I'm concerned, I've never really had a relationship with him. He's always been there, but emotionally remote.

As I'm writing this now, tears are flowing from my eyes. I feel so scared, so very scared and alone.

Posted by: benjaminfry Jul 31 2004, 08:49 PM

You articulate quite well why just existing is so hard for you. It seems quite vital to your life and health that you move on from being the family's emotional dustbin. I suspect that is why you have moved back. So that you can find the impetus to take this step.

It's a really hard place to be in when you feel that you either lose yourself or your family. There's no easy answer and certainly without a network of support its very hard to take that gamble. You say that you trust your intuition and I think that your idea to talk to your brother may be a good one. He is on some stable ground himself and as long as you present the subject without blame (after all he was a child too) then perhaps you could get a breakthrough for each other.

I hope you don't find this invasive, but given your physical symptoms and lack of adult sexual history, I think you should try to be specific about what happened with your brother and particularly with your father. I sense a reluctance to engage with the detail which suggests a possibility of deep trauma there. This may explain your lack of an adult sex life. I understand that what happened with your father is hard to explain or define, but perhaps you can give a subjective account.

Another thought I had was that perhaps you accumulated terrible unconscious guilt about enjoying the sexual interaction with your brother. Perhaps you had sensations and desires in the vagina that you thought were wicked. This could explain the development of sexual difficulties both physically and mentally in later life; you would be unconsciously punishing and trying to rid yourself of this troublesome organ. Sexual feelings often result in guilt when not supported by society norms. Certainly at that age you would have been very confused.

Your family are unfortunately an emotional prison for you. I'm glad you've been crying. That's probably one millionth of what you need to do to recover your true self. This may be very hard to achieve at your parent's home, but clearly you are there for a reason, and if you'd like to rehearse that reason here, please do.

Posted by: bluesky Aug 1 2004, 10:57 AM

Dear Ben

I seemed to have been crying all this week – feeling up and down, emotional and angry. But I've also been crying "secret tears" for much of my adult life – when there were things that I just couldn't express, especially in front of others.

My father had left to move abroad and then I moved back into the family home. I didn't plan it this way. I wanted to leave London and go travelling – and needed to let my flat. 5 years on, my father is coming back and I feel that it's time to leave – there seems to be a kind of synchronicity in this.

I began thinking of ways in which I could scale down the business and associated costs. I've put on hold plans I had to develop the business further – will aim to keep it at very much a holding level – there's more important stuff to do. I've also begun to detach myself from my home emotionally. Of course, it's never really been my home, having been associated with too many negative memories.

I also spoke to a friend, who can offer me a "safe haven", if I need to go away for any length of time.

At times I feel like an adolescent, which isn't surprising, as I never went through the adolescent rebellious stage – so I'm 39, going on 14 at times. I look younger than what I am as well, so when it comes to relating to people, feel neither fish nor fowl. I have an age and life experience of a sort, but not the kind of life experience that defines and has shaped people of my age. Although looking at people around me, I wonder if we ever truly grow up, so much of our behaviour, even in adulthood, you can see the origins of the children we once were. But I'm digressing here.

So what is this leading to............in a way I feel it's about gathering the strength and courage to do what needs to be done to strengthen and bolster my courage. It's an exit strategy, I guess.

Re: the abuse/sex play with my brother and father. I really don't feel that I can mention it publicly, or at least describe it – or not yet. But I am getting there, I feel – it's taken me a lot just to get this far. I realise that not doing so is probably contributing to ongoing trauma and disassociation (I also remember stuff about my mother too – it's all coming out of the woodwork now!). I was going to write that I could respond to you privately, but that would lose the point. But the more I write, the more things come clearly to me – so I feel that it will come in time.

5 mins later...........

Maybe the time is now.

My brother and I used to indulge in heavy petting. I don't remember any play re: my vagina, but I certainly remember touching his genitals – so I guess he must have touched mine, sucking my fledgling breasts, french kissing and so on. I don't remember if there was any actual oral sex, but do remember kissing his genitals. This seemed to be fuelled by curiosity and as well as emerging sexual feelings. This took place over a period of about two years, I think – from about 9 – 11. I remember thinking that our parents shouldn't know about this. It felt (and was) clandestine. But I did enjoy it. I find it hard to think of this as abuse, as I was a willing partner. Also he was 13/14 at the time – not an adult, but he was older. But I guess it was inappropriate and obviously been a big influence on the way that I feel now and my lack of sexual experiences and relationships to date.

In fact as a child, I was highly sexual, by which I mean that I had and recognised that I had very strong sexual feelings. In my oldest brother's bedroom, he had a selection of soft porn magazines which I used to read. I got my sex education from there. Like many parents, my parents weren't too hot on the sex education stuff. I got a sentence from my mum about how children were made after I got a dirty phone call (at 11). What an "in" that was!

I used to fantasise a lot even then and still do now. I was also very curious, I put a button in my vagina, when I was about 8 just to see where it would go. There was a lot of mirth in our family about that! I can't remember though who found it or how it got out, probably my mum.

So it's no coincidence that this brother is the one who sees me more as a sexual being. I also think he sees more of my potential as well. I once put an ad in Time Out for a partner several years ago. It was him I invited to see the responses and check through them – we had quite a fun time doing that. The rest of my family (with the exception of my mum, occasionally and with disastrous effect) ignore the fact that I haven't had a relationship worth writing home about. There were times when he tried to set me up with one of his friends. I was too scared because I wanted to meet someone not connected with the family – all those associations. Although I quite liked the guy.

My sister in law once said that they discussed why I hadn't

had a boyfriend and came to the conclusion that I wasn't interested. I got annoyed when she told me this, but at least she told me. It was the wrong conclusion and I didn't have the heart to tell them the truth (I didn't really know it myself at the time).

But also he sees more of my potential. I think he often wonders what I'm still doing in the family home, (he's never explicit about it, but I sense it) in a way that my other brothers do not. I do identify more with him in lots of ways. I see my other brothers as being rather safe and staid. He's more of a risk taker and I see that he probably enjoys life to a greater degree than the rest of us. He certainly has a broader life, it's more expansive. In his drive and motivation, I do see a lot of myself – a part of me that hasn't been truly realised or acknowledged.

My father........this is a bit hazy. My mother used to work nights as a nurse. So my dad used to sleep alone at night. Here I'd better explain that we grew up in a three bedroom terraced home. It's a very small house. My two youngest brothers shared one bedroom and the eldest brother had the other. I shared a bedroom with my parents till I was about 9/10. For a while all three of my brothers shared one bedroom, before my eldest brother bought a house. None of the bedrooms are very big. Looking at the house now, I wonder how we all stayed together. It seems impossible. I think that I spent a lot of the time in my bedroom, trying to escape the crampedness and chaos. So one of my biggest fantasies is of space. I'm very territorial. Because my boundaries have been breached so often.

So, my mother is on nights and so I'm sleeping with my dad. Now as I'm writing this, it feels kinda weird – but we were short on space, I guess I'm trying to justify this. I don't remember any explicit sexual activity – but I used to kiss his backside gently (he had his pyjamas on) and that was about it. He used to pretend that he was asleep, but I knew that he wasn't. He never suggested that this was inappropriate and that I shouldn't have done it. And that is all I remember, I honestly don't remember any more activity than that. It could be that I don't want to remember – but as I'm replaying these scenes in my head again, I honestly don't remember.

My relationship with my dad is a strange one. He is emotionally illiterate and lacks social skills. Even when he was abroad, he lived a very isolated life. Now I realise that he used to suffer from depression. I can only think of my dad in two ways: brooding, depressive and angry. There never seemed to be any in-between. My mum confirmed this, she said that he used to brood on things and she'd ask what she'd done wrong, but he'd never tell her.

I didn't think that there was much joy in his life. I feel that he did what he had to do in raising his family, but he never took much interest in our social/emotional development – only in getting a good education. I really suffered from that. My brothers seemed to cope much better with this lack of interest. He was very much the practical dad, giving me lifts to college, helping to decorate my flat. But also the stern father as well. I don't think we've ever had a conversation that really meant anything to me.

It's odd but out of the four of us, my eldest brother and youngest brother (with the mental illness) missed my dad the most when he left. My second brother (the New Yorker) and me, I don't feel we did. In fact, I think my mother blossomed when he left. We completely revamped the house, which my dad had neglected for years. And she really came into her own, as an independent woman. She found out what her tastes were. That's not unusual, especially for many women of her generation.

I'll also point out that I'm from an immigrant family and that is obviously a big influence. Although we had family around when we were growing up (had an Auntie who lived up the road). It's always difficult trying to establish yourself as a first generation. My parents didn't have support from their parents. By the time they moved to England, only my maternal grandmother was alive. My parents weren't the kind to think about social and emotional development. I don't think that it's purely cultural either. But everything was about education, education, education.

The other stuff of life didn't seem to be so important. Money was tight (although I never recognised it at the time) and life, in lots of ways, was fairly functional. Their priority was trying to survive and raise their kids in a sometimes hostile and discriminatory atmosphere. As a result, I'm completely the opposite. I have a highly tuned aesthetic sense and hate the thought of life being lived on purely a functional level.

I often felt that my mum had been denied or had denied herself the chance of a happier life. My dad was not an alcoholic, wife beater, gambler. He was just emotionally absent. He rarely socialised so my parents rarely went out, he was happy just to read the papers, do the gardening and watch TV. My mother is or was more naturally outgoing, but didn't really have many friends that she would socialise with. The more I think about it, the more I realised how isolated as a whole our family has tended to be.

As for my mum. Well, it's hard to know how to explain this, but at about the same age 7-9 (?), when I was getting ready for school. My mum used to wash me "down there", quite roughly. She had this thing about making sure everything was clean (still does, very houseproud). It wasn't overtly sexual, in the way my brother and father was, but did make me associate my genitals, and especially my vagina with pain and not pleasure. I also remember that I was feeding from a bottle when I was 4! It was my second brother, who told my mum that I was too old to still be using a bottle.

And so she stopped. I'm not sure what was going on for her

(she also used to wipe my bottom when I was way too old for her to continue to keep doing so). I think that she wanted to keep me as a child. Maybe it was her own powerlessness within the marriage (I often don't think that my dad treated her very well, he was quite mean with money and I think with his emotions). I was very, very overprotected and have always been trapped by feelings of powerlessness in my life. And hence the emotional dustbin aspect. People always feel that they can talk to me, even strangers, particularly strangers. At first I got flattered, now I just get annoyed, it's like l have this vibe which makes me seem all warm and understanding – but rarely do I get this in return.

For a long time, I was scared of men. Scared of the power, the freedom, their physical strength. I was taught to acquiesce to my brothers. I was scared of getting involved and went all out to become Miss Independent – covering up my vulnerability and needs, because I felt that they couldn't be met, but in the end, the needs and desires, get bigger and bigger and it becomes an aching chasm. The centre caves in eventually, hence the depressions.

Now I've written all this, I feel a sense of relief, but also very strange and I'm hesitating about pressing the reply button. But just fuck it, I'm sick and tired of feeling sick and tired, acknowledging and accepting my truth will set me free.

Posted by: benjaminfry Aug 1 2004, 04:12 PM

I'm so glad you did just fuck it and press the button. Your post is so touching, eloquent and intelligent. I can see you perhaps one day writing about these issues. I look forward to seeing "Just fuck it and press the button" on the bookshop shelves one day! It perfectly sums up where you are in your process right now and I hope that this little exercise in the forum has reinforced your courage to deal with these issues.

There are many complexities with issues of sexuality from childhood. One is the controversy over "recovered memories". This is alleged to happen when a therapist repeatedly suggests that sexual abuse may have taken place and the client agrees. It is true that clients will often try (unconsciously) to please their therapists and this could be a reason for the confusion here. Hang on tight to your version of reality. Don't worry about labels. Just do what you have to do to get the facts straight in your own mind. Writing them down is a great way to start.

Another complexity here is your ethnic origin. It has been recognised by the mostly white community of therapists that, particularly with sexual issues, cultural differences can lead to emotional complexities that are hard to understand across this racial border. You may need to bear this in mind when trying to explain your background to others.

There are a multitude of issues which related to your family here, but because you started your question by flagging your virginity and genital health problems, I suspect that you are now at a cross-roads of bringing the dark sexual secrets of your family out into the light. I don't think that you need to worry too much about what counts as what, but instead just focus on recovering your emotions from these difficult episodes.

Certainly though, it is clear that what happened between you and your brother was incestuous. That is just a definition of the word. Generally speaking, anyone who has been in an incestuous relationship is at risk from psychological problems associated with sexual abuse. This doesn't make your brother necessarily an abuser or abusive. But it is just the category that these issues may fall into.

It certainly seems as if sexual issues were too much, too strong and too early for you. On top of this your mother seems to have given you the message that sex was dirty and not respected your body. Putting this together with perhaps a natural, healthy interest in sex may have been a powder keg. I suspect that you ran from your sexuality at a young age, overwhelmed by guilt, shame and a feeling that it was dirty. This may be a psychosomatic reason for the vaginismus. You can recover from this and you are only 39 so it is well worth doing so. But in order to do so you will have to go through the middle of all of this. There is no way round it.

The crucial thing is that you find some support for your need to release all of this from within you. There are support groups for the survivors of incest and sexual abuse. There are also therapists that specialise in this area. There may even be ones from your ethnic group who can help you. Try contacting the UKCP for a list of suitable referrals.

Posted by: bluesky Aug 1 2004, 08:28 PM

Dear Ben

Thank you so much for all of your insight and understanding, but most importantly your compassion. It helps to feel accepted, especially when I've felt an ongoing sense of guilt and shame and airing a miniscule part of my story has been a first stage of clearing out the emotional baggage and clutter.

Funnily enough after sending off the post this morning, I went to the gym - which I love doing - and felt quite sexual - I felt that I was giving off something potent. For months (years?), my libido has been fairly dormant, but it feels as though it's returning, but what it's tied into is a sense of beginning to feel alive again more than anything else.

I actually left a part time job recently to (ostensibly) devote more time to my business; but things never work out the way you think they will. It turns out that the business I needed to pay attention to was myself.

Once again, many thanks.
Namaste.

FOUR

Projection

Projection. The result of the ignorance of the conscious mind. Choices, fate and destiny. The path of the wise unconscious mind.

Theory: Projection

So the conscious mind turns out not to be so great after all. Granted, it keeps us alive very satisfactorily, but it does so at a huge cost: imprisoned in a state of permanent trauma. In this state it is impossible to feel the happiness that life should automatically bring to us regardless of our circumstances. So we start to live a life that is based only on circumstances. Our aims become those of our basic survivalist instincts: to acquire more security and comfort around us. The part of us that remains miserable is rationalised to us by our conscious mind as unsatisfied with the extent to which we have gathered re-sources around ourselves. We deduce that if we become better provided for then our troubles will cease, and that happiness will then somehow miraculously ensue. Never mind that it is quite obvious that rich people are not necessarily happy.

Being miserable and rich is better than being miserable and poor. To be genuinely happy, however, is better than both. Then we wouldn't mind so much whether we were rich or poor. The mistake that we make is to believe in our conscious mind, and to rely only on the information that we are aware of in our conscious mind. If only we could see beyond that, into the wisdom of the part of our mind that we are not conscious of, then we could allow ourselves to be guided automatically to happiness.

So, since happiness is the obvious goal here, the question that needs to be addressed next is; how can we access our unconscious mind; how can we see it, listen to it and learn from it? Since it is defined as the part of our mind that we are not conscious of, it is clearly no use just trying to look at it with our conscious mind. That is self-evidently impossible.

We could engage in various ancient practices (many of which are connected with the various religions of this planet) to attempt to expand, or (they say) raise, the consciousness. However, this is the work of a lifetime and it's unlikely that you picked up this book to be told that everything will be just fine so long as you move to the Himalayas and chant eighteen hours a day for the next twenty years. Much as we would benefit from doing so, life has to go on. So instead we will need to understand what our unconscious mind gets up to when we are not looking, and to start to develop the awareness and experience to notice.

Our unconscious mind is far more powerful than we think. It is working all the time to progress our existence on this planet. It just doesn't see "progress" in the same light as our conscious mind. The part of our mind that we are conscious of tries to follow our conscious mind's resource based agenda. This might be a job, house, woman, man, school for the kids, new car, etc. However, our unconscious mind works towards a higher goal, with a higher function and a higher understanding of life's priorities. Our unconscious mind in its wisdom is trying to move us into a life of greater understanding and connection with our true selves and with our rightful place and function in this universe.

That's bad news for our plans for the new car. These other aspects of our journey through this life constitute what is often referred to as our "spiritual" journey, and it is not necessarily supposed to be a comfortable one. It may even be at great odds with our conscious efforts to ensure our survival and the survival of the next generation. It might not care about the new car. It might actually need us to experience the pain of not getting what we want for a while, or indeed perhaps for ever. And why? Why would a part of our own mind want us to suffer? It doesn't necessarily want us to suffer any more than we already have done, but it needs us to release the frozen emotions from the suffering that we have already accumulated in this life (and maybe even, some say, many more lives before).

The unconscious mind needs us to let go of the trauma that we have stored up in our mind-body system, and in order to help us to unfreeze that well of pain, it introduces us to experiences that can help to trigger this thaw. Unfortunately (as we have seen) the conscious mind resists this thaw, and so the cycle continues and the trauma is unresolved. As long as it remains unresolved, the unconscious processes in our mind that represent our true wisdom will guide our lives into places, situations and people that will help us to find a way to resolve this outstanding trauma. Unfortunately this is done by mimicking the original stimulus for the original traumatic feeling.

If we don't like the way our lives are, or the way that certain feelings, situations or even people seem to keep repeating themselves, then we are going to have to learn to quiet the influence of our conscious minds. We'll have to let the unconscious mind guide us into situations that will help us to release the emotions that we repress. If we don't, we will be depriving ourselves of our one real chance for automatic happiness.

We can observe the unconscious mind at work quite easily if we can become adept at noticing its effects. To do this we need to develop a very dispassionate, honest and clear view of what is actually happening in our lives: rather than what we think is happening, or what we would like to happen. Usually this is just too hard to do without a good deal of practice and help. For example, if we hated our father or mother, but married a man or woman who is a lot like him or her (and many people do), then we may find it too hard to recognise that our spouse, with whom we are due to spend the rest of our lives, has many similarities with the parent we spent most of our lives trying to escape. However, perhaps this would be less hard to bear if we could realise that we are to be congratulated for this choice. We have done well.

We might not be living in a Calvin Klein advert any more, but we would be enjoying the opportunity to resolve some of the trauma set up in our childhood by the difficult experiences that we may have had with our father or mother. Therefore by marrying someone who has similarities to our parents, we would be helping the project of our truly wise mind to thaw out some of our impacted trauma. We must ask ourselves why we were attracted to this man or woman in the first place. If we can do that, we can start to look at some of the delicate work of the brilliant unconscious mind.

There seem to be two components to attraction. First, there is the animal instinct to survive. This works well and its consequences are evidenced in glossy magazines where good-looking, healthy people look like they could breed forever. However, another dimension kicks in when we actually have to spend time with another human being for much longer than a photo shoot. There is an X-factor that is so hard to define in human attractions. It is what makes one person so attracted to someone whom a third person might find completely revolting. For those of us who won't be marrying supermodels, this is the dominant factor and therefore a very important one.

If we think carefully about this, the reason that we might be attracted to someone that another person does not find attractive can only be for two reasons; (a) that we simply desire different things, and/or (b) that we actually each see a different person standing before us. Both do happen, but they are connected in a much more subtle and interesting way than might at first be obvious.

One of the most important mechanisms of the unconscious mind is projection. This is a term that stems from the pioneering work of Sigmund Freud on the foundations of psychoanalysis, which today has developed into a multitude of healing processes, largely grouped together under the banner of psychotherapy. The identification of a projective mechanism of the mind goes back into history, myth and culture. Projection simply means the difference between what is actually there, and what our own mind sees to be there. It is most often used in relation to our reactions to other people.

When we relate to any other human being, we are inadvertently projecting on to them stuff that is actually coming out of our unconscious mind. This helps us with our unconscious mind's greater ambition of healing our unresolved trauma.

This might sound confusing. The idea that we are actually projecting out of ourselves some qualities on to another person perhaps doesn't quite do justice to the subtlety of the process. Really the way it works is more like a filter. It is a bit like the old saying that some people are looking at the world through rose-tinted spectacles. The rose tint filters everything they see, so that the world actually looks like a more charming place to live in than it really is.

Now imagine that from birth you had been surgically implanted with rose tinted corneas. As far as you would know the world really is rose tinted and really is a charming place to live in. You might find yourself disagreeing with others on the essential qualities of the world, and find it hard to understand how they could paint such a drab picture of their own environments when you were all looking at the same thing.

What if instead of using a tangible physical filter, such as a rose tinted spectacle, the effect that was causing this difference of perception was actually generated by us in a different way? Perhaps it was our own unconscious mind that was somehow throwing out onto the world this pink hue, projecting on to it our own version of reality. Our conscious mind would again observe a charming pink landscape and be similarly affected by it.

The difference in this latter example is that somehow it is our own mind that is both creating the distorting effect and then also observing, recording and validating it as actually real. That is the result of having our wise and subtle unconscious mind working in opposition to our more coarse and unsubtle conscious mind. This also gives us the clue to how we can begin to observe our own unconscious mind in action.

For example, we may dislike a person who is popular with others. It may be very hard for us to be able to understand why they see someone likable in a person that we see as being un-likeable. How could friends who otherwise have much in common disagree on something like this? The answer is that we are all seeing someone slightly different. For us, this person may have strong resonances with another person or situation from our past that was experienced by us as traumatic. It is useful for us to be able to project on to this new person the characteristics of the person in the past and the traumatic reactions that we had to this person. Thus when we experience this new person in the present, we simultaneously experience the other person in the past.

This sets up uncomfortable feelings as old emotions are thawed and start to try to be expressed. As we have seen, it is likely that we will repress these feelings again and simply find the whole process somewhat irritating, uncomfortable, unpleas-ant or downright maddening. We have all known someone who could just drive us mad for no particular reason, just by being there and opening their mouth. Did everyone else react the same way to them? Probably not. Therefore there was something particular, something unique, about the way that we were experiencing this person. That unique component was our projections, projected out on to them, and then observed and reacted to, as if that projection was real.

Projection may seem like science fiction. But it's not. It's science fact. It has been a central plank of the science of the mind for over a hundred years. What is extraordinary is how little awareness there is of it outside of the study of psychology and psychotherapy. Very knowledgeable, responsible and intelligent people take it very seriously indeed. They work with it daily. They research it, write about it, and help people to understand it. It is part of the basic fabric of their business of treating people with mental problems. And yet it remains a big mystery outside of the sphere of mental health professionals.

If you could absorb an understanding of the mechanism of projection, your own unconscious mind and the processes that you are yourself the unwitting cause of, then you could use this understanding to make your life a whole lot more bearable.

Case Study: Heather

I lay on the deck of a fifty meter motor-yacht in the Caribbean and watched the Sheik's Gulfstream jet fly low overhead waving its wings to us in a parting gesture. I had just arrived on that jet from London in the company of his wife and daughter. We were going for a cruise. After all it was Easter and the kids needed a holiday.

All was not exactly as it seemed however. The glamorous exterior belied a strife strewn reality below decks, a metaphor for exactly the kind of person that I had by then become. The "kids" were not kids anymore. We were in a teenage wilderness marooned between childhood and adulthood, between school and university. I was on my "gap" year and it was the year in which I was finally going to be reintroduced to the memory of my mother.

After leaving school I had reconnected with a previous girlfriend following the summer holidays. We had been each others' first serious relationship for nearly a year in our teens. Heather had come up to live and work in London after school and somehow the suggestion was made that she could stay in a vacant flat below our house that my parents had just bought. I suppose it was inevitable that we would find ourselves back together again. It was the age of sexual inquisitiveness and our arrangement was just too convenient. She had a boyfriend at the time and I wasn't exactly looking to settle down, having just been recruited to be a male model in London, but we were irresistibly drawn to one another. I found in her a gentle, feminine comfort that I had clearly been missing for many years. It was intoxicating and addictive.

Not surprisingly perhaps for someone of that age, I lacked the skills and perhaps even the will to manage to have a serious relationship with her. I was frequently away on modelling trips or holidays and our paths and plans casually intertwined during much of the rest of the year. Our approach to contraception was perhaps naïve, perhaps irresponsible, but mainly the result of received wisdom. We were careful when we could be and tried to be as careful as we could when we couldn't. This was a pre-Aids era and education then was not what it is today.

In February I went to Milan for some work. Heather missed me and I was homesick despite my success there. As it happened, one of her best friends, Antonia, was also the best friend of the daughter of the a very rich Sheik with an English wife. They had some family connection and had been close since childhood. I had not met Princess Cassandra but was good friends with Antonia since we would frequently hang out as a gang. Cassandra had invited Antonia to visit her for some skiing in Zermatt where she was at school. Antonia suggested that Heather go with her and that I come over from Milan to meet up with them. It was a great plan and I was wildly enthusiastic about it. I had spent my recent summers in Corsica where this Sheik was a well known figure of great influence. To be welcomed into the inner sanctum of his family was an irresistible notion.

Work was a little slow, so I set off a few days early, kindly accommodated by my new hosts. There was only one problem. Heather's period was late. She had become increasingly concerned that she might be pregnant. I really had no idea how to react to this. I manifested this by simply ignoring it and setting off for Switzerland by train to see how much fun I could have. The scene that awaited me was dazzling. On my first evening there many of Cassandra's friends came round to her chalet and we were all served champagne cocktails by the butler. The boys were suave and urbane. The girls were sophisticated and generally beautiful. The world was their oyster and Zermatt was their playground.

One of the girls there caught my eye instantly and there was a story to go with it. Oleanda was the daughter of a billionaire and she had a "history" with Heather. There had been some issue with a mutual boyfriend and Heather had won. I knew instinctively, perhaps cruelly and calculatingly, that this young woman would be game for revenge. I had placed my mind in a bubble, like one of those Zermatt landscapes in a snowenclosed glass ball. This new stage had taken me over and I suppose I wanted it to become the limit of my reality. I managed to blind myself to the fact that Heather was arriving in a few days and that she was probably pregnant. It didn't take Oleanda and me long to get together. There was nothing much to do but fine alcohol, parties, skiing and guest bedrooms. However, it certainly upped the ante for Heather's arrival. After all, there was already enough tension between these two.

Heather arrived on the train with Antonia. The first thing she said to me was that she was pregnant. After that we were bundled into the chauffeur driven Mercedes jeep and we hardly had a moment alone until much later that night. The gang had gathered to welcome the new arrivals. I was sipping champagne cocktails between my recent conquest and the woman carrying my child. I was still only eighteen. I had exceeded my capacity to cope. I went into denial. The following long weekend was alternately extraordinarily difficult, fun, tense and drunk. Matters were complicated by the arrival of two extremely handsome French lads from Paris. Jean-Paul was inscrutably cool but Eric instantly fell in love with Heather. He was a phenomenal skier. I was not. He spoke French. I did not. He paid a lot of attention to her. I did not.

The climax of our stay was a night out in the club beneath the Palace hotel, the most glamorous and expensive spot in town. Eric made a pass at Heather on the dance floor. I fell drunkenly into the arms of yet another girl at the bar. It was not a big place but somehow we managed to ignore all of this. In the morning I made arrangements for Heather to collect some money from my bank in London on her return. She would have an abortion and I would pay. It seemed very much that the relationship was going from bad to worse. In any case, she was shortly to depart for a holiday with her parents to America and from there to travel with a friend up the East Coast of America "backpacking" through the Amtrak system. I knew I wouldn't be seeing her for months and we were preparing our goodbyes.

On top of this, I was now totally in denial about the pregnancy. I couldn't think about it. I just ignored it and hoped she would solve the problem for us. Neither of us told our families. That just didn't seem to be an option. We'd both grown up at boarding schools and I suppose learnt to deal with our own problems. We had the support of our friends and in many ways that was what we had come to know as the place to find help in crisis. However, in this instance what we needed was the wisdom and compassion of maturity to understand the significance of a pregnancy. I totally lacked either. Things might have gone smoothly to plan, in so much as an abortion ever could, but for the fact that upon our departure from Zermatt, Cassandra and her mother invited us to rejoin them shortly after for a cruise in the Caribbean: all of us.

Our automatic reaction was to accept (we were practiced spongers), despite the difficulties that this would cause. Heather was to spend the next two weeks on a family holiday in California, and this new plan would then bring her straight out to the Caribbean for another two weeks before going to meet up with her travelling companion in Florida. When was she going to have the abortion? She must have already been six weeks pregnant. But of course we had no experience or knowledge of these matters and little understanding of what a delay might mean. She decided to deal with it on her arrival in Florida. Meanwhile I returned to London. School was now out for Easter and as it happened, Oleanda's mother lived in London literally within view of my bedroom window. Our liaison there was inevitable.

I was inexplicably and irresistibly drawn to her, not so much out of our own sexual chemistry but more as a defence against the reality of what was happening with Heather. I remember taking Oleanda to a club where many of Heather's friends were. One of them knew her well enough to know about the baby. She took me to one side and just asked me what I thought I was doing. She reminded me that Heather was pregnant with my child and yet here I was partying with another woman in London. What was I doing? I simply had no answer. I had no idea. I didn't know. I really didn't know. I had disappeared into an emotional void and the only instinct that I had was to grab at uncomplicated female company.

It was a reaction that was to characterise my young adult life. I lacked the emotional apparatus to cope with the reality of my situation and found distraction from this in the superficial pleasures of a superficial liaison with a young woman in a superficial society. I went plastic. It was a coping mechanism. I knew that what I was doing was wrong, but it was all that I could do at the time. It was as if I lacked any ability to behave differently, like an addict.

Soon it was time to head off to the Caribbean. I left Oleanda in London and incredibly had already made plans for my next liaison in New York. I had met a girl, Rachel, on the beach at Christmas during a family holiday in Antigua and was fascinated by her tales of life in Manhattan. I had been attentive enough to her to get her to invite me to stay with her "anytime". The Sheik's plane was to stop at New York at the end of our holiday. I therefore took this opportunity to schedule my own arrival in the Big Apple. But first there was the small detail of two weeks about to be spent on a boat with Heather, who was pregnant, Antonia, who knew what I had been up to in England for the last two weeks, and Cassandra, who probably knew even more and liked it even less.

As we regrouped in St. Thomas, it rapidly became clear that this wasn't going to be a carefree cruise. There was the small matter of my behaviour over the last three weeks to be brought to account. Antonia wasn't going to be able to spend two weeks on a boat with Heather and not tell her what had been going on. She had however given me the opportunity to explain myself first. I had a guillotine dangling over my head. If I didn't tell her, the girls were going to. And with tensions thus delicately poised we set off on our superyacht from St. Thomas, the jet screaming home overhead, looking for our first sunset and martini.

With the distractions of outside life removed, my affections for Heather returned. With this came the awful realisation of how badly I had been behaving. I wasn't even sure now why I had been doing it. It was as if I had been in a trance. Ensconced here on this luxury gin palace, safe in her company, it seemed madness to want to be with anyone else. And now, just as I began to reconnect with my feelings for her, I was required to deliver to her the death blow to our relationship. In fact it may have only been because I knew that I had to tell her about Oleanda that I was prepared to feel the warmth and security of my connection to her. I'd been unable to appreciate these pleasures when they weren't under threat. Now they seemed the most important thing in the world to me. I prevaricated. I put off telling her. This boat was large but it was still just a boat, and a boat is no place to keep secrets.

Meekly, whimpishly and with great self pity I eventually came clean. Heather kicked me out of the room and I assumed that that would be that. I'd be stuck on a boat with her for the next ten days, adoring her but shunned and hated by her. However, about an hour later she came back to me. She was pregnant, not feeling well, far from home, about to embark on a journey through America, commencing with an unknown abortion. She just didn't have the heart to hate me yet. She had too much to deal with to be pushing me away. So we cried and stayed together. We focused our minds on being on holiday and let life be about the picture postcard illusion that betrayed the rotten reality of our situation.

Once again I dealt with separation badly. Heather went on from there to Florida where she met up with her travelling companion and together they went through the yellow pages to urgently find her an abortion clinic. I went onto New York with Cassandra and their jet. A limo took me from the tarmac at White Plains airport and drove me into Manhattan. I had left Heather to her fate at breakfast in Antigua and by tea time was being welcomed into the waiting arms of Rachel in her upper east-side apartment in New York.

I think that it was during that limo ride into Manhattan that I probably first truly lost my way in the midst of all that madness. I became a character in my own drama rather than a real human being. I had so much that I wanted to forget about. So much loss both past and present that needed to be abandoned. I used the surreal circumstances of my journey to allow my ego to make a journey of its own. I migrated from the reality of common human interaction into the illusion of superhuman invulnerability. Somewhere between the gin-palace, the Gulfstream jet, Heather left behind on the beach and Rachel welcoming me to the upper east side, I made a bargain with myself and it was not one that I was going to lose. I decided that I was special. That I was worth all this. That I was above other people. That I was cool. Alone finally for the first time in days, cocooned in the comforting limousine interior, I watched as the horizon swapped the flat suburbs for the awesome canyons of New York's jagged skyline.

I was being swept into the capital of the world, for the first time ever, on a wave of self-delusional hype, promotion and self-satisfaction, concealing my deepest, darkest feelings of rage, frustration, loss and despair. Nothing could have been more appropriate for Manhattan in the dying days of the eighties. We were both world beaters with nothing to fear, undermined by a grisly underworld of grime. It was a match made in hell and we fell for each other instantly, hard and with a passion.

I was a male model, in New York, young, good looking, English, rich, connected and unsupervised. Nothing in my short life had ever been so easy. I started to replicate my London life very quickly in New York. By day I would hang out with the rich kids on the upper east side. By night I would allow the modelling world to absorb me into its rich tapestry of parties and characters. There was also the odd moment spent working. I think I worked five days during the six weeks I was there. It paid for the entire trip. I was also able to access some of the other scenes in town through a friend from London who was now working for Vogue in New York. However, Catherine was also a friend of Heather's. Again I made no effort to disguise my situation. Again it was put to me that I was a disgrace. Again I had no defence. New York being what it was in those days, my bad behaviour was not enough reason to end a promising social liaison, and so Catherine and I remained friends. However, there was a clock that had just begun to tick, counting its way down to the resolution of this drama.

Heather's plan was to travel up from Florida slowly to New York. Her arrival was at least a month away and I had some plans of my own. I had hooked up in New York with a school friend. Alex was keen to go on from there to meet some more friends in India and finish our summer there. Travelling in the far cast was a gap year staple, and one that I had shunned in favour of the international glamour available to me through my modelling. However, things were getting too hot even for Mr. Cool to handle and India seemed to me to be an ideal escape from everything. Nonetheless something compelled me to stick around in New York to see how things would pan out. I'd like to think that it was out of a sense of duty, fairness, compassion or decency: an obligation to see Heather when she got to New York and to try to make things right between us. But the reality was that nothing was going to be alright and I was staying in town partly for the same reason that people can't look away from an impending car crash and partly frankly because of the women.

I'd met someone else I really liked in Manhattan, Abigail. But I was running out of favours in New York. Heather had accelerated her plans to arrive in town. Catherine was going to tell Heather about my affair with Rachel. Tickets had been booked to India from London and in the meantime Alex and I had nothing to do but wait. It was a toss up whether we'd be leaving to connect to our flights to India, or have to leave because there was nowhere left in town that we could go. That balance was severely tilted when Catherine told Heather what I had been doing a few days before her somewhat precipitous arrival in New York.

Heather had had enough. She refused to be drawn back into the lunacy of my behaviour and simply cut herself off from me. This had a predictable effect. I was now desperate to see her. I bombarded Catherine with pleas to intervene on my behalf. I couldn't cope with being denied. I had spent the last few weeks living in New York where every door would open to me if I just so much as looked at it. "No" wasn't a word I was used to any more. Finally I went to Catherine's office at Vogue and begged her to get Heather to see me. I don't remember what I said but it worked. We met up one afternoon under a cherry blossom tree in central park. It was really nice to see her. Somehow the last few months seemed to fade away and the genuinely supportive and loving connection that we'd first found together was briefly reinstated. However, despite us wishing that we could roll back the clock on a blanket of cherry blossom, the reality was that we had been damaged by the recent events. We both shared a pain that we longed to resolve but now that we were together sharing that experience merely amplified the pain, and that was something that I had not even begun to try to deal with.

I had a tried and tested method by now for dealing with this overload and it wasn't hard to find the opportunity to escape. I managed to see Abigail a few times. I well remember, just at the moment when we would have otherwise shared our first kiss at the end of long evening of electric and exciting chemistry, instead I found my lips telling her plainly that I already had two girlfriends within ten blocks of her home. She was polite but firm. She showed me the elevator.

I think that this was the beginning of the end for me. I

began to accept the insanity that had engulfed me since the first hint of Heather's pregnancy. I needed to straighten up the mess that I had made. I knew that I had to do some straight talking with Rachel and Heather. Rachel was relatively easy. It had not been a heavy romance and we'd clearly been drifting apart. Nonetheless she was relatively unimpressed. Her friend who I was staying with had a huge row with her mother about getting me out of her house. In the end I was given a few days to pack my bags. I had run out of favours and had nowhere else to go. Most people I knew in New York weren't speaking to me any more. Heather was soon added to that list. I had to be straight with her. I had realised that I couldn't have a relationship with her at that time. Even though I had been desperate to see her and delighted to find myself once again in her company, something else, something wild and ungovernable, was willing me to run as far away from her as I could. A profound discomfort was tearing me away from the soothing embrace that I had always longed for.

It made little sense to me at the time, but to her it was nothing other than the final insult. She had steeled herself to come to New York and to cope without me by ignoring me. I had begged her to see me and made my way back into her affections. Now I was withdrawing once again. With the stage thus set and New York turned from my fruit basket into a barren wasteland, Alex and I made our exit.

Understanding Why?

How many times did I reconnect with and then lose Heather? Isn't it true that each time I lost her I was devastated and yet it was entirely a separation of my own making? Did I not actually do everything I could to kill off our love? How similar this is to the original loss of my life where the first woman I ever loved actually did die. I repeated the scenario a number of times with Heather within the space of only a few months.

Consider what projections I was placing onto Heather. When I first met her she seemed to me to embody all that was warm, angelic, comforting, feminine and secure. She had been granted the mantle of my lost mother. The early stages of our love affair filled me up from within with a magic that I couldn't have ever remembered knowing. It was the echo of the unconditional love that my mother had been able to give to me during the few months that we had had together. Without Heather I felt listless, unable to imagine finding happiness and any satisfaction in life. There seemed little point in an existence that was not spent pursuing a love affair. That was my sole source of engagement.

I didn't understand then that I was using this projection onto otherwise what was a very nice, kind and pretty girl (but just, you understand, a girl) to create a perfect fit for the mother-shaped hole that gapped so yawningly in my mangled heart. Having recreated my mother in Heather's projection, my unconscious mind was trying to use that image to stimulate my recovery of my memory of my love for her and my devastation at her loss. Losing Heather became a cipher for the experience of losing my mother. It is important to understand that she was not the catalyst herself, but it was the projection that I had created and placed over her that was working on unearthing my lost trauma.

Why her, you might ask? Why not? Who knows? There are some of the mysteries of the universe that I am not privy to. However, I remember some time later when I was at Oxford that I hung a treasured photograph of my father and mother on the wall of my bedroom. It was taken of them by my uncle right after their engagement. My mother is radiant in it, and young, perhaps only twenty years old. I was struck as I hung it by a sudden similarity between her in that picture and Heather, who by that time was the same age. I actually thought to myself, "my God, I've been going out with my mom". At that instant, the picture fell off the wall. I guess even dead parents require a certain modicum of respect too.

Theory: Fate

Projection is a very powerful mechanism of the unconscious mind that directs us towards emotions which can help to resolve our trauma, but it is not the only mechanism of the unconscious. To be truly effective, it needs a partner in crime. The unconscious mind is also at work in the way that we manifest our free will: in the way that we make choices. This can been seen from the very broad to the very smallest detail. If we think about how many choices we make in a day, they run into the hundreds of thousands.

We might have really big choices to make, like whether or not to accept a new job or propose marriage, but while we are considering these choices we will be performing the normal mundane acts of living, such as getting up, getting dressed, eating breakfast etc. We make choices at every stage of this process. Our bodies don't just move about on their own. They require direction. It is in these many acts of choice that our unconscious mind has the opportunity once again to reveal itself and so influence us towards situations that will help us to resolve our trauma.

We often notice certain patterns in our life recurring. But we rarely accept responsibility for the fact that we chose for these things to happen. Most people see life as something that happens to them. This can be a starting point for bitterness and dissatisfaction. But worse, it can leave us feeling powerless against the overwhelming task of keeping the universe at bay while it buffers us with its tides of fortunes.

This is not necessary. If we review our lives, we can begin to understand that everything happened because we made a choice that led us towards that situation. This may be very hard to do if the situation is very extreme or random. For example, if you have suffered from a seemingly unrelated event, such as a tree falling on a car, then it is hard to see how this could have anything to do with you and the choices you have made. However, if you were driving at the time, then you were solely responsible for guiding the car to that exact spot at that exact time. If you were a passenger, then you can see that you chose at some point to get into that car. In other words no-one else made the choices that led to us being in that car at the time and place coincident with a falling tree.

It may seem absurd to suggest that someone would on purpose make choices that result in them driving under a falling tree, not least because they would have had no idea that the tree was falling in the first place. However, as we become more adept at understanding the true power of our minds, we may come to accept that the unconscious mind knows far more than we think: much more than we can possibly comprehend within the tiny confines of the conscious mind. It is in fact possible that the unconscious mind has all of this kind of information available to it. We may just be unaware of it in our conscious mind. Ironically, the unconscious mind may intuitively know exactly the consequence of every action (every cause and effect) that the conscious mind would struggle to understand and to predict. On this assumption, fate and circumstances can be reduced to the choices that we are making unconsciously.

It can be very hard for us to understand, let alone to accept, that we might be making unknown choices for ourselves, particularly when these choices seem to harm us or to stand in the way of us achieving what our conscious mind wants in life. However, we have to remember that the unconscious mind's agenda is not our survival and prosperity. It is to help us to resolve our trauma and thus to expand our conscious mind so that we can return to a state of automatic happiness.

Our unconscious mind knows better than our conscious mind how to make us happy in the long run. It knows how to guide us into a state of permanent happiness. It knows that this takes many years, perhaps even a lifetime (perhaps, some say, many lifetimes), and it's not looking for a quick fix. The conscious mind by contrast has now confused contentment with survival. It looks for ways to quickly make itself more likely to survive, and assumes that happiness will follow when more resources and power have been accumulated. Its base desires and short-term agenda are often in direct conflict with the wise guidance of the unconscious mind. That is why life can be so frustrating at times.

We have two parts of our own integrated mind-body system working in different and opposite ways to influence our lives in different directions. It's no wonder that we end up stuck. It's like having two powerful trucks trying to pull a vehicle out of the mud. It doesn't matter how strong they are if they are pulling in opposite directions. The net result of this is that they will expend an awful lot of energy and probably just end up back where they started. Remind you of anyone? Sure, things change. But they change slowly, and it often seems that however much we change our outside circumstances, the dissatisfied states of mind that we have carried with us for many years persist through these changes in circumstances, which we thought might have eased them.

Many people report that it is when life has brought them hardship and real difficulty that they grew emotionally, and thus ended up more stable and happy. The reality is that resources alone don't make you happy and it seems that the path to happiness can often lie through places of great suffering and pain. Nonetheless, we all orientate our conscious mind to the path of minimum suffering and pain; that's what survival is all about. What we can't seem to reconcile ourselves with is that survival doesn't make us happy. In fact, circumstances that actually threaten survival can often in the long run lead to a more balanced and contented state of mind.

This is where the unconscious mind does its best work. The choices that we have made which seem to us to have been unlucky, or unwise, or jinxed, or cursed, or just plain stupid, are most likely to have been the actions of our wise, unconscious mind hard at work, hidden away from our conscious mind. Rash decisions, moments of madness, acts of lunacy that we bitterly regret (anything that seems to be at odds with our calm, logical agenda of accumulating wealth, power, a mate, a better job or whatever satisfaction we crave) these are all choices made by us, and there must be a reason why we made these choices. We are not out-of-control automatons. We are brilliant minds in extraordinary bodies. When we did these things or made these choices, there was a reason. Something inside us caused these things to happen. There was a cause for the effect.

Our conscious mind may be terrified of this process because it doesn't understand it, and fears that it may threaten its own agenda of survival and prosperity. But nonetheless, whether we can bear it or not, the fact remains that everything that we have done in our lives we did for a reason, and when we can't understand how that could possibly be true, that's when we have the chance to notice the influence of our cunning unconscious mind at work.

We might fear it because we know it can ruin us, but the reality is that it can actually save us. It is our one chance to find real, lasting, automatic happiness.

Case Study: Heather regained

I left Manhattan for India via a few days in London. I'd been back home about ten minutes before my entire frame of reference seemed to shift to an entirely new perspective. Perhaps being back in the relative safely of my home environment allowed me to see things differently. It was as if a veil was lifted from my eyes. Probably for the first time since Heather had suggested that she might be pregnant, I saw the whole situation and my resultant behaviour with some objectivity. I knew immediately that I had behaved terribly and that I had treated her unforgivably. I still missed being with her in the innocent and happy way that we had known before, but I knew now that I had succeeded in doing everything that a man could ever do to push her away. But I didn't yet know why. All I knew was regret and confusion. I became terribly upset and depressed and left with Alex for India with the awful realisation that I was going to be very far away from where I should have been to attempt to make some retribution for my sins. India at that time was a country almost without any form of international telephone system outside of the main cities. I was not going to be able to make any dent in the apology I owed from there.

We met up with our old school friends and went on a dizzying journey with them through rural northern India. At first Alex and I were dispatched to Dharamsala where the Dalai Lama lived. I'd never previously heard of Tibet, but enjoyed the harmonious company of the many Tibetans that we encountered during our acclimatising stay there. From there we went to stay in a small house in the foothills of the Himalayas, high in the Kulu valley. We cooked our own meals and really just ran amok in the shadow of the snow dusted mountains. India had an intensity that was unimaginable to me before my arrival. I'd never been to the third world and didn't even really understand what it meant. The potent combination of crowded cities and a land so large, open and striking left my illusion of a firm grip on my reality dangling by a thread. I saw a new world in India and it made me not entirely sure where I stood in that world any more. We finished our journey staying on Srinagar lake in Kashmir, a giant basin on a high plateau, surrounded by the snow peaked caps of the Himalayas and terraced with houseboats left over from the days of the Raj. The lake had very few motorised craft in those days and passengers were ferried around in punt taxis. Perhaps as a result, the lake itself was unnaturally still.

That vision of the water at night reflecting the myriad of houseboats unseasonably adorned with Christmas fairy lights remains with me as the most beautiful landscape I have ever witnessed on my travels. The deep tranquillity of the water surrounded by the impassive mountain range is set as a backdrop to this remarkable man-made anachronism of Victorian pleasure barges. It is as whimsical and magical a combination of the sublime with the ridiculous as I could ever imagine. It took my breath away. I know it's a cliché, but India changed me. In a few short weeks I travelled so far away emotionally from where I was accustomed to hiding that I would find on my return to London that I would not be able entirely to go back. That was when I would first encounter the legacy in my life given to me by the love and loss of my long forgotten mother.

I returned once again to England and home. Somehow things looked very different to me. I had begun to get some perspective on my behaviour with Heather. I owed her a deep apology, but I also somehow wanted to persuade her that my actions had not been out of malice. It was a hard argument to try to make. I was aware that she too by then was back in England. It was clear though that she would not countenance any contact with me. However, we had many friends in common and such is the social structure of teenagers that it was inevitable that we would meet eventually. It happened in a London nightclub. I'd been there for a while and was a bit drunk. Someone told me that Heather was coming. When I saw her it was a shock. She'd cut her hair short and wore a new, tougher expression. The blond angel was gone. In her place had emerged a new, damaged version, rugged with lost innocence.

We spoke briefly. It wasn't successful. I tried to suggest that I'd never wanted to hurt her. It didn't go over too well with a slight slur. She left soon after. Some days later I spent the weekend with my parents at their country house. I felt lonely. I missed the closeness that I'd had with Heather and yet understood that I'd done everything I could to sabotage that. I was left wondering why. As I lay in bed that night, waiting for the comfort of sleep, I got my answer. I was quite suddenly overwhelmed by a terrible yearning for my mother. I'd not thought about her, much less spoken about her, throughout almost my entire remembered life. She was buried both literally and by the invention of our new perfect nuclear family history. Her existence had been consigned to the mythical borderlands of a reality that must have been, but now never was. But that night, for the first time, I remembered her.

It wasn't the memory of the mind, but a memory from deep inside my soul. I felt wracked with the grief of her loss and in an instant had an intuitive understanding of the genesis of my recent drama with Heather. I knew that I couldn't love Heather because I had so traumatically and tragically lost my mother. The repressed well of pain that had accumulated from my childhood and through all of these more recent experiences of love and loss opened, and the tears ran freely across my pillow. I tried to cry myself to sleep but the reservoir ran too deep, too long and too strong. I was alone with a new me, frightened, shattered by grief, terrified of a new understanding of my own capacities to destroy the one comfort that I had so long missed and now so dearly craved.

Somewhere between New York and India, Pandora's box had been opened. How I would come to miss those idle days before when its lid had been so firmly shut. I woke up to a new reality and a new genealogy. It was one that I knew wouldn't work with the family that we had become. It was a full ten years before these two competing versions of who my mother was would be able to be aired for discussion. For ten years fear kept me from mentioning my parents to my parents: such was the investment we had all made in the system of denial that had now burst for me in the watershed of that night. But first, fate had one more last trick to pay on me. It was time for the kids to go on holiday again.

It was the end of the summer and that was usually our time to go to Corsica as a family. Oddly enough, this year our usual hotel couldn't accommodate us. Instead, we were booked into a sister hotel in the nearby port. The Sheik had a house in this same town for his family. Corsica was bandit country and their security fears kept them from going further afield to some of the other land that he owned on the region's stunning beaches. As it happened, their house was next door to our replacement hotel. I was being taken on holiday to a hotel next to Cassandra's summerhouse. That was going to be a bit weird, but I was young and thick skinned. I would survive. However, the plot would dramatically thicken, and thicken. I learned before I left that once again Cassandra had invited Antonia and Heather to holiday with her. They were to arrive there days before me and to leave at the same time. We were to be neighbours on holiday again for two weeks through absolutely no design of our own. We were separated in time and space by no more than four hundred feet, by sheer coincidence. I arrived with some trepidation.

Of course I desperately wanted to see Heather and indeed have the company of my other friends on the holiday. Oddly enough, I was able to get their phone number out of the phone book and I rang them a few times on our first day there without success. Then on the second day I had news of them. They were out on the Sheik's yacht and would be back later in the day. I left a message that I was at the hotel next door. This was a message that I would later discover sent shockwaves through the assembled company upon its delivery. It turned out that not only had Cassandra invited Heather and her friend for a visit, but also a few other old friends as well.

The house party included Oleanda, Heather's nemesis and my old flame, and the two French dudes who never liked me, Jean-Paul and Eric. Eric was still enamoured with Heather and had invoked the memory of her rejection of him in Zermatt to initiate a holiday romance. Jean-Paul, who was ridiculously brown, muscular and good looking on a beach had easily won over Oleanda. Heather wasn't speaking to Oleanda. Eric wasn't letting Heather out of his sight. Jean-Paul was well aware of my history with Oleanda. None of them were prepared for the effect of me turning up in the middle of a soap opera that I had largely created for them. There was mutual attraction, suspicion, hate, envy and copulation in just about every corner of the otherwise regal guestrooms. It was a stage perfectly set for my entry, had I the strength any more to participate. But I didn't. I was spent. I stayed away.

Heather and Antonia came over to the hotel to see me and they found me in the pool. I must have changed a lot since I'd last saw them. I'd lost a lot of weight in India. I'd seen a lot of new reality. I'd met a new and terribly fragile aspect of myself. And most recently I'd watched as a dear friend and fellow travelling companion in India had gone mad upon his return. I was a shell of the proud, arrogant and cock-sure youngster than had torn up the night life of New York. I had discovered a new mode, vulnerability, and was very surprised to see it so well received. We swam a little in the pool, literally circling each other like wary animals on the savannah. We caught up on the equally dramatic events of our respective summers. It was a tranquil and genuine moment. Beyond everything that had happened, our bond of companionship remained. Despite everything we were somehow deeply nurtured at that age by each other's presence. Heather invited me to go out with the gang later for drinks and so I agreed to step back into the lion's den. It was clear upon my arrival at Cassandra's house that I was to receive a very mixed welcome.

There were so many individual dynamics at work that it was impossible to really know where to avoid offence and where to shelter from assault. Already both Jean-Paul and Eric were giving me the evil eye, unsure of when I might attempt what with either of their women. The reality was that I had no intention on either. I was finished with that game and I knew it. Later we moved on to a club, ushered in by the magic doors that opened when Cassandra's entourage left town. The drinks were all on the Sheik's tab, and since they otherwise cost about twenty pounds each, we made good use of the hospitality. I ended up quite drunk and quite alone, using a wall to keep me vertical. During the evening there had been a palpable chemistry between myself and Heather. It was hard to be there with all that was going on inside me and to see her with her new boyfriend. But I understood that she owed me less than nothing. She found me standing there alone by the wall. She had been looking for me.

I wanted to try to explain to her why I'd done all that I'd done over the last few months. I wanted her to understand as I felt that I now understood; but I lacked the emotional apparatus or courage to begin to know how to tell her. I told her that I thought that I couldn't love anyone, that it wasn't possible for me to love another happily. She asked me why. I couldn't say. I couldn't even speak. I'd never spoken a word of my mother's memory to another person and didn't know how to begin to start. But she wanted to know. She had that right. We were very close by then, both quite drunk and I think feeling very vulnerable, open and connected. She said that perhaps she thought she knew. I was just frozen with fear. She asked me if it was because of my mother. I collapsed in her arms from a mixture of gratitude and grief. She was the first person ever to have articulated my deepest pain; the first person to share it with me; the first person to help me.

She couldn't explain how she had known this. She was as perplexed about it as I was. She just felt at that moment, in that instant, that she knew and she understood. We had been thrown back together by circumstances just when we were at our farthest apart, and now we had found together the deepest thread of our mutual torment. Neither of us could understand it, but neither of us any longer wanted to try to. We were just grateful for each other and the understanding that we were beginning to reach.

By the end of the evening Heather and I were firmly back together, not to be parted for another two years when the natural course of our relationship ran out of steam. For the last year we had weaved in and out of each other's lives on an international roller-coaster with a stellar supporting cast. That was our "year off". A lot was learned, but also a lot was lost. Innocence was handed over in return for the beginnings of understanding. We both had our separate paths yet to follow, but we'd graduated to these new journeys together. The wisdom of life and the people that it had brought to us had combined to give us not what we had wanted, but perhaps exactly what we had needed at that time to prepare us for life's next steps to university and beyond.

Our conscious ambitions and decisions had thrown us into uncharted and unwanted territories where we had never wished to go, but our unconscious minds were working overtime to deliver us to exactly the place where we needed to be. It was my first taste of my own fallibility. The fruitless, arrogant delusions of my conscious mind were shattered. I was no longer able to construct a scenario of a glossy life of perfect accomplishment allied to a pristine state of inner contentment.

Something had to give and I'd been given a lesson in how and why.

Understanding Why?

Look at all the coincidences and choices in my story with Heather and how finally, perhaps psychically loosened by my experiences in India, I was able to make a breakthrough into some new understanding of my self and my behaviour. Trauma had found a way to emerge, using my yo-yo relationship with Heather as its stimulus. After that we were able to stay together.

In a way, it all started with the coincidence that my parents had just bought an empty flat below our house and she had just arrived in London with nowhere to stay. However coincidental that was, we still made choices. I chose to suggest offering her the flat and she chose to accept. There were many other logical reasons for these actions that the conscious mind would readily grasp hold of to justify itself, but perhaps underneath this was an unconscious realisation that there were dramas to be unfolded here which would be helpful for the release of trauma and therefore beneficial to my long-term happiness.

I was in Milan when she was invited to Switzerland. She was pregnant, just at this point when we were geographically to go our separate ways. We were invited to the Caribbean and this coincided exactly with a two-week hole in her own travelling schedule. I was dropped off in New York where she was to arrive less than six weeks later, spurred on there earlier than planned by various other circumstances along her way. Oleanda, Eric and Co. had their own roles in our drama which seemed to be perfectly interlaced with our own efforts to weave in and out of each other's lives. And the final grand coincidence was the location of our respective summer holidays that ended our "year off".

It is reasonable to suggest that there could have been no design of our conscious minds here. She was invited by Cassandra and I was taken by my parents, and to a different hotel to our usual one at that. However, the resolution that followed and the sheer scale of the coincidence that set it up leaves me wondering. Too many unusual factors were at work for me to accept that it must have all been entirely random. Even the lack of space at our usual hotel seemed in retrospect to have been designed to bring us back together. (It turned out that after one call from the Sheik's butler to our preferred hotel, we were immediately collected by limousines and ushered there into two rooms, miraculously suddenly available for the rest of the duration of our stay.)

Perhaps we knew all along, unconsciously, that we would be meeting again that summer. Perhaps we somehow cleverly, unconsciously, engineered it. Perhaps is was the work of mysterious forces outside of our comprehension. Perhaps it just was the cold consequence of random events. We will each have to audit for ourselves the role that coincidence and fate has played in our lives and make a judgement in retrospect about how these seemingly random paths along life's journey have contributed to our own development, learning and resolution of the past. Only then can we begin to guess at the wisdom that our unconscious mind might hold and the subtle ways that it expresses itself though the unseen consequences that our supposedly conscious choices reveal for us.

Cure: Our Response to Others

When we find someone really getting on our nerves, we have a choice. We can either react in the typical way that we are used to, or we can stop and try to think about what it is about that person that really annoys us. Then we can consider carefully what that emotion feels like, what other emotions might be present with it, and who or what, if anything, could remind us that of from our past.

We can make considerable progress towards an easier life by connecting the feelings that arise from this interaction with something from the past. This could be a memory, however distant, of an event, person or feeling.

First, we will begin to allow the feelings to come out (letting e-motion happen), and this will thaw our trauma, and therefore start a healing process.

Second, as we bring into consciousness the connection between these feelings and something in the past, our unconscious mind will have less need to project these qualities on to the person standing in front of us, and we will actually begin to see that person differently. We will find them less annoying, be more in touch with their real self, and experience different emotions in relation to them.

All this has the benefit of allowing us to interact with other people in a way which is more likely to be understood by the other person. They are not party to our projections; therefore they cannot understand why we bite their head off just for mumbling a polite good morning as they pass us in the corridor at work.

Observing and working with our own projections is a hard skill to learn, and an even harder one to master. What we need for now is something simple that we can hang on to, to try to start to turn our lives around and sort out what's wrong with us. We need a beginners' guide to dealing with the influence our projections have on our daily lives. The bad news is that it can't be directly defeated, because it is us that is doing it, and our unconscious mind is much more powerful than our conscious mind with no respect for its agenda.

However, the good news is that we can collaborate with our unconscious mind to help it to get its work done more quickly. Then we can get on to interacting with other people in a less weird way. The first step is to learn and to understand the logic of the causal process that sets up projection in the first place. You are already gaining that understanding by reading this book.

Cure: Our Response to Circumstances

We can make a choice to accept our fate, embrace our luck and delight in our circumstances. If we are able to momentarily turn off the boring mechanism of our conscious ambitions, we can tune into what is being said to us by the circumstances that we actually find ourselves in, rather than what is not being said to us by the ideal circumstances that we spend all day thinking about. The people we see around us, the life that we are living, the disappointments that we suffer, the frustrations that we experience are all there for a reason. They all contribute to the important process of trying to pull us out of the deep freeze of our traumatic past.

Our unconscious mind is trying to help us to encounter the difficulties that we need in order to provide the catalyst to trigger a thawing of our impacted, frozen, traumatised feelings.

Once we embrace our reaction to all of these troubles and let our feelings flow without judgement or censure, then the cycle of these circumstances can shift as the unconscious mind is able to move us on to different challenges, to release different feelings, and to resolve different traumata. If in the end we can let go of everything then we will be finally at one with ourselves. Our conscious mind and our unconscious mind will start to pull in the same direction, and our understanding, power and happiness will know no limits.

Until then (and frankly that is a goal that very few of us may reach in our lifetime) we can ease our struggles in life by approximating to that state.

It is the firm resistance of our circumstances, the daily battle that the conscious mind makes against our unconscious wisdom, that crushes us down into our rutted lives. This is what it holding us back from finding an easier path through life

This constant struggle against the unconscious mind, which guides our choices and gets us where we need to be, is one of the cornerstones of what's wrong with us. Maintaining that high-octane tug-of-war between these two mighty engines pulling our lives in opposite directions is the exhausting dynamic that both tires us out, and gets us nowhere.

Our reluctance to let go of the conscious plan (and instead to trust that the unconscious plan will lead us to a greater happiness than we could imagine) is the absolute key to understanding why life is such a struggle, and why the choices that we make seem to frustrate even the simplest plans of our own conscious minds. It is our adherence to the plans and reactions of the conscious mind and the priority that we give to this over the elegant actions of the unconscious mind that maintain the enduring structure of what's wrong with us.

Step 4: The 1st Conclusion

the Unconscious use of Projection and Fate

The unconscious mind wants you to allow your trauma to be resolved by letting go of the associated feelings that were originally repressed with it. The conscious mind won't let this happen directly, so the unconscious mind has to bring some heavy guns to bear. To do that, it uses its ability to augment the reality that your conscious mind believes that it experiences; and it influences your subtle and unconscious decisions, guiding you in directions that lead to circumstances that satisfy its objective.

In creating these projections and influencing these decisions, the unconscious mind is hoping to lead you into reactions to people and circumstances that complement your unconscious need for trauma resolution. Your reaction to the behaviour of others and to your fate in life will be a catalyst to spark off the e-motions that are currently repressed in your mind-body system by the trauma mechanism. These feelings need to be released so that your trauma can be resolved. This will allow you to expand your consciousness and move on to a life of true happiness regardless of your treatment or circumstances: a much more permanent state of contentment than the one sought by your short-sighted conscious mind.

By reminding your conscious mind to allow the unconscious mind to do its job, you will actually get closer to achieving the goals that you currently hold dear in your conscious mind. Just hang in there. Don't fight the e-motion. Let the feelings come and go. Understand that they come from you, and they originated in your past. Free from blame the person onto whom you are currently projecting. Free your present circumstances from judgement and action based on these feelings. Hopefully, you will then come to a new understanding of your relationships and circumstances, and therefore have an easier life.

It's a hard thing to do well and very hard to do completely, but you can easily start to do it a little. Just notice your feelings in relation to other people, let them be, and ascribe them to the past: not to the present. You'll find the present changes for the better, and you'll find that you are more resolved to your past. In short, you'll begin to get some real insight into why life up to now has proved so frustrating and difficult, and you'll actually begin to experiment with a hands-on understanding of what's wrong with you.

Exercise 4

Did you get what you need and not what you want?

To look a little at the projections that you may have already encountered, let's try to reveal them in the differences between what you thought you wanted and what you actually got from both people and events.

Write a list of significant people and what you wanted to get from them. Like this:

Heather   *Wanted love, warmth, companionship and happiness.*

And write a list of significant events and what you wanted to get from them. Like this:

Trip to New York   *Glamour, life in the fast lane, women, success.*

Then try to be really honest with the same subjects and make a list of what you actually got. Like this:

Heather   *Got pain, heartache and emotional chaos which led to grieving for my mother.*

Trip to New York   *Went on ego trip and was brought back down to earth by poor treatment of other people. Ended up alone and hating myself up a mountain in India.*

Now the question is did you get what you needed? How did the actual outcomes of your desires move your life forward? Did you learn anything from what really happened rather than what you had wanted to happen? If so, then this is where you can recognise the wisdom of projections.

For example, I had pointed my life in the direction of being young, cool and successful and in fact ended up emotionally broken, humbled and honest. But this breakthrough was very important for my development as a person and healing for my worn out psyche.

Finish off by trying to articulate the projections that you are beginning to discover. Wherever there was a result that got you what you needed, but not what you wanted, there was a projection that led you down that path.

Can you see now the difference between what is real, and what you are convinced that you see as real? If so, then this will give you a huge advantage in understanding your personal relationships which is what you will explore in more detail in Step Five.

Central Practice

Teaching the Conscious Mind to Understand the Cause and Effect of Trauma

- Remember that the conscious mind only respects what makes sense to it. You have to teach it to believe in the logic of the argument contained in these pages, so that it begins to accept the experiences of projection and fate as normal, valid and above all non-threatening.
- Remember that you are an animal on a spiritual journey.
- Remember that your great survivalist tool is your conscious mind.
- Remember that the conscious mind allows you to understand your environment, by linking cause to effect.
- Remember that this need to understand effects in relation to their causes results in a great fear of the unexplained.
- Remember that when trauma thaws in your mind-body system, your conscious mind can't make sense of it, because the logical and temporal connection between cause and effect has been lost.
- Remember that this lack of explanation freaks you out, and the opportunity to resolve the trauma is lost.
- Remember that the unconscious mind is much wiser than the conscious mind.
- Remember that the unconscious mind is searching for ways

to help you to resolve your trauma so that you can move towards a fulfilling and automatically happy life.

- Remember that the unconscious mind has the power to affect everything that you think that you see, hear, and understand.
- Remember, therefore, that when you experience an emotion in response to a person or situation, it is a product of your unconscious mind, working to help you to release you from your trauma.
- Remember that the unconscious mind is using your real experience as a screen onto which to project another layer of experience.
- Remember that the unconscious mind is filtering reality back to your conscious mind though the projection from your unconscious mind.
- Remember that the unconscious mind is deceiving you into reacting in a way that begins to allow your trauma to be released.
- Remember that the unconscious mind is helping you to heal.
- So let it.
- Remind your conscious mind why this in happening.
- Remind your conscious mind that it does actually make sense.
- Remind your conscious mind that it doesn't object to this happening, because it now understands it.
- Remind your conscious mind that although the emotions might not make sense yet, they are real, valid and must now need resolving (e-moting).
- Remind your conscious mind that there is no effect without a cause.
- Remind your conscious mind that therefore there must have been a cause in the past to connect with the effect of these emotions in the present.

- Remind your conscious mind that letting go of these feelings is healthy, healing, and helping you.
- Remind your conscious mind that once you let these feelings out, the unconscious mind won't need to project this experience any more and you can get on with life and people more easily, more harmoniously, and more successfully.

Q&A

From the wwwyou?forum. You can see the original text and ask questions at whatswrongwithyou.com.

Is it me?

Posted by: marina Jul 16 2004, 05:41 PM

I'm an intelligent 30 year old, I have just taken a large step in my career. I have a 6 year old boy and I own my own home. I just cant find a decent man!! Is it me? I go on loads of dates and nearly always come back with someone's phone number from a night out, but I just cant seem to find anyone that's 'right'. I've been on my own now (this time!) for 2 and a half years and to be honest, I am quite happy doing my own thing most of the time, but I do get really lonely at times. When I meet someone, they always seem to open up something in me and I feel insecure. Then I think they don't really like me, are using me or just wont make me happy and finish with them. My friends say its cos I pick the wrong sort, but I feel it is something I do...this situation is eating away at my self-esteem and I know I haven't given you much to go on, but you may be able to give me some general advice on how to cope with the disappointments. I feel like a 14 year old sometimes when it comes to relationships! Feeling Hopeless!

Posted by: marina Jul 16 2004, 11:37 PM

I just wanted to give you a little more background to go on and reading through some of the other columns I touched upon jealousy. I have experienced jealousy issues with boyfriends which is one reason I finish things so soon. I got jealous with the last boyfriend after a week as he had a number of female friends and invited them along when we went out in a group on our fourth date. I became jealous and left early and decided I didn't want to see him again. I have one friend who says I was a little hasty and another who says I was absolutely right. I feel I do have unconscious issues affecting my ability to have happy relationships in the present. My father had affairs throughout his marriage and left my Mum when I was thirteen. My Mother reacted very badly to this and started drinking, she also didn't spare us the gory details of her disappointing marriage. About six months later my Father moved in with another lady from our local church and ten months later committed suicide stating that he had made wrong decisions in during his life. I could not tell you what exactly was in his mind at the time and it has taken a long time to get over his death. I don't know for sure if I have fully, but I don't cry everyday anymore and since I had my little boy I have something far more positive to focus on. But I still wonder if all those events are standing in my way. I feel angry at my Father and my Mother and feel they tried dumping their mistakes on me and my brother. How can I tell if these are the real issues affecting my current single status?

Posted by: benjaminfry Jul 19 2004, 10:45 PM

Anything that repeats itself in relationships is about you and not the men. That's just a logical reasoned conclusion from the fact that you are the one constant factor in these relationships.

Yes, it could be coincidence, but it seems clear from your second post that you know otherwise.

You seem to have answered your first post with your second one better than I could have hoped to do. You have suffered a great tragedy in your life. Your prototype for relationships is one of separation and death. As an adult, you find that relationships "open up something in you and you feel insecure". I would suggest that they open up the spectres of death and abandonment. Not wanting to deal with these heavy issues, you will find any way to avoid them. This means finding reasons to end the relationships before they start.

There's always a good reason to end a relationship. Every man has his flaws. If you are going to give up on men without even talking through what concerns you, then you will be able to go through the rest of your life saying you want a man, but never having one. On the other hand, if you stick with a relationship, then you may have to continue the grieving process for your nuclear family and your father.

You shouldn't minimise what happened to you. It is about as rough a deal as you could get from the point of view of setting you up psychologically for healthy relationships. My mother died very young so I can assure you that if you are to allow yourself a long-term partner it will be at the expense of some hard inner work.

There's one crumb of comfort I can offer you and it is this: that which we most fear has already happened. For you, each time you begin to deepen in a relationship, particularly at your age when long term commitment is a headline issue, you will be coming face to face with tragedy. However, the tragedy has already happened. The future is still possible, but only if you face it with courage about the past.

You show this courage admirably in your second post. You also show an innate insight into your own issues. You might really enjoy the opportunity to talk this through with a therapist or counsellor. I suspect that you would make rapid progress on an inner level and this could relieve the pressure on the outer symptom of the sticky relationships.

Posted by: marina Jul 31 2004, 10:53 AM

Yes, this does seem to be what has been occurring in my 'relationships' for the last 18 months. It didn't really happen like this before as I had other ways of repressing my pain (I used alcohol and drugs for 8 years). Then I had a breakdown when I heard news of a friend killing himself – I had only known this person for a month whilst I was travelling, but it opened up a large wound. Again, this was the power of the subconscious at work as when I met this guy I knew he would kill himself – quite freaky that I knew this, but there was nothing I could have done to prevent it and I realise that, as he had a lot of problems. Anyway, I was hospitalised for a couple of weeks after hearing that due to my psychotic reaction (I was unable to speak for several hours and was expressing myself on paper – all this weird angry stuff came out. Cant remember it all now but it was stuff like 'You made me pay' in red ink' – very disturbing as my Mum and Brother had to watch. I was 'ok' the next day, but then (after a joint, which I don't smoke now) had all sorts of panic over my Mum thinking she'd had a heart attack etc. Anyway, I was hospitalised for a couple of weeks and I didn't have any medication as I thought I'd end up a zombie in a psychiatric hospital and never deal with my feelings. When I came out of hospital, I was in a very deep depression for a year. I didn't work and I had no money, I had to break away from all my friends as they all used drugs and that wasn't the answer for me. I moved into a bedsit and didn't really know where to go from there. Eventually I started helping out at a Nursing Home which my Mum ran, talking to patients and washing up etc. I started to get better and met someone I had known from hospital one day when I was shopping. He took me for coffee and he said that he had nowhere to stay. I said that he could stay at mine and he slept on my couch for a couple of weeks. Things developed between us and we slept together and I became pregnant, almost straight away. My life started to turn around from there. Unfortunately my partner had real problems which he was unable to overcome. Again, I had found someone who attempted suicide twice – This of course fits your theory of seeking out ways to resolve a trauma. I split with my boyfriend a week after my son was born and don't have much time for wallowing in my grief anymore!! I lived with someone for nearly two years and that relationship was ok although subject to silly squabbles, but I am still good friends with him today. But I have been single again for 2 and 1/2 years and it seems I am faced with overwhelming feelings of abandonment, anger etc even when someone doesn't text back straight away and I have finished all dating within about 3 dates!! I realise these issues is mine and I also realise that I am somehow picking guys that bring out those feelings in me – guys that are emotionally unavailable etc. I just hope that when I have resolved my issues I will be attracted to someone who can love me back.

Do you think I am attracting the wrong people to resolve my past traumas or is it because of the relationship that I had with my Father? Before my Father left home, I had a good relationship with him. He used to take my brother and I out swimming to the beach and all things like that. Maybe if I could reconnect with this healthy bond I had with him instead of the trauma he (I think unintentionally) left us with I could have more healthy relationships with men or hopefully one man!

Any suggestions as I find your insights very useful and have managed to connect to some quite deep and painful feelings in the last week. I have got the doctors to refer me for counselling on several occasions but have not followed through. I am starting a new job and will probably be able to afford private counselling then, so that is a possibility. Although useful to me, I don't really want to use my romantic relations as a form of psychotherapy!!

Posted by: benjaminfry Jul 31 2004, 05:07 PM

Thank you for that eloquent, touching and honest contribution. You certainly seem to be well equipped emotionally and intellectually to help yourself to recover.

I think you are attracting the "right" people to resolve your past traumas. That's what we all do. Trouble is they are the "wrong" people to create a Mills & Boon story line with. You see this clearly in the connections that you make with suicidal people.

Yours is a very clear example illustrating the simplicity and yet all pervasive depth of what I explain in my book and try to make relevant through this forum. You had a very sudden and extreme trauma relating to the man in your life. This is then played out through men that you know. This replaying of the circumstances that so wounded you actually provided the opportunities you need to emote. It's not the life you want, but the life your emotions need.

So, if you want a "better" life, get stuck into the emotional work on a voluntary basis rather than waiting for the next good-looking suicidal stranger to bounce you into a break-down. If you get into the real psychotherapy, then perhaps your unconscious mind will give you a break with the relationship workshops that you have been enduring. I always recommend mixing therapy with a bit of non-verbal healing, such as yoga or meditation, just to keep a balance and shift the energy in different ways.

Congratulations on your sobriety and your brave enduring attitude. I am sure that if you are prepared to take conscious steps back into the past, then your unconscious need for dysfunctional relationships will ease a little. It will be a long hard slog, but it should be worthwhile and definitely good for your son.

FIVE

Relationships

Relationships. What happens when two people indulge in simultaneous mutual projections.

Theory: Mutual Projections (a.k.a. Relationships) and Lovers

Much of the most serious pain in life for both men and women is experienced in the baffling environment of the peer-to-peer mutual projection: nowhere more powerfully felt than in the romantic or sexual relationship.

There is a reason why intimate relationships are so explosive. To understand it, we have to return to the example of the frozen gazelle and the thawing of its traumatic state. It only comes alive again once it is safe. One of the qualities that we crave in another person (in the context of intimate relationships) is someone with whom we can feel safe: or at least a little bit less scared, alone and vulnerable. One of the reasons we crave people and particularly that special someone is that it increases our basic sense of safety. When we find someone we really connect with, particularly if there is a level of real emotional or practical commitment, then we begin to experience the kind of security that we may have craved since our early childhood.

However, when we start to feel safe, that's when the trauma

thinks it is safe to come out. Our threshold for the total threat that we can face remains the same. Therefore, if our external world becomes safer, we can tolerate more internal threat. So finding that special someone, making a commitment and feeling more secure externally prompts a vicious compensatory reaction from our psyche. The honeymoon ends. The unconscious mind sees its chance to release trauma via projections. Soon, the euphoria of recently discovered love is replaced by the confusion of projection. These projections stimulate the thawing of the trauma. The emotions of the emerging trauma are overwhelming. The conscious mind freaks out, unable to understand what is going on.

The conscious mind tries to control these feelings as much as it can. One of the conscious mind's best defences is to blame our partner for causing this rampaging tide of emotion surfacing within us. While we are freaking out with our partners, they are also likely to be taking their opportunity to project plenty back on to us. They too get caught up in the thawing and fear of their own long neglected traumatic feelings. They start to see us as the cause of all the problems. While we are both simultaneously eviscerating our emotions from a thousand childhood injustices, it's touch and go whether or not the relationship will survive. The good news is that trauma is thawing. E-motions are moving out. The bad news is that this may be accompanied by such a degrading of our relationships that we will start to feel unsafe again. That would trigger all of our childhood concerns about survival again and may create and accumulate yet more trauma.

Some relationships reduce your reservoir of unresolved trauma; some add to it. This fundamentally separates the good relationships from the bad. All relationships will trigger deep and complex emotional patterns, projections and unresolved emotions. If this can be processed in a mutually respectful manner, and the underlying conditions of the relationship remain supportive, committed and safe, then it can be very positive and healing. However, if the interaction degenerates into something that threatens the very fabric of the relationship itself, then it is unlikely that any healing will occur. In the latter instance it is more likely that the belief system set up by the original trauma will be reinforced and that the accompanying emotions will sadly become buried more deeply than before. We may even just give up on relationships all together.

It is hard to differentiate exactly what makes one scenario more possible than another. Most relationships will experience a shifting balance of the two as trauma ebbs and flows. The fundamental intention of genuine compassion and respect between two individuals is a good place to start. And if on top of that there can be some conscious understanding of this process, an acceptance of the fact of the projective mechanism, then there is a chance that our emotions can be experienced without blaming and pushing away the person who is helping us to experience these feelings in the first place.

The nature and intensity of our emotional experiences often make this very difficult, but if we can see our current situation and partner as merely a catalyst to stimulating emotions frozen from our past, then it can help us to relate to them with more equality, understanding, compassion and respect. If however we dump the responsibility for the whole of our past and all of our impacted trauma onto our partner in the present, then we are giving them an impossible burden to bear. We are therefore unlikely to reach a meeting of minds before bedtime.

It is hard for the conscious mind at first to comprehend this. How can something that is happening to us (our strong feelings) because of what someone else is doing to us (our partner's words or actions) not be their fault? If they are in our face calling us names and saying hurtful things that they know will upset us, then surely they are in the wrong? We convince ourselves that we are in the right and they jolly well better learn to understand this and apologise or else. The trouble is they also think exactly the same thing.

The easiest way to see that this is not correct thinking is to imagine two different people responding in two different ways to the same stimulus. (Or we could imagine ourselves responding in two different ways to the same stimulus at two different times.) Clearly if we accept that this is possible, then we understand that it is not simply the stimulus that causes the reaction, otherwise the reaction would always be the same. The stimulus has to combine with something in us. That something is our own projection. It is a function of our trauma and our own buried feelings which sometimes will surface, and sometimes will not. We will let them out when we feel safe enough or are just too tired, or too hot, or too bothered, to be able to keep them in any more. (Why do hot countries have such passionate populations? Does this seem to improve their relationships and cohesion as families and couples? It might be hard to generalise, given many other factors at work, but cultures that seem to place less emphasis on repressing emotional expression do seem to have some attractive societal qualities.)

It is difficult to live with someone who makes us feel emotionally safe. Both partners will be unconsciously using that safety to place projections on to each other nearly all the time. The only time that we may be somewhat free of this kind of projective mechanism is perhaps after a big outpouring of e-motions. We are familiar with the sweet quality of kissing and making up. Often it can seem as if we are particularly open, present and radiant right after a strong and emotional disagreement. This is because we are actually seeing each other more or less as we really are, temporarily without any need for our projections: simply as a treasured fellow human being. But this state is rare and fleeting. The rest of the time we will simultaneously struggle with the difficulties of relating to the ideas that: (a) the other is a fellow human being, who loves and cares for us, and (b) that they are also manifesting qualities of the experiences in our past that we found most difficult to bear.

This makes the dynamic of relationships especially charged and hard to negotiate. Opposing qualities may seem to simultaneously exist in our partner, and our partner may never agree with us that these qualities are there. We have augmented what we really find there with the projections that we have placed over their objective reality. Once this starts happening at the same time on both sides, then it becomes impossible for anyone to know what is really going on. There is no longer any objective reality. The truth becomes a battleground. Finding a simple consensus on who is doing or saying what becomes maddeningly impossible. Both parties genuinely think that they are right. Both parties have different versions of reality. Hence the conflict. That's why lovers fight.

Case Study: Scarlet

At that moment I knew for the first time that I wished I was dead: not in the metaphorical way that people often dramatise their stories, but in the terminal moment of despair. There seemed to be no other way to curtail the agony contained in the mind other than by destroying it and stopping, even just for a moment, the unending torment and misery within. It's quite something to experience. It goes against all the instincts of a million years of evolution to actually recognise the clear and valid thought that you wish you were no longer alive. It was the worst moment of my life.

There was a new woman and a new drama. I was beginning by now to understand in a rudimentary way how the projective mechanism was at work in my life: bridging the gap between the love and loss of my mother in my earliest months to the chaos in my personal life in the here and now. I was trapped in a cycle of loving deeply and then destroying that love, repeatedly battering it to death until I felt the terrible, desperate pain of once again being back on my own: naked, vulnerable and infantile in the face of life's many threats. Scarlet was my latest object of attachment, and had been for quite some time.

I was alright with the split initially. We had been together for most of our young adult lives. We had shared a great deal of love and life's experiences, but at the end we had grown apart in the way that young couples do as they emerge into the real world. There was no fault, no-one to blame. We had had the best of each other and the best of a mutually supportive relationship at a key transitional time in our lives. However, when the balance turned from the positive to the negative, we began to do what all couples do at the death. We fought more. We loved less. We made plans separately. And yet we stayed together.

I was hugely reluctant to accept the inevitable physical separation that our growing emotional distance would require. We both had difficulty finding the kind of support that we had enjoyed from each other at the outset of our relationship. I had lived in a secret exile from my own family: gradually coming to terms with the reality of my mother's death while pretending to the world that my step-mother was actually my mother. Scarlet's father had left home just after I first met her, leaving her mother with their children and no money. And so we were both on the run from loss in our own families. We had coped by finding each other. Now I had to face the reality that this was only a temporary port from the storm, and that I would soon have to deal once again with loss: and deal with it alone.

For a long time it didn't seem that either of us could imagine any alternative reality other than the one in which we were a couple. Perhaps it also seemed that way to everyone else. We had many mutual friends and we were in some ways well matched. We looked quite similar, both tall, fair and good looking. I owned nightclubs and made films. She was in the media. We bought into our perfect life together and tried to continue to do so long after its sell by date. However, it was not to be. I was beginning to notice our fundamental differences as we began to face more mature influences and issues in life. We naturally grew to want and like different people and things. The trouble was that we just couldn't bear to face reality.

In the end, after a particularly miserable summer holiday, I brought up the subject of "us" and she was relieved that finally one of us had said something. We agreed that we weren't happy together and should try being apart. Of course, with that weight off our shoulders we suddenly found each other much more bearable. We split up, but remained quite close. We didn't have the same intensity of relationship, but talked a lot and met up often. It was as if we were returned to our carefree student days. We could appreciate again our natural compatibility without dealing with the difficult realities of maintaining a relationship against the backdrop of maturing into an adult life.

But there came a point where the reality of the separation began to dawn on both of us. It happened in different ways at different times. For me it seemed to come as part of a general malaise that introduced me firmly to the other side of my psyche: the damaged, desperate, lonely, freaked out inner-child.

I descended into what I would later understand as a depression. However, at the time I was unable to recognise being depressed. I didn't do depressed. I lived alone and spent my days writing a new film script. I had been commissioned by Disney to write a screenplay for them. This would be a dream for most UK based writers, but I couldn't see it that way. I found the script difficult and I was very lonely. I thought that I was simply unhappy and refused to accept or to recognise the growing, more serious, mental malaise beginning to engulf me. Somewhere in all of this, my route back to success, happiness, the admiration of others, away from the inner-directed loneliness that consumed me, was to get back together with Scarlet. It became like a one-stop shop to solve all my problems.

It seems amazing to me now that I couldn't remember that, only six months before this decision, I'd been miserable in our relationship and relieved when it ended. Scarlet for her part was beginning to move on from the relationship. She wasn't interested in becoming my emotional crutch. The more that I seemed unable to re-engage her in the excitement of having a life again with me, the more I'd become fixated on it as a quick and easy solution to the emotional torment that engulfed me every day. I failed to realise that the feelings that I couldn't shake were part of me, were embedded in me and coming from me. I began to see them all as only related to her absence from my life. They did stem from an absence, but not hers: my mother's. Failing to see this, I put all the blame on her. I began to review every aspect of our relationship and to blame Scarlet for everything that I was suffering. I made her into the bad one, and yet all that I was thinking about was how to get back together with her. I was becoming obsessed and driving myself a little bit mad. I was driving my friends to distraction too. And then the panic attacks started.

It was while having lunch with a friend in a city wine bar that I had my first panic attack. It was a mild one although at the time I thought I'd lost my mind. My senses all became extremely sensitive, as if in a moment of true life or death emergency. The room was brighter, louder and more crowded. Standing, talking about the relative merits of different careers was impossible and made no sense. I had to get out. I had to move. (I began to learn that accessibility to open spaces and using exercise to begin to drain some of the spare adrenalin was a vital crutch to coping with panic.)

I'd been overwhelmed by anxiety for months now and here I was having a panic attack. I was coming to the end of a long downward spiral of internal collapse. The worse it got, the less

I felt capable of doing anything about it. Inside me was nothing but a barren plain of emptiness which I'd avoided experiencing by using all the props of externally perceived success. My life had many opportunities but was currently insecure. This real external insecurity resonated deeply with the profound emotional insecurity that I had been keeping at bay since I'd lost my mother. My circumstances were beginning to trigger a connection with more of my abandoned unconscious memories and feelings. I'd been on the run from this my whole life. And now I was finding out why.

The next time I had a panic attack, it was a real one. It was the middle of the day and I had been writing at home. I felt overwhelmed with a crushing sensation of anxiety and loneliness. I desperately needed to get these thoughts out of my head and just talk to someone. The only person I could think of to talk to was Scarlet. I could think of no-one else I could share this kind of misery with. In reality she was attempting to rebuild her life and move on from supporting me emotionally. I called her at work.

The moment I heard her voice it was like a dam burst in my head. I was overwhelmed by the panic attack. I tried to talk to her but I soon began hyperventilating. My vision blurred. I was crying and gasping for breath. I couldn't see. My heart was pumping a million miles an hour. She kept me on the phone and tried her best to calm me down. The last bond between us was the shared awareness of the horrific nature of a panic attack. We were prepared to be there for each other for some limited assistance.

Scarlet phoned my step-mother who suggested that I go round to her house for the afternoon. I walked there through Hyde Park, which took the edge off my panic. I arrived at my parents' house a shattered wreck. I had no idea how to look after myself in this situation and was very grateful for my step-mother's support. We talked a little about what was going on.

It was then, for the first time ever, that I brought up with her the subject of my real mother.

I had sunk so low and felt that my sanity was in genuine jeopardy. It seemed like there was nothing left to lose: nothing left to fear. I somehow knew that if I didn't start to deal properly with the issue of my mother, then I wasn't going to recover. The fear of the consequences of not talking about my mother had become greater than the fear of the consequences of doing so. I suggested that maybe I had unresolved psychological issues from my mother's death. She didn't disagree. She suggested a nice doctor who lived down the road and I went to see her that afternoon.

The doctor wisely suggested that I might consider seeing a therapist. I jumped at the opportunity. Once the idea had been mooted I was keen to try to find an escape from my emotional inner prison. I had no idea what to expect or whether it would help, but at that point anything constructive was welcome. However, I was a wreck. Every minute was an ordeal to get through. I was now alternatively overwhelmed by real anxiety or manufactured anxiety about having another panic attack. On top of all that, my life was a mess and needed a great deal of courage and action to sort out. But I could hardly even fix myself a meal, let alone my life.

I made an appointment with the therapist, Lois, who kindly agreed to see me urgently, but even that was not for three days. I wondered how I would get through them. I struggled to keep my spirits up and my mind stable but the effort was totally absorbing. Very little could penetrate. If I went for dinner with friends, I was on edge, expecting panic, unable to connect well or communicate freely. There was no relief in the company of others, entertainment, work or relaxation. There was only the crisis in my mind. It was this I think that became too much to bear. I was desperate for mental rest: even for just five minutes of not having to think about the state of my mind. Having the mind on constant red alert monitoring the mind is an exhausting, lonely task.

One evening I simply realised that I'd had enough. I couldn't bear it any more. My mental resources were spent. My courage run through. My appetite for existing like this was gone. I knew in that moment that I would actually rather be dead that live in this crisis of mental illness. It wasn't a flip thought. It was a real evaluation of my options. At that point there was no immediate alternative to the hell of the experiences that reverberated through my own mind. Death was literally the only way out. I was in a passively suicidal state. I suspect that that is how it starts for those who actually go on to take their own lives. It was an awful experience. It crushed me to realise that my reality was so bad that I would trade everything that was wonderful about life and every relationship that I had with everyone who loved me for the dark fate that we expend every energy to avoid. I knew that I'd hit yet another new low.

I fell onto my sofa with a framed picture of Scarlet in my arms. I imagined my body being found like that, prostrate and alone with no solace but a photograph. I got quite excited about the guilt trip that I could send Scarlet on and how this would be suitable revenge for her abandonment of me. However, I also knew that it was a fantasy. There must be another big step to take between a passive desire for death and the state of mind that actively takes some action towards it. I wasn't yet near taking that step and I don't know if I ever would have. However, it crushed me to admit to myself that I was so far gone that my life was no longer a better alternative to me than death.

That night I woke up with a start in the small hours of the morning alone in my flat. I was wracked with anxiety. Panic was welling up. I didn't know what to do. I needed someone to be there with me. I called Scarlet. It must have been three or four in the morning and she was not happy to hear from me. I had another full blown panic attack. Then we had a blazing row. She needed her sleep, but I needed her, anyone, more. I told her that I was dying: that what was happening was killing me. I told her that I felt like I wanted to die. It was a low blow and a terrible responsibility to lay onto someone else struggling to rebuild their own life, but that was a measure of how desperate I felt. Scarlet was obviously really worried. She called my parents straight away and they phoned me. I told them that I was alright. The argument had got some of the tension out of my system, but I obviously needed a lot of help. Fortunately I was soon to get it.

Understanding Why?

Once again, I was in the grip of a projection of a benign mother figure that I had placed onto Scarlet. I had conferred on her the capacity to give me unconditional love. When this was not actually supplied to me, I became very angry with her for not giving me what I wanted: or perhaps more significantly what I felt that I deserved and was owed. That was the basis for my mental decline.

Scarlet's version of reality was quite different. I would speculate that she had set up a projective mechanism of her own that placed onto me the role that was missing since her father had left. To some degree, I had played that role during our relationship, but after our separation I became increasingly needy and incapable. I was reverting to the behaviour of an infant because that was the age from which my own trauma was being released. She saw the person that she had relied on for some strength and protection become as useful to her in that regard as a small baby. I saw the person that could tend to my infantile needs abandon me just when I needed her most. She had recreated the abandonment of her father. I had recreated the death of my mother. We were both using the relationship as a backdrop to projections which helped us to resolve the troubles of our past. It is clear in retrospect that there were two dimensions to our reality.

Looking back on it now, I can see that our mutual projections were beginning to wane. The reality of our lives was moving on and the gulf between that reality and the projections that we had set up at the outset of our relationship was becoming too great. This was eventually what caused us to separate. In reality, it was the right thing to do and a positive move forward into our respective futures. In projection-land it remained as complex and difficult as possible. I had deep and significant projections at play here and they were tied to my most painful personal issues. I began to become more and more absorbed in the world of my projections and less and less anchored in reality. Thus it was that I began to find it unbearable to be separated from Scarlet and told myself with my conscious mind that the solution was to return to her.

We can see how real and how strong these unconscious projections are in the number of crimes of passion. Outside of acts of war, this is statistically the greatest source of homicidal impulses in our society. Often these murders are done by people who would never be considered violent or dangerous. Usually they kill people whom they have previously loved, sometimes for a lifetime. Almost always they bitterly regret their actions and find it hard later to understand why it happened. We can see this in my brief suicidal fantasies and the implied associated blame that I enjoyed forecasting for Scarlet. It was quite mad in retrospect and quite at odds with the idea that I held her in high regard as my perfect partner in life.

Unfortunately, the projections that become associated with our partners can trigger such powerful emotions from our pasts that we believe our best option to control these feelings is to destroy what we erroneously perceive as the source of the emotions. The reality though is that these emotions remain frozen inside us whatever external action we take; trauma is not resolved and our efforts to repress it can spill over into regrettable negative behaviour, or even tragic irreversible actions.

Theory: Mutual Projections
(a.k.a. Relationships) and Parents & Children

The pain suffered in our romantic and sexual relationships may be the vehicle for a million different opinions a week aired in conversations and the popular mainstream of society's publications, but the sum of our problems is not just in these peer-to-peer relationships, but in all human relationships. These start in the family.

Early on in our lives, we began to project on to our family members. They in turn will have had their own projections which they were placing over us. As a result, our earliest experiences would have been the confusing aspects of how people related to us and how we related to them. We may have received very mixed messages from our parents or other carers. At times they may have loved us and made us feel warm, safe and secure. At other times we may have lived in fear of them as they chastised us, disciplined us, raged at us or just ignored us. This would have made little sense to our young minds, but over time the conscious mind may have been able to develop patterns and link some cause to these effects.

Thus we may have begun to believe that we could start to have some control over our environment by altering the causes of these effects. We may have noticed, for example, that when mummy was tired she would usually end up yelling at us, regardless of the circumstances. So when she was tired we may have tried to be extra good, or extra invisible. Along the way we would have started to place our own projection over her. She for her part may have been projecting on to us qualities that were borrowed from memories of her own childhood. Perhaps we took on something of her father, or brothers, or mother, or sisters. Clearly, though, there must have been a reason for change of behaviour towards us. The reason would have been deeper than simply fatigue. Tiredness makes us less able to control our emotions. It doesn't create new ones.

A parent whose behaviour changes from a benevolent safety zone into a threatening adult is undergoing a change from seeing a child as a baby, needing attention, love and comfort, to a parent seeing something else that triggers off their own frozen emotions. For example, the screaming of a child might trigger the thawing of frozen emotions, which the parent experienced traumatically as a child when he or she screamed for the help that never came. This thawing of early childhood experiences can be experienced by the adults' conscious mind as deeply threatening and uncomfortable. Mistaking the screaming child in the present day as the cause of their own extreme distress, a parent might need to leave the child alone, or in the worst cases actually shake, hit or damage the child to shut it up. Thus the cycle of trauma for the child continues to the next generation, from parent to offspring, through abandonment or abuse.

There is a very good reason why the worst treated members of our society are children. They are in the unfortunate position of being able to trigger the thawing of adults' most deeply repressed and highly uncomfortable unconscious trauma. They do this because, simply by being young children themselves, they are easy catalysts for triggering the emotions that adults repressed at those same ages.

The thawing of trauma sustained in infancy can be the most threatening of all for adults. This trauma is pre-verbal. It means that the strong feelings of infancy don't have any words to go with them. These thoughts are not yet framed by language. There was no language available in the infant's mind when it experienced these overwhelming and traumatising feelings. To have these feelings presented again to the adult mind-body system is highly uncomfortable. In fact when this happens (and it does a lot) we might think that we are in danger of going mad. Imagine having the kind of strong feelings witnessed in a screaming infant, feelings that take over the whole mind and body, and imagine that there are no thoughts to go with these feelings, no rationalisations, nothing but pure overwhelming emotion. That kind of experience can be totally terrifying to an adult, especially an adult who has grown up in a culture which is not very emotionally literate and is afraid of strong displays of emotion.

So, an adult may often feel overwhelmed by the emotions stirred up by the proximity of a child, and often even more overwhelmed the younger the child is. The adult who is over-whelmed by the thawing of trauma triggered by a young child (and who does not understand why) may need to withdraw from these overwhelming feelings. The conscious mind will be freaking out, unable to understand its own context. The child will often suffer trauma as a result. This contributes to the societal neglect of the needs of children, and the attitudes that say that children need to be controlled, disciplined, suppressed and ordered to conform. This contrasts with the way that people might treat a disorientated adult like, say, a respected foreign visitor (which is how children might be more fairly treated); letting them develop their own sense of what they need; trying to listen to them even though you don't speak the same language; and where possible accommodating their separate needs, or at worst trying to explain carefully why this is not possible.

The irony is that the child cannot help but be a child. What is really agonising for the adult is not the child itself, but the projection that the adult has placed onto the child. In many cases, it is even a projection of themselves. The adults' own identification with the experience of the child creates something psychotherapists call a projective identification; it is as if we become the child, and then their experience becomes our own. We are then likely to treat the child as we were ourselves treated in that situation when we were a child, because that is what is familiar to us and was acceptable in our own family.

This is why parents so often treat their own children in the same way as they were treated by their parents: even when they hate the way that their parents treated them and have vowed never to be like them. Once again, the unconscious mind is taking over from the conscious mind. The conscious mind wants to create a better childhood than our own for our children, but the unconscious mind wants only to heal our trauma. The unconscious mind's agenda is to expand our conscious mind. It doesn't matter if it uses a small child as the object for our projections. It will leave others, however young or vulnerable, to sort out their own problems.

The child also creates its own projections which it in turn places on the parent. The reality of childhood is that it is a time of great vulnerability. It may seem like childhood should be the one time in our lives when we feel safe, loved and protected, but of course this is not always the case. Even in the most benign of environments, the child is acutely aware that it has very little resources of its own. It relies on its parents or adult guardians for its very survival. This has terrifying consequences if there is any interruption in the perceived good intentions towards it of those adults.

Absence is probably the greatest threat. If the adults simply disappear, then the conscious mind is terrified about its chances for survival. So the threshold for trauma is pretty low. Anything that creates the momentary impression that the big, strong, powerful creatures that support the child's life are not going to be there (or are not going to be kind, loving, warm and nurturing) will be perceived by the child as a possible life-

or-death situation. The antidote to this is an environment that feels safe. That is what children really want.

This safe environment is what we try to create for ourselves as we get old enough to gather our own resources around us. It is usually a futile effort undermined by the greater ambitions of our unconscious mind, directing our lives back to the very experiences that we are running from. Many adults reflect on their lives and wonder how, despite all their promises to themselves and their sincere efforts, they seem to have ended back in a family that is almost identical to the one that they wanted so much to escape from as children.

If the child can not find a safe environment then there is no relief from trauma, because life is constantly lived on a knife-edge of survival anxiety. The child begins to accumulate the trauma of its short life and its own unconscious mind starts to get to work, trying to resolve this trauma. Unfortunately, because the threshold for what seems safe to a child is so easily breached by the magnitude of everyday events, it is really hard for a child to ever find the space to begin to achieve this kind of resolution. Usually if mummy is angry the first time, then mummy is angry again the second time, and so on for years, and years, and years, and years. This repetition of what feels so unsafe is what creates the impacted, frozen reservoir of trauma. It is also what creates the permanent, deep illusion of reality ascribed to the projections formed by the child to deal with this trauma.

We project on to our parents from a very early age. The traumas that these projections attempt to release remain sedimented and concretized, so these projections become our only version of reality. That is why parents have such a unique capacity to disturb their children. Sometimes it only takes a look or a comment from a parent to thrust you back into a kind of pre-adolescent funk or rage. No-one else has that power to stimulate so much so quickly by doing so little. This is often a source of distress to parents as well as their children. They wonder what they did wrong as their grown-up offspring go into another meltdown. The problem is that the parents obviously can't see the projections that the child may have thrust upon them, and the child can't remember a life without these projections.

Thus the deep conflict is born between us and our parents, as both the providers and guardians of our lives and as the monsters and dementors of our psyches. This is a hard conflict to resolve. Much of the commentary on the focus of modern psychotherapy centres on the process being about our parents and our childhood. This is an unfortunate popularisation and one that many therapists themselves are too prone to absorb.

It is very seductive to believe that we can simply blame our own parents for everything, and absolve ourselves of our own responsibilities. We have been projecting onto our parents all of the qualities that our own unresolved trauma needs us to encounter for as long as we remember. It would be a great relief if these problems were really out there in others, rather than within us and placed out there by our projective mechanism. It is therefore very seductive to believe that there is some sort of healing to be done just by identifying what's wrong with the generation before us, but that's not an accurate view of the situation. What we really need to understand is what's wrong with us, and the answer isn't just what's wrong with our parents.

The reality is that we will have set up our parents to be distorted beyond their original failings. They become very hard to see as real, ordinary human beings. (They have themselves lived through infancy, childhood and adolescence and are themselves simply trying to do their best through their own confusing, frustrating and difficult lives.) Instead they become superhuman, infused with the terrified projections of our lives' earliest experiences. They were in a unique position as the guardians of our existence at the time when our existence was most vulnerable. Consequently, we have lost all proportion of the scale of the projections that we may have subsequently placed over them.

It is a great shame that we have lost some of the skills of the societies that we now call primitive. It seems some of their techniques for encountering and respecting the unconscious mind were far better developed than our own. Rituals reinforced these connections throughout the year and throughout the community. For example the male and the female forces that contributed to survival were routinely ascribed to some aspect of God and nature respectively. The power of God and the bounty of nature theoretically dwarf the ability of our father or mother to ensure our safety and survival. Therefore a real connection with God (whatever that means) and with nature would relieve our parents of those impossible demands. This in turn would lessen the intensity of the projections that we place onto them.

However, in a modern industrial society, all the old rituals of God and nature have been airbrushed from the fabric of our culture. Hence, there is nowhere else for the burden of our needs to rest than on the shoulders of those other equally freaked out human beings: mummy and daddy. This sets up such an intense projection that it closes down the nurturing family system that otherwise might enable us to feel safe enough to resolve our trauma. Instead, it simply generates more and more trauma in our lives as we grow up with nothing to sustain us but the erratic benevolence of our well-meaning, but inevitably flawed, adult guardians.

Case Study: Scarlet lost

My life turned around as soon as I started to see my recommended therapist, Lois. I was so thankful that there was someone for me to talk to who seemed to understand. She didn't view what was happening to me as a freakish, dangerous phenomenon to be avoided. She was American, like my mother, very matronly and old enough actually to be my mother. We instantly adopted each other. I felt a rush of gratitude that finally I had a sense of what it would be like to be understood and accepted by a maternal figure in my life. My relationship with my step-mother had always been devoid of real intimacy. She'd cared for me best she could, but the natural connection was not there and my suspicion of her from the early years of being on the wrong end of her moods never subsided. I longed for maternal comfort and felt like here I was beginning to get some. With it came professional skills and advice about how to begin to pick up the pieces of my life.

One of the first points Lois made was that this wasn't Scarlet's fault and I should not be asking her to fix it. With this new support system in place, I was able to recognise the truth of this and I didn't call Scarlet again. Lois pointed out that if I wanted to get better, it was time to start talking about the real issue: my mother. But I was very reluctant to let go. In Scarlet I had someone to blame for not giving me what I needed, and it was a real comfort to continue to locate the problem outside of myself. Lois reminded me that I had had the choice simply to accept that my relationship with Scarlet hadn't been working any more, and should have therefore accepted this and moved on. After all we were young and not married: this was the typical dynamic of growing up. I realised suddenly how I'd put myself through much of what I had subsequently blamed Scarlet for. It was a difficult realisation because it was so much more comforting to blame her than to see myself as undermined by my own clingy, insecure personality, but almost as quickly as I had that realisation, I had another epiphany that if it had been my fault, my responsibility, then it was something that was in my power to change.

Throughout all of this spiral into mental decline, the most difficult aspect for me to cope with was that I seemed to have no power to change anything. I had focused all my efforts on changing people and circumstances outside of me, such as my relationship with Scarlet, or my career. I had never once attempted to change the reaction that I had had to these circumstances, or indeed even considered it possible to change the actual reality that I ascribed to them. I was illiterate in the language of the mind and therefore knew nothing of projection, nothing of the unconscious and nothing about how I'd been using both to bring me back into contact with my lost feelings. I now needed to unearth these emotions in order to move my life on to its next stage. I'd reached the worst point of my life, just before I began the most valuable phase of my personal growth and education on this planet. I'd have done anything at the time to escape it, but now of course consider it to have been the best thing that ever happened to me.

From there I began to look at what had happened in my family, and more particularly what I really felt about it. Initially I felt nothing. I had no complaints. My family was perfect. My parents gave me love and support and everything was fine. There was this small, irritating detail of the fact that my mother had died when I was a baby, but I couldn't see how this could be a problem since I didn't remember it. One of the things my father had always said was that children were very adaptable and that nothing that happened to them when they were very young really mattered since they didn't remember it. Of course, looking back, I see why he would want to believe this. I suppose it made it bearable to see his son lose his mother. However, here I was in a state of mental collapse. This hadn't happened without reason and intuitively perhaps I knew it was related to my mother's death. I'd hoped so far in my life to avoid dealing with the reality of both her life and her death. But now I just knew that if I wanted my sanity back, the genie would have to come out of the bottle, regardless the other consequences.

Gradually, the denial fell away. At first, I was defensive about any possibility of the issue having been badly handled by my family, particularly by my father. But then I began to see that it was not normal to bring up a child with no remembrance of his mother. I had to accept that in an emotionally literate and functional family, people would talk to a child about a dead parent. Indeed I'd seen it happen elsewhere. So what had gone wrong for me and why? At the time I was too afraid to talk to my father or step-mother directly, but I began to dig about a bit with family friends and relatives. It was hard work. I experienced a huge reluctance to bring up the subject of my mother with them. I had felt for possibly almost all my life that this was dangerous territory to get into. But I recognised from my work in therapy that I needed to push through this emotional barrier, because it was behind it that I suffered in my prison of overwhelming fear.

The response that I received during my investigations was overwhelmingly unanimous. When my father remarried, it became very difficult for my mother's friends and family to talk to me about her around my father and his new wife. It seemed that particularly my step-mother gave a very clear impression to all concerned that she was not going to be living with her husband's dead wife in her house. She wanted my father to be her husband and me to think of her as my mother. She'd been adopted herself, so for her family connections were few and far between. As far as she was concerned, they could be rearranged with some fluidity. She had never known for herself the innate connection of a child with its mother.

At first these realisations were hard to take. I had been denied a real emotional connection with my mother, and I gradually had to accept that the person who'd given me my only maternal sustenance was responsible. Everything that I had missed in my relationship with my step-mother seemed now to me to also have been stolen from me in the possibility of knowing that it had once been there for me from my mother. By all accounts, my mother had been delighted to have a child, and remained very close to me during our few months together. These gradual revelations in the external world combined with gradual realisations in my inner world. Slowly they started to peel away the years of concretised repression and denial. However, I largely protected my father from any censure. I managed to organise my mind in such a way as to keep him out of the picture. In fact, he was of course more responsible for me than my step-mother. He was my blood relative and had been married to my mother. (My step-mother never even knew her.)

It suited me to keep the negative emotions fixed on one half of the camp. Then at least I could tell myself that me and my dad were fine, while the step-mother remained the villain. This was relatively easy, since I had always had to some extent an antagonistic relationship with my step-mother. She was the one with whom I had the rows. My father made things better. So, it cost me little to park my anger and resentment with her. I preserved my father so that he could remain my knight in shinning armour.

An interesting thing began to happen during this process. As I moved my step-mother into the place of blame, so my fixation with Scarlet and her failings in my life began to wane. I realised that as I got closer to the core of my own emotional backlog, the more peripheral characters in my life took on less and less superhuman significance. Scarlet was no longer the central woman in my life who had let me down. I was now beginning to try to push this projection back into the midst of time, back to my dead mother. So far I'd only got as far as the obstacle of my step-mother.

In any case it did seem that Lois' prediction was beginning

to be shown to be true. By starting the work of emotionally unearthing my mother's memory and my grief about her loss, I was beginning to lose the intensity of my difficult internal crisis about Scarlet. And so I began to be able to let go of her as a receptacle for dumping all of my anger, grief, abandonment and blame. She gradually became just another person again: someone much like me in fact: the same age, background and with many of the same problems. It seemed such a shame in retrospect that someone who had so often been a close ally could so quickly have become to me such a source of distress. But I hadn't been living in the real world. I was relating to her through some very thick projections. And it was these projections that had led me into therapy, and thus towards an authentic effort to release the great well of trauma sealed off inside me after my mother died. So I'd lost Scarlet, but in her place I was beginning to find myself.

This self-knowledge though was itself beginning to threaten a new crisis. In my therapy and particularly in a group which I had joined, it had become clear that one of the stranger facts of my life was that I had never talked to my father about my mother. It seemed such a simple thing, but for me it remained a great mental barrier. I had always been afraid of mentioning my mother but it wasn't clear why. It just terrified me. The only explanation that I could muster was that I had picked up from my father, step-mother, or both, a sense that I wouldn't be acceptable as my mother's son. It felt to me very much like a stark choice between having my father as a living parent or remembering my mother as a dead one. I can't explain why this was my impression other than simply because my mother had never been mentioned at home. Like all children, I had a great sensitivity to how much of me would be tolerated and this seemed to fall outside of that remit. The resistance that I experienced to discussing my mother with my father felt to me in some urgent way like a matter of life and death. It was as if I had realised as a child that my survival depended on keeping quiet.

This couldn't last forever. I had focused my attention for responsibility of this issue on my step-mother and forgiven my father's involvement. This helped me to avoid going to the core of the issue, but there came a point when this distortion could no longer be supported. I had to accept eventually that my father had a very significant part to play in the loss of my connection to my mother's life. Gradually I realised that it was far more threatening for me to begin to accept being angry at him than it had been to open up to some negativity towards my step-mother. He was my one surviving parent. I had always felt a natural connection and his unconditional love in a way that had been missing with my step-mother. My evolved survival mechanism had decided that keeping him on-side was paramount to my survival. When I was one-year old, perhaps this was true. Now, however, this no longer applied. But the feelings remained the same.

I agonised for months about getting these issues out into the open, but somehow just lacked the courage. It became a recurring refrain of my therapy. I knew that I needed to talk about what had happened because without it I was struggling to enjoy a relationship with my parents. There was so much that remained unsaid that I felt it almost impossible to say anything. Time spent in their company would make me on edge. I started to feel the internal pressure of needing to re-solve these issues, but simultaneously somewhere in me a safety valve was shut tight. The conflict became overwhelming, particularly when I was actually with them.

In the end, it was not until I went to the therapy clinic in Arizona that I began to move on. There I was allowed the space to explore these issues in greater depth and with the emotional continuity that residential therapy allows. Slowly I began to move on from my step-mother and my father and work even deeper on the issues relating directly to my mother. At the same time, I was engaged in an environment that was at harmony with both its natural surroundings and a spiritual outlook on life. As I leaned into this backdrop psychologically, I began to experience a diminution of those strong feelings about my father and step-mother. I particularly noticed that as I brought my mother into the frame, my step-mother became more forgivable. True, there were still objective matters of fact relating to the choices she and my father had made about which I still had feelings, but the intensity of my reaction to them lessened as I made more contact with these deeper wounds that came from my mother's loss.

I was moving once again into a new realm of emotional reality. In this safe zone, I was finally able to touch the core of my distress. From that perspective, ordinary people once again became more ordinary. In the same way that Scarlet had ceased to become such a thermonuclear emotional trigger once I had begun to explore who my mother really was, so as I delved deeper into the emotional pain of the loss of my mother, both my father and my step-mother seemed to be less guilty, less flawed and less culpable. I was able to attain the state of mind that understood and recognised that they were just normal people doing their best. And so, I scheduled a meeting with them when I returned from the desert.

High on my new found consciousness I opened my mouth and began to speak for the first time about my mother. I had forgotten however that they hadn't spent the last three weeks on the therapy farm. I was disappointed by their response which was highly resistant to recognising the issues. My step-mother immediately interjected that my father couldn't remember anything about my mother and when she was finished my father said that he had never mentioned my mother because he had never thought about it. I was brought back down to earth with a bump from my workshop high. I shouldn't have been surprised. They had invested thirty years in an order of reality that I was now challenging: this wasn't easy for them either. But at least it was progress of a sort The first step had been taken. It was up to us to see what we could make of it from there on.

I had come a long way from the day that I first entered Lois' consulting room full of my grievances about how Scarlet had reduced me to a nervous wreck. Scarlet was no longer on my emotional radar. Instead I had begun to engage in an honest interaction with my parents and recover some of my forgotten emotions that I had frozen away after my mother's death. Layer upon layer of experiences had followed, and each one needed carefully peeling away. They didn't necessarily come in order, but as they were brought into my consciousness and emotionally processed, I felt a little lighter, a little easier, and a little less angry. Slowly I began to notice projections in my family and relationships transmogrify before my very eyes. I recognised patterns and marked their ebb and flow.

Through all of this the one remaining constant was the difficulty of seeing through my projections. The most painful thing of all perhaps was to start to recognise that all of these feelings that I had had about others, the ones that I took comfort from blaming them for, were in fact located inside me, and as long as I continued to give into the illusion of my projections, I was destined to remain locked up on my own with this pain.

Understanding Why?

Projections in the family can be utterly baffling. They start so young in our lives that any suggestion that they are not entirely real can seem risible. However, I experienced the slackening of their strong grip on both my father and my step-mother as I dug deeper into the recesses of my own psychological baggage.

Long-term projections can become amalgamated like layers of film over a screen. In therapy, part of the process is to peel away these layers by articulating directly the emotional distress that these projections are trying to reach. This is very clearly seen in the progress of my attention moving from Scarlet to my step-mother and finally to my mother. It is quite possible that there is further to go. Most of the great and ancient spiritual disciplines describe this process as almost interminable in depth, until we reach a point of ultimate nirvana: of enlightenment.

I used both my father and my step-mother as screens onto which to project qualities which were at the time highly unsettling. However, these qualities provoked emotions in me that were echoes of the ones that I needed to uncarth from my past. In no short measure, these emotional reactions to my projections gave me the grist for my therapeutic mill. During my time in Arizona, I was able to work on these suggested emotional avenues more fully. As I did so, these feelings began to migrate to my conscious awareness. There became less need for the unconscious mind to stimulate these feelings within me because of my parents. Slowly, therefore, this shade of reality began to shift until there was nothing left but the ordinary quality of petty grievance that one human so routinely has with another.

Upon my return however, I realised that I was no longer contained within such a safe accepting environment. My consciousness retreated. My projections returned. At least I'd had a sneak preview of the state of mind that I should try to attain, and it was clear where the route to this tranquillity now lay.

Cure: Resolution

In disagreements with lovers and families, we should take comfort from the fact that it is quite possible for both parties both to be right, and yet to disagree. Each are simply stating their mutual experiences. These do not necessarily have to correlate, since each brings their own projections into the relationship. Once we understand the mechanism behind this disagreement and why projection is so important for the unconscious mind, we can begin to let go of the logical positions that our conscious mind holds so dear. Most importantly, we can let go of the absurd idea that reality ought to make sense. Then we will free ourselves up to a whole new level of being able to relate to other people: be they lovers, family, friends, co-workers or even complete strangers.

The key to conflict resolution in relationships is to be able to report our experience with reference to another person without demanding that this experience is exclusively located in and caused by them: to be able to refer to them, but without blaming them. This is actually really hard to do without using some quite contrived language and processes. When people do start to learn to express themselves in this way (often through seeking help in psychotherapy or self-help literature and groups) they can initially come off as a bit whacky.

For example if someone working for you says, "when you criticise my work I feel lonely and depressed," you might be tempted to respond by asking them to guess how much you really care and whether or not they can remember where the door is. Just as we find it very hard to experience anything in relation to another person without blaming them, we find it equally baffling to hear about another person's negative experience in relation to ourselves without feeling criticised and guilty. This is what so quickly sets up the oppositional emotional architecture of a disagreement, even when one side is only expressing their own emotional reaction without actually allocating blame or responsibility.

(To avoid this almost automatic confrontation, there are techniques that are used to slow down the exchange of information and the assumptions made from it. One such technique is to write a balanced account of our experiences. This account lists your experiences, both good and bad, and releases the other from blame. When this is done mutually it can result in some very informative communication and bridge this oppositional divide.)

The root of the problem remains the same as the root of all of our problems: unresolved trauma. When we find ourselves experiencing strong emotions in relation to another person, if we can remember that these emotions are the product of our past and only triggered by the present (not caused by the present), then we will have the opportunity to allow these emotions to come and go without using them to batter the other person. The more that we can do that, the more we will be able to enjoy a safe and harmonious relationship with the other, and therefore the more trauma we will be able to access, to thaw and to release.

This could take many years, if not a whole lifetime. The aim is not to complete the process, but merely to begin it. Imagine changing the focus of those terrible arguments into something constructive, bonding and healing. Could you really bear to feel so hurt, resentful and angry with someone and at the same time accept, remember and understand that those feelings are coming from you, not from the other person, whom you love and who professes to love you? The answer is usually no, for the good reason that no-one really wants to believe or accept that these horribly difficult, upsetting and disturbing feelings are within us. We want to blame them on someone else. But we'd be wrong to.

These feelings are inside us and they need to come out. The people that we are close to, work with or otherwise need to relate to are doing us a favour if they are bonded enough with us to allow us to use them as a projective targets for triggering our trauma. Why else would we have our worst fights with the people we love the most? Why else would we do and say the worst things to those people for whom we care the most? That just couldn't make sense any other way.

The pain of dysfunctional relationships, whether with a lover, in the family, with friends or just with colleagues, is among the most acute and widespread in our society. It is often a lonely, concealed pain, and equally often the source of hours and hours of discussion and self-examination. It is very much the fabric of our lives and occupies a great deal of our time, attention and energy. This is because it is the work of our very soul (the work of our deepest, wisest, unconscious self) to extract ourselves from the frozen state that we live in, to release trauma, to expand our consciousness and to spread our spiritual wings, emerging from our huddled, rat-race pupa into the beautiful harmony of a fully realised life. Relationships are one of the key catalysts in assisting us in that struggle. Unfortunately, they are usually accompanied by our sense of being out of control and overwhelmed by what they bring up. They can become unmanageable, and we either give up on them, or find a mutual stasis where, though the relationships survive, any meaningful sense of relating in a full, open and honest way is itself given up to another layer of frozen zombie-like existence.

Our inability to wake up from this trance and to use our relationships wisely for both the establishing of a safe environment and the concomitant manufacturing of projected experiences is a very large part of what's wrong with us.

Step 5: The 2ⁿᵈ Conclusion

the Unconscious use of Mutual Projections

You make heavy use of projections in both your intimate relationships and in your family. This disguises the reality of your circumstances. You attach negative qualities to the same people that you feel most safe with and supported by. You create a baffling conundrum of security and persecution. You do this by placing over a person a screen onto which you project qualities that you find useful to trigger a thaw in your own impacted trauma.

This screen is often so thick and has been there for so long that you no longer notice it. In the case of your family members, you have placed these projections over them since you were too young to remember anything else. With lovers, you probably can remember a time when they were seen by you in a very different light. Both can lead to great confusion and confrontation. However, that's exactly what the projective mechanism is trying to bring about: e-motion.

It is important when relating to others to remember that they have two qualities: their own independent real existence and the screen that they provide you for your projections. If you can remember from time to time to pull that screen to one side and look beyond it onto the face of the real other human being, then it will assist you considerably in maintaining valuable relationships.

You need relationships because they provide the emotional (and sometimes material) security to allow more dangerous feelings to be processed. This is precisely what happens when your relationships provide for you this screen and the opportunity to project onto it. You are likely to make good use of this to unearth all kinds of deeply challenging emotions and issues from your past. You would make bad use of this if you let the confusion that it creates spill over onto harming the real, separate person that lives and loves you from behind the projection's screen.

If you begin to explore your relationships as a road map to understanding what's wrong with you, then you have a chance to use these opportunities for deep healing and insight. If you can liberate others from blame and start to take responsibility for the genesis of all the terrible thoughts and feelings that you have when interacting with others; if you can cope with the paradox that those who you love and those who love you trigger in you the most powerful hate, hurt and distemper; if you can begin to peel back the layers of projection and see others for the beautiful beings they really are, full of love, life and compassion; then you will be well on the way to some significant healing and very far advanced in the process of beginning to really understand and to work with what's wrong with you.

Exercise 5

Do you really know your friends?

Look at the people in your life: lovers, family and friends. Who do you turn them into and what do you get out of it?

Draw up a list of the significant people in your life right now (or from another time that you would like to understand better). Partner them with the qualities that you ascribe(d) to them. Like this:

Scarlet

Was angry with her for the reverses in my life and how miserable I was feeling, yet still thought she was the solution to all my problems

Step-mother

Blamed her for the loss of my mother's memory in my life.

Now take a look at this same list of people and qualities. See what use you are making of these qualities. If you can, see how these thoughts and feelings are preferable to something else, something hidden deeper, probably something more personal and difficult. Make a corresponding list of what is really going on, even if it is speculative. Like this:

Scarlet

Couldn't face the pain of separation. Tried to reverse the separation to avoid dealing with emotional consequences. Tried to locate all of these problems in her to avoid recognising my own deep issues with separation.

Step-mother	*Used her as a foil to protect myself from my own emotional reaction to my mother's loss and absence. It is easier to be angry than to be hurt.*

If you peel back the layers in this way, perhaps you can begin to see why you might have been experiencing difficulties in these relationships. Can you come up with a strategy to improve things? Do you think you could bear to look at these people without these projections? What, or who, would you see?

The task here is to separate our the person from the projection. Then you must look deeper into what the projection tries to communicate to you. If you are experiencing anger in relation to a person, then you must look deeper for the source of that anger and try to work with it directly. If you can do so, then you can forgive the person onto whom this projection of anger has fallen. You will be able to relate to the real person more easily.

Try to finish this exercise by identifying any emotional themes that come up for you in relation to projections on others. These are the emotions that your unconscious mind wants you to stimulate fully and to release. Can you remember why? If you can find the source of these feelings then it is often easier to understand, to bear and to release.

Q&A

From the wwwyou?forum. You can see the original text and ask questions at whatswrongwithyou.com.

Self-centredness, Other-centeredness

Posted by: crystal Jul 13 2004, 06:52 PM

Hi Benjamin,

What you said to JLS45 about "self-centred" and "other-centred" was very interesting. I am interested to hear that they are opposites.

I'm sure it can be possible to be both self-centred and other-centred. I worry about other people's opinions a lot – probably because I have never been popular so they must think some horrible things about me. Also, sometimes my partner points out that I have said things that are unkind – when I think I'm only answering a question truthfully!

However, I am self-centred in that one of my greatest fears about social encounters is that I may not get my own way! I so hate it when one of my ideas or my suggested course of action gets rejected that I often don't risk an opinion these days! If I suppress my desire for a certain outcome then it will be bearable when I don't get it! If I voice my desire then not getting my own way will be unbearable.

As a child, it was often pointed out to me that it was bad that I always wanted my own way. Trouble is, I have always felt that I know best, and therefore fear the outcome of having to follow the lead of anyone who has challenged my suggested course of action. I always feel that the course of action suggested by the person whose opinion has been favoured over mine is doomed to failure. And often, I am right! So why didn't everyone listen to me in the first place? Answer – because I'm not popular, due to poor social skills, I suppose. Which is why I have social phobia.

I have identified that one of my earliest memories was of mistrust of people and a realisation that authority figures were often wrong about what was best for you. I can even identify the event that seemed to really trigger it. But that doesn't help me any.

Is there any way I can learn to be one of those outgoing friendly people who always like people when they meet them, don't mind not getting their own way and able to take vicarious pleasure in other people's happiness.

Posted by: benjaminfry Jul 14 2004, 09:32 PM

Crystal, can you tell me more about the "event" before I reply? It might help.

Posted by: benjaminfry Jul 24 2004, 02:15 PM

Here is an interesting observation; you have sent me a private message which explains a great deal about your state of mind. It is eloquent and elicits much sympathy. You were worried to post it here on the board in case it might identify you. By contrast, your post here describes what you want. As such it is less sympathetic since it lists your self-cantered

qualities and judges others. Would it be too much to hypothesise that this perfectly represents your private and public per-
sona?

Inside, you are a person who has suffered much unhappiness in your family. There has been little stability and love. All
of the goodness that you received as a child came from fragmented resources and you were locked into a central drama
with a mother figure whose values and ideas you did not share.
Trapped in that situation, you would have created a wall between the outside and the inside. Beyond that wall was where
you would wrestle with the authority that you had lost respect
for. This is where you can't bear to not get your own way and
are so tortured by having to follow others' less able plans.
Within that wall is where you kept and stored up your own
private reservoir of pain. This is the part of you that craves
company, is desperate to be accepted just for being who you
are and feels so lonely behind your walls.

The importance of these walls to you is demonstrated by
your reluctance to make your inner-self public even behind the
anonymity of an internet forum. Yes there is a risk that your
self-disclosure could identify you to a family member. But you
have to also ask, what is the harm in that? Nothing that you
wrote to me privately indicates anything other than an intelligent and able person who has not received the love and nurturing that you deserved. More than anything, you give the impression of a childhood spent not being understood by those
you were closest to. Now you deny this same opportunity to
your present day family members by not revealing who you
really are.

When people retreat behind walls and obscure their true
selves, they may find some safely, but they also find even more
loneliness. To other people, you may come across as missing
something. This could be the cause of your poor social recep-
tion. Since you have buried your true self, you have no option

but to put on a mask. Your mask isn't engaging others. People don't trust it. People don't listen to it. Even when it is right! That's not wholly unreasonable. If you won't trust other people by presenting them with a three dimensional version of yourself, then they will intuitively and unconsciously know that you are disguising something from them. This inevitably leads others to disengage from you personally and intellectually.

The emotional isolation that this sets up can be unbearable. You need and crave more than anything else to be understood and accepted (even perhaps praised) for who you really are. However, by holding back your true self from the outside world you are making this very hard. You may conspire in this process for good reasons. You currently have an intellectual awareness of where your problems come from. If you were really reached and touched by human empathy and understanding of these problems, then you would begin to feel the pain that goes with these memories. You say you can identify the source of your problems, but as yet appear to have resisted using this comprehension and a bridge into releasing the emotions that were frozen within you when that happened. This is probably because you lack the human safety net around you to keep you supported as you emotionally fall apart. The cruel paradox is that you can't find this human support while you isolate your true self, and you can't reveal your true self without this support.

You therefore need to take small manageable steps to "outing" yourself. Try to begin to share personal details and information in those situations where you would least like to. Be aware that your fear of doing so comes only from your actual pain experienced in the past, not from the present where being more open with others will make them warm to you .

You may have leadership skills, but lack the magnetic leadership quality. Here's a challenge for you; post here in this topic the private message that you sent to me. By taking that risk to be seen publicly for who you really are, you will make a statement to your unconscious that you want out of your inner walls. You will also build trust with other members of this forum and perhaps then they will be more inclined to do what you say!

Posted by: crystal Jul 26 2004, 11:18 AM

Eeek! A challenge.

I have to say that your post was spot-on, Benjamin. Thank you very much. It did help.

I was going to post an edited version but then decided I couldn't. When my mother was alive, she felt it was important not to speak unkindly of the dead. It just feels too disloyal to leave a set of criticisms of her online for all to read. I also consider that somehow or other, I have to forgive her, rather than continuing to moan on about it forever.

This weekend I attended a party where there were a lot of people from my childhood present. I found it stressful to see them but one of them (who I had always felt was very much on my mother's side and whom I have been avoiding for years) suddenly said to me that he imagined my childhood had been very hard but he knew that everything was done with the best of intentions by parents who didn't really know what they were doing. I felt much better after this – that someone who had known me all my life and been my mother's good friend had noticed what was wrong with my childhood.

I think, when contemplating your childhood and the failings in your upbringing, it is easy to feel that you are being ungrateful for resenting it and this can make you feel guilty. We all know from the media that broken homes, unpleasant events with relatives, traumatic events in childhood etc easily lead to mental health problems in adulthood. And yet it can be hard to admit that your parents, who you know did their best, provided you with a poor quality childhood. And family friends won't want to admit they saw it either. So how do you verify that you really went through some bad times and are not just being self-pitying? I felt a lot of relief from getting that verification this weekend.

Posted by: Hilary Jul 27 2004, 03:07 PM

Hi Crystal,

I'm following this exchange with interest as I have some of the same things in my own story. What Benjamin says is right – it takes enormous courage to reveal your true self if you are not sure there is someone waiting to welcome you, but I promise you it's worth doing. And we are waiting to welcome you!

Perhaps there's a way you can meet Benjamin's challenge without being unkind.

If you use wording like this: "When my mother did/ said .... I felt ...." you are giving a true account of what happened and taking responsibility for your feelings without blaming your mother for the outcome. This will allow you to acknowledge your own pain, which is the first step towards forgiveness.

Hope this helps.

Love, Hilary.

Posted by: benjaminfry Jul 31 2004, 04:52 PM

You identify an extremely interesting theme here. It is a tremendous conflict and one that stems from our survival instincts growing up. We are loathe to "criticise" our parents for all sorts of reasons, but a key one is that when we were small we literally needed their approval to survive. We needed them to protect and feed us so we both decided that they were "the best parents" and also didn't want to piss them off with criticism.

As you get older and need them for survival less (around the teenage years) this block wears off and we are all familiar with the behaviour of teenagers to their parents. The repressed criticism comes up and is often quite vitriolic. Then as you mellow into adulthood, and particularly if you have your own children, there is a quality of guilt that develops with a sense of maturity. You get to understand that your parents did "their best" and that being mean about people is itself a bit mean.

So what's the answer? Well firstly it is vital to separate your negative experiences which happened as a result of other people with blame of those people. You had a hard time with your mother. This was acknowledged to you and you felt a great sense of relief. However, this doesn't mean that you have to blame or "criticise" your mother. If you frame your comments in the subjective, such as has been suggested in the last post, then you are talking about yourself. If you move into the objective then it is about the other. The remarkable thing is that subjective statements hurt us and cause us pain. Objective critical statements usually cover up that hurt with an attack of our own.

Guilt is a big problem in our society. It is endemic to the western world and perhaps derivative of a Christian mindset (or vice versa). Apparently, it is largely absent from the eastern mindset and there isn't even a word for it in Japanese. Their honour is the key. However, if you feel guilty, then just work with it. It is another emotion that you need to deal with. You have repressed it by not posting the information you mention. This is the enemy of good mental health.

There is a way through this sticky trap. The reason that we place so much power on our parents' behaviour is that we project onto them the power of nature to sustain us and the heavens to guide us. That's a lot for ordinary frail humans to bear and so inevitably they fail us. We have lost the rituals as a society that connect us with the earth and the Gods, so we look to our parents unconsciously to provide these great overarching paradigms of male and female archetypes. Having placed our very existence in the palms of two people who themselves are equally lost, we usually end up very angry with them for not living up to this expectation. So try this:

Get up in the morning, go to a church or any equivalent that you can bear and then spend the morning in a park or with a strong connection with nature. Then see how you feel about your mother's "failings". I'd hope that the intensity of your disappointment would be lessened because you would be relating to her more as a fellow human being, without the God and nature projections. Then you can frame your comments on her impact on your life more evenly.

Then you can share it with us…

SIX

Society

Society and life. What happens when six billion people all project together.

Theory: Two Tribes go to War

The projective mechanism, which works to resolve our own individual traumas, can be seen to have a much wider influence than simply working one-on-one. There is a tribal component to this projective mechanism that moves us to form strong opinions and to have strong emotions about what is safe and what is a threat. We project on to those who are similar to ourselves the qualities of safety, and project on to those who are different from us the qualities of a threat. We gravitate towards the company of what is familiar and similar because we survived best among members of our own tribe, but also we unconsciously desire safe places in which to resolve our own frozen traumas. Thus we are able to differentiate between where it is and where it is not safe to experience our difficult emotions.

We often project negative qualities on to the individuals we are closest to, but it seems that it is not practical to project, in the same way, threatening aspects on to the whole society that we live in and which we believe keeps us safe. Instead we seem to project that threat out onto anything that is different from

the society that we understand. We create the myth of the
bogyman.

This idea of the bogyman is formed very early in childhood.
It is a useful function for the unconscious mind to project onto
unknown individuals all of the frightening qualities that are
really found within ourselves and in those closest to us. Our
unresolved, darker feelings which lie repressed within us, both
as a parent and child, are moved out of our own sphere of
responsibility, projected on to the identity of others. Children
have a great fear of being left to die by their adult keepers.
Much of this fear remains buried in the unconscious mind and
is accompanied by their own murderous retaliatory fantasies.
Throughout childhood and life, these fantasies and the accompanying fears are amplified, worked on and expanded until they
become the basis for all of the negative projections that people
cast out on to the other tribes of the world. The most obvious
consequence of this is the tribalism that has been such a hall-
mark of human society since it has been recorded. Modern-day
mankind continues to vigorously manifest this in its racism,
nationalism and wars.

It clearly doesn't make any objective sense to judge negatively someone you haven't even met and know nothing about,
but equally clearly, evaluating people on the basis of race is
deeply rooted in the way that our minds work. Many people
may have mastered their own thought process sufficiently to
remove from their behaviour actions based on racial prejudice,
but few people will be free from automatic, unconscious assumptions based on the fact that a stranger is not from our
own tribe.

We stop noticing these kinds of differences with other
people, once we begin to establish a relationship with them.
We may even make comments like we don't think of so-and-so
as black/white/yellow/green any more. The bogyman projection doesn't work once we get to be familiar with another

person as a human being. The whole point of the bogyman is that he takes on the parts of ourselves and our social system that we wish to disavow. That falls apart if the object of our fear, and therefore our hatred, turns out to be a really nice person.

Tribal differences dissolve very quickly when there is a real human connection. Nonetheless our entire planet, governments, societies and constitutions are driven by the collective projection onto other tribes of all of the threats which actually exist within ourselves and within our own homes and neighbourhoods. It is useful to put these threats on the outside. It helps to allow for the present time and place to be used safely for healing. At the same time, through the projection of our own internal threatening qualities onto others, we can still feel the fear and hatred of these aspects of ourselves and our own society.

Look at how the American psyche adopted a projection for part of the Arab world. It demonised it to the extent that it judged it wise to spend over a hundred billion dollars (and thousands of lives) on an invasion of the region. A similar sum spent at home combating cancer would have instead saved thousands of American lives. (More Americans die from cancer each month than have ever died from terrorism.) But cancer doesn't work for the collective unconscious. We can't project onto a disease. We need a tribe.

This is the basis of all conflict among tribes. Just as the projective mechanism promotes conflict between lovers, who in their calmer moments would state that they would rather not fight, so the projective mechanism promotes conflicts between societies that claim that they would rather live in peace. This projective mechanism has been very successfully stoked and manipulated by political leaders throughout history to help them to alleviate their own unresolved traumas.

Hitler used it in his successful manipulation of his tribe

against the Jews. They were portrayed as an enemy at the core of the nation and society. In fact, they were metaphorically representing an emotional enemy in the heart of Hitler himself: one which resonated with the emotional conflicts in many of his compatriots. Tragically, the consequences of his unchecked projection was his attempt to exterminate the Jews. But on another level, he was just trying to do what we all want to do: to kill off the unexplained and difficult feelings that arise within us when trauma starts to thaw. He lacked the wisdom to do it internally, and unfortunately had the absolute power to attempt to do it externally.

The reality is that all of our emotions are located and ignited from within. They are not in themselves brought upon us by other tribes. The other may stimulate it, but it begins and ends in us. The unconscious mind makes good use of the mechanism of projection to help us to explore and to resolve some of the traumas first set up in childhood by these bogyman-type fears. The unpleasant consequence of this is the racial and tribal bias that it uses.

We see this pattern of the collective quality of projections every day. For example, in the recent second Gulf war, the preservation of any American life was celebrated in the American media, while the routine killing of many hundreds of Iraqis was given cursory, statistical mention. The reverse occurred in some of the Arab media. Politicians and journalists, who would bristle with rage at the merest suggestion that they were racist, would routinely describe people they had never met as the "good guys" or the "bad guys", based on nothing other than knowing their nationality. There is clearly no objective balance to this equation, since all human life is equally valuable, but it is the same in every nation and every conflict.

The people being described as "good" or "bad", and cherished or disregarded accordingly, would be entirely differently evaluated if the viewer could actually meet them. These same media reports on both sides could have been rejoicing at the saving of a wife-battering rapist, whilst delighting in the death of a well respected poet. We just don't know. From such a distance, we have no way to evaluate another human being other than by understanding whose side they are on: or in other words, which tribe they belong to.

When there is a great deal of fear being put out into the collective projection, individuals will delight in the preservation of any member of their own tribe, while revelling in the destruction of any member of another. This is entirely at odds with most people's behaviour towards those people that they get to know and experience personally. Usually we would not wish, even on our worst enemy, the kind of hellish destruction that we might be happy to see inflicted on a complete stranger in time of war.

Those political leaders who march steadfast and determined towards open conflict with a different tribe are probably therefore those who have within themselves the most unresolved trauma, which they then try to destroy with this metaphor of war. But it doesn't work. The conflict remains intact and so another conflict is always needed. Conversely, those leaders who advocate peace between nations and a connection between their individual inhabitants are likely to be operating under conditions of less internal threat. Both styles of leadership will always find a consensus of support somewhere in a population. Everybody lives with the constant struggle of trying to balance their own desire to destroy their unconscious projections and the equal desire to be reconciled to them, and thus resolve their trauma. It is the same for nations.

But these are broad examples set off by extreme events. As the global temperature of fear declines so the distance to the bogyman diminishes, and we may find that the other who we become so afraid of and hateful towards is no further away than our own next-door neighbour.

Within all societies, this same dynamic that brings nations to war works at every level in ever decreasing concentric circles. Any difference can be a trigger to the fear and hatred that lie repressed within us. Thus, we can also come to project our negative emotions into and among our own society as we shrink our perception of what counts as our tribe. In the workplace, the village, the neighbourhood, the community, the school or on our block, the collective unconscious is at work pushing back the threshold of reality and placing in front of it the force of our own projections. That is how we create the dynamic of life's real soap operas: village gossip, petty rivalries, blood feuds or duelling neighbours.

It is no accident that this distillation of our global projective mechanisms finds such popularity with television audiences. These forms of entertainment all rely on the one basic premise, that the audience thrives on a constant diet of conflict. Our unconscious mind recognises this conflict as a metaphor for the one that it is itself trying to resolve itself within us. The conscious mind tries to maintain the resources of our survival (key among which is its ability to make sense of phenomena through a logical connection of cause and effect), while the unconscious mind tries to resolve our trauma and to free us from the limits that it places on the scope of our consciousness.

Thus all conflicts in society from the local and petty to the global and devastating stem from the same source. These conflicts are created by the unconscious projection of threatening qualities from within ourselves on to those in whom it is easier for us to locate these threats. From the alien race, person or culture, to the neighbour who just hangs her curtains a different way, anyone will do.

This projective mechanism highlights our differences and marginalises the similarities that actually bind us to one another. It creates enmity between people who have not yet even had the chance to become friends. It separates nations whose populations all face the same basic challenges and aspirations in life. It divides all the peoples of the planet, who are actually startlingly united in their similarities. It is the source of the greatest acts of human violence, pain and misery our world has ever known.

Case Study: Eton

"Plebs" wear white socks and are called Kevin or Sharon. That's what I learned on my first day at Eton. It was the start of my unofficial education at this great institution. Eton was very different from my previous boarding school because it was geographically out in the open. Where my prep-school had hidden young boys away on a private estate, Eton was not just a school, but also a real place. It was just a short walk from the large historic market town of Windsor. Lots of real people lived and worked there. Not much further away, but out of range for us boys on foot, was the large urban wastelands of Slough. At Eton, we wore a uniform of a tailcoat and white tie. It is otherwise used as the most formal dress available for state and private functions, very rarely worn in public life these days. We wandered about these public streets dressed like this every day of our school year. We paraded privilege down the high street of other people's ordinary and difficult lives. We invited envy and we received enmity.

It was drilled into me very early on as a thirteen year-old new-boy that the plebs were a danger. Plebs were people of somewhat similar age to Etonians who were not Etonians. The age-old collegiate drama of town versus gown was well understood by the boys. Plebs were easy to spot by the curious fact that they really did always seem to wear white socks. Etonians never wore white socks.

Going to Windsor was about the only diversion to be had

from school life at Eton. It was allowed some afternoons of the week, but the main exodus would be on a Saturday. There was a MacDonald's in Windsor towards the top of the high street. This route from Eton to MacDonald's pretty much defined the area that was in bounds to Etonians. Venturing further into town was not allowed and therefore highly exciting. The only official way into Windsor was across the pedestrian only bridge over the Thames. It was here that gangs of plebs would gather on a Saturday for some sport. Our school uniform requirements were slightly slackened to allow us to blend in Windsor. Instead of a full school uniform we could go to town in a sports jacket and tie.

Not many thirteen year-old boys routinely wear sports jackets and ties on a Saturday afternoon. We might as well have painted our heads bright red and had a sign round our necks begging for a kicking. We were easy targets for the locals. However, as long as we stayed in bounds and moved about in daylight, the threat was mitigated by the relative difficulty of anyone attacking us unnoticed. Nonetheless, the stories were legion. Time after time we would hear and retell dark takes of plebs kicking the shit out of Etonians. This was really quite frightening for a young boy. At the age of thirteen, a sixteen- or seventeen-year old is a huge physical presence. It is the difference between man and boy. A new boy could not defend himself from an attack by local youths. The only hope we had was that we would not be a target in the first place. I remember being amazed by the scale of this threat. Not once in my life up to that point had I ever encountered overt physical danger from strangers. Now, simply for having gone to a new school, it seemed that I was living with the real possibility of a frightening physical attack any time that I ventured out of the safety of a well lit Eton venue. It was really quite a shock. Survival became paramount.

The first technique for this survival was to identify the

enemy. Thus the pleb moniker was born. The elitist snobbery that Eton encouraged informed the choice of label, but it disguised the real fact that we weren't naming the locals as plebs because we looked down on them. We were in fact attempting to denigrate them because we were so scared of them. As with most conflicts, fear was the initiating cause of our own provocation. Who knows who started it? Who cared? They wanted to kick our heads in and we wanted to despise them because of it. There was a subculture of on-going warfare at the heart of the nation's most famous school. Our next manoeuvre was to become less Etonian. Clearly what angered the plebs the most was our elitist posturing: young boys going to Mac-Donald's in ties and jackets, while the locals queued up in their shell suits. And really who can blame them? Not only did we have all the possible advantages in life, but it seemed like we wanted to ram down their throats how different and superior we were.

The reality though was that we wore the uniform because if we didn't, we couldn't get across the bridge into Windsor. We would be stopped by the teachers who manned this convenient gateway at peak hours. So we developed tactics to be less obtuse. We could move off the beaten track so we could remove the tell tale signs of our Etonian roots. But we would never blend. There's still a lilt to the Etonian gait, a quiff to the Etonian hair and a drawl to the Etonian voice that no kind of dirty jeans and open neck shirt is going to disguise. However, simply making the effort to appear to be in some respects less institutionalised seemed to mollify the local population. Shop keepers would be less diffident, locals would be less hostile, plebs in white socks seemed slightly less menacing.

If Windsor carried with it a risk of a beating at the hands of marauding plebs, Slough was genuinely rough. (Think Ali G in real life.) You had to take a train or bus to get there, which itself was a tough call since you had to get to the station or bus stop unnoticed. Then on arrival in Slough, you could lose yourselves happily in the crowds. However, the pub scene and the youths who hung around the shopping districts were unforgiving and there were quite a few stories of near escapes from those daring souls who had ventured this far. I don't think that we really had any idea quite how conspicuous we all were despite our efforts not to be. At least in Windsor, the tenor of the town was gentile and people were faintly amused by renegade rich kids. In Slough they were just grateful for the rare opportunity to deface the establishment by doing in its most privileged sons.

Perhaps the most frightening episode during my time there was the invitation, which was accepted, to rumble on the golf course. On one side of the notional campus of Eton town there is a large golf course exclusively for our use. Beside it ran the train line to Slough. You could make your way into Slough on foot by following this train line. Some boys had ventured that way and come across a gang of plebs from Slough. There had been an exchange of verbals, but no fighting. The local boys challenged the Etonians to bring their friends and sort this out properly. A date was set for a rumble on the golf course the following afternoon.

This was highly unusual, wildly cinematic and of course greatly exciting to the prisoners of Eton. The word spread like wildfire and about fifty of our number gathered to make the march on the golf course. We were all about fifteen years old. Fortunately for us, word also spread to the teaching staff. The boys arrived at the golf course to find that the locals were taking this seriously. They'd done this before and had come prepared. They were well tooled up with baseball bats, knuckle dusters, studded gloves and planks with rusty nails. The teachers arrived just in time. The grateful Etonians were given a terrific excuse to run for their lives. It was a quick and painless lesson in the relative severity of life faced by the rich and the poor. No-one went looking for trouble again in a hurry.

I personally came face-to-face with marauding plebs only once in my time at Eton. It was early on in the summer of my first year. We had very little to do in our down time and lived on the edge of the town. All around us were fields with handy bushes where students congregated to smoke cigarettes and joints, or sniff glue and aerosols. It was the summer so the days were long and warm, perfect weather for outdoor high-jinks. One particularly boring Sunday afternoon, someone had heard . that there was a way into the abandoned church in Eton high street. It backed onto a large field that also shared a border with our house. We only had to make it a few hundred yards across this open field and we were at its back gate. If we could make this territory our own once we got there, then we would have our very own private den of iniquity. We could smoke, drink, do whatever we liked, and all with a roof over our heads.

The information was good. There was a way in. It required some climbing and initiative but we quickly found ourselves inside the disused church. The doorway to the stairs was open and we went up to see what else we could find. The stairs led all the way up to the roof of the spire. It was a flat topped spire, not a steeple, and so we could stand up there and survey the whole town and school laid out beneath us. Some of the slates were loose on the roof and were knocked off as we cavorted about. The smokers had a cigarette or two and we basked in our incredible freedom, found so near to our own boarding house and yet so far from anyone's thoughts or experience.

As time drew on, we determined to go back to our house and return again as soon as possible. We made our way down the spire, out the back door, over a fence and into the rear enclosure behind the church where a flaw in the fencing had allowed us in. There we found two youths in white socks waiting for us. It was our worst nightmare: plebs with numchuckas. There were seven of us and only two of them. But they were older than us and armed. They seemed a little taken back at our number, but what they didn't realise was that we were never going to fight. We were just small frightened boys who had grown up in privileged schools. We hadn't a clue how to really fight. We were street dumb.

These youths told us that they had been sent by the vicar to see what was going on in the church and that the police were on their way. That seemed to us to be highly unlikely. It couldn't possibly be true that the police were coming. We feared the authority of the school. We feared being caught by the Lower Master with odd socks. We feared small transgressions of simple, trivial rules. The thought of actually being apprehended by the nation's constabulary was mind blowing. The consequences of being arrested were just inconceivable. And so it was with a surreal horror and temporary detachment from reality that I saw the policemen's hats come into view over the fence. There were two of them.

They relieved the threatening plebs of their jailors' duties and asked us what had been going on. They'd had a report of someone throwing tiles off the church roof and terrible crashings about inside. None of us spoke a word. We were marched single file back across the field that we had so freely scampered through an hour or so earlier. The field was in full view of the longest side of the house and since it was late afternoon, many of the boys were having tea sitting in their windows enjoying the warm weather. I'll never forget looking up and seeing a broadside of open windows crowded with our housemates gazing open mouthed as almost the entire first year was led back to the house by two uniformed policemen. It was just unthinkable.

No charges were brought, but the leader of our gang was expelled and another rusticated until the end of term. No-one could ever remember a boy being expelled in the first year before. It was quite something. We were famous in the school and the story of our face-off with two numchucka-wielding plebs added further fuel to the burning furnace of our suspicion and fear of the omnipresent local menace.

Understanding Why?

Look at how we Etonians used the "plebs" as our projective tribe of choice. At boarding school, we faced constant threats from one another, and yet we were able to bond in the face of an external threat from random acts of prejudicial violence meted out by local youths. We judged and branded an entire socio-economic class on the basis of the colour of their socks. We formed an oppositional relationship with them which we exploited to keep all of the "threat" on the outside.

The reality though was that Eton was an environment where internal competition was stoked incessantly. On top of the usual jockeying for social position that is ubiquitous among teenagers, we were constantly assessed, graded and publicly rewarded or shamed. In academia and sport, it was a matter of public record who was a success and who was a failure. Our system of compulsory dress codes reinforced this. This rubbed off onto our social interactions with one another. We would persecute the weak and consolidate with the strong. Our lives were lived permanently under the scrutiny of judgement and the fear of punishment for the same. We were there, without our families, twenty-four hours a day, seven days a week, for months on end. We had to find a way to make our environment safe and our mental escape route was to project the routine dangers of life out onto the less frequently encountered menace of the local youth. The plebs were our way of finding a worse, external threat to make our environment more bearable. It was highly effective.

So we created the "bogeyman". Our world was very small, so the threat was placed on what was local and yet outside of us. We found a different tribe on our doorstep and it was there that we were able to locate our projections of all of our fears. It would never have occurred to us that we were alone away from our families at the age of thirteen and therefore our fears may have been related to what we were going to find much closer to home. It is so much easier to locate a threat in some shadowy presence that we don't really know or understand. We had no idea when we would come up against a "pleb" or what threat that person would bring. We really knew nothing about them or their lives and could not have understood what would have been going through their minds in relation to ourselves. We seized upon a few acts of violence to brand an entire group of people defined by their "difference" as an enemy and a threat, when really all along we faced much more threat from within our own selves and from our neighbouring school chums down the hall. I was actually once literally stabbed in the back by an fellow Etonian, puncturing a lung and putting me in hospital. By contrast, no pleb ever laid a hand on me.

Cure: Love versus the Rat Race

The unconscious mind's relentless quest to find its way to a resolution of our own trauma has the unfortunate consequence of swamping our natural predisposition to manifest the more attractive qualities of our mind-body system. Beneath all that trauma lie the love and compassion that are the natural birthright of all human beings from their own deep well of divine and spiritual understanding.

Unfortunately, we are routinely deflected away from any contact with this experience by our unconscious projections, which attempt to clear away our trauma so that we can once again connect with this experience. If it wasn't for the conscious mind getting in the way, then we could fairly quickly move through the agenda of our unconscious mind, and we would eventually return to a state of grace where we would be comfortable with both our circumstances and our emotions. We would know and trust that everything was exactly as it should be.

Instead, the conscious mind interrupts that process with its own fear of our own emerging trauma and we end up stuck in the middle. We end up living permanently with our projections and thus experience life in a state of constant confusion and fear. This fear is generated by the reaction of our survivalist instincts to threats, but the threats themselves are not real. They are our projections.

We probably no longer notice this constant state of background fear. This is the fear that fuels the rat-race. The decisions that we make for our lives and that we make for our society might seem like they are taken for positive reasons, but really they are just a flight from what we fear.

We all seek to protect ourselves, like animals working to ensure our survival, but we also go far beyond that. We continue to act the same way even when our survival is not at stake. We develop advanced, safe societies, and yet push for even more progress. We attain material wealth, and then continue to strive for even more. We constantly challenge ourselves to move one rung higher on the ladder of life, mindful only of the rung above and the rung below: never seeing the bigger picture of a vast ladder, on which all three rungs are really in exactly the same place. We maintain a dull struggle for survival against illusory threats projected onto our society by our unconscious mind.

By locking our unconscious mind and our conscious mind into a stasis (where they pull and push in equal measure) we become stuck in this state. We lose contact with our higher functions of love and understanding, the same qualities that

would create a truly safe and harmonious planet. These qualities are available as the natural consequence of moving beyond
the prison of trauma. They can be attained by letting go of the
conscious mind's agenda and letting the unconscious mind do
its work. Without an awareness of our own compassion, we
remain living like rats in a cage, constantly striving to improve
our chances of survival relative only to what we think we see
around ourselves. We fail to see that we face very little real
threat and see only our projected reality. We respond to the
world as if it is constantly bringing us face to face with life and
death scenarios. In doing so, we actually create our own
greatest, real threat: the threat of the dysfunctional human
society. In pushing to constantly improve our progress and
wealth, we degrade our natural habitat and overwhelm our
planet with ever demanding needs. We develop weapons that
have the potential to obliterate life as we know it.

It is the conscious mind that has allowed us to develop the
tools and understanding to build our safe society. But it is also
the conscious mind that paralyses the vital work of our wise
unconscious mind, and thus holds us in a prison of fear, out of
contact with our higher spiritual functions which would show
us how to enjoy and sustain this safe society. Ultimately, the
tool of our greatest evolutionary triumph may prove to be the
cause of our extinction. That would not be unusual in the
history of evolution. Nature finds a balance in the end.

We live trapped in a state of unrivalled material security
combined with incomprehensible emotional insecurity. We face
less threat from the world than any species at any time, ever, in
the history of the planet; and yet we never feel safe. Our fear
fuels our anger, which drives our conflict, which sustains our
discontent. Our conscious mind constantly fights against the
wisdom of our unconscious mind and we remain stuck in a
psychic battle that no-one is winning.

That is why our lives are so often experienced as stuck,

frustrating and unrewarding. That is the reason why, despite our dissatisfaction, we accept the rat-race, and nothing seems to change. That is why our society is so successful, and yet so fundamentally unrewarding. That is why there is nothing wrong with our lives, and yet there is something wrong with us.

The source of our discontent is our inability to use our relative safety, circumstances and projections to promote the emotions that would heal our frozen trauma. If we could stop judging our emotions, if we could allow our feelings to flow, if we could stop rejecting our circumstances and if we could stop taking our projections so seriously, then we could start to feel the real and immediate release from the stasis of unsuccessfully fighting the unconscious mind for control of our lives and our feelings.

Once that starts then the deadlock is broken. Once we start to move through our emotional residue, then it is like releasing a boulder down a hill. It will move us, slowly at first, but inevitability and relentlessly towards a different point of view. Once we begin to experience how our projections shift and adjust according to how our state of trauma is reduced, then we will begin more and more easily to accept that our projections are just that (fictions that we project on to reality) and that our circumstances are indeed the product of our wise, unconscious mind leading us where we need to go.

The unconscious mind casts its net far and wide, trying to manipulate our world to give us opportunities to resolve trauma and expand our consciousness. If only we could assist the unconscious mind in its work, rather than letting our conscious mind resist the resolution of our trauma; if only we could let go of emotions as they arrive, rather than trying to control them; if only we, as a society, could bear to examine our own fear and rage, rather than project it outwards to other similarly afflicted nations; then the unconscious mind would have less work to do, and the forces that separate mankind would diminish. All this just because we made better and more genuine efforts to work to resolve, to contain and to understand what's wrong with us.

Step 6: The 3rd Conclusion

the Unconscious use of Tribal Projections

You project onto those people whom you determine to be different to you an assortment of negative qualities that actually exist in yourself, your relationships, your family, and your own society. This allows you to manage your existence in a state of greater security which in turn allows you to begin to unearth your own impacted trauma. These negative qualities which you have disavowed are placed onto other tribes. This can be across racial stereotypes, national borders or just the garden fence. It is impossible to entirely dispose of these negative qualities since they exist in you and around you. Therefore they have to persist in your image of the other tribes. Your desire to get rid of these threatening aspects to your experience can lead to all the unpleasant symptoms that we associate with tribal confrontation: prejudice, racism and war.

The reality though is that all people on your planet are remarkably similar. They are so much more united by what they share than separated by their differences. They all want a bit of peace and security in which to attempt to see their trade prosper and their families survive. No-one wants war. However, the whole planet remains in the grip of its tribal projections and very few people look behind the screen of those projections to notice the reality of our true human solidarity.

You can step out of this cycle of aggression if you choose to use your projections as a tool to better understanding yourself, rather than as data on which to judge and to persecute other races. Those world leaders who have the least trauma in themselves, and therefore the least need of projection to help them to cure themselves, are probably the most able to dispassionately and objectively see the ties that bind our respective nations, rather than the projected threats that separate them. World peace and societal harmony start in your own mind through the resolution of your own trauma and in the minds of every other individual on this planet.

If you can explain to your conscious mind that it can achieve its goals in life by releasing you from its emotional control, then you will be able to reach your ultimate aims of happiness in life more easily, more fully and more deeply than you could have hoped for simply by using only the base material and survivalist agenda of the conscious mind. You will understand and experience what real change is. You will influence those around you to change. You will effect real change in your society. And you will become a true force for bringing happiness into not just your own life, but also the lives of those closest to you, and eventually the whole world.

You will have begun to absorb, begun to work with and begun to broadcast, through the manifestation of your own changes, life and satisfaction, the fundamental power and simplicity of being able to understand and to change the reality of what's wrong with you.

Exercise 6

Do you really know your politics?

You might fancy that you are free of prejudice but can you put that to the test? Write down a list of groups that you might think of as being "other" than your own; such as a race, nation, organization or political party. Then write next to them what qualities you automatically associate with the individuals that are part of those groups. Don't judge yourself. Just let the adjectives flow. Like this:

> *Plebs*   *Common. Dangerous. Envious. Threatening. Violent.*

Then take a long hard look at these qualities. Can you find them rather closer to home? Now take the same list of groups and write along side this list another set of identifiers, but this time they must be people that you know, including yourself who are actually the real source of these emotional projections. Like this:

> *Plebs*   *Other Etonian school boys. The boys I live with. My class. My form. Myself.*

If you are successful, you should be able to reduce the entire list of "others" to experiences and people much closer to home. Perhaps this sheds a whole new light on your views about the society you live in. For me, it illustrates how unconsciously I experienced Eton as a constantly hostile and threatening environment, which isn't unreasonable for a thirteen-year old living away from home among a very competitive set of other boys.

It is likely that you can learn a great deal from this exercise about your own political inclinations. Do you oppose those parties that represent the parts of yourself which you are most keen to avoid?

If you find yourself on any issue at the extreme of any political and social spectrum, then this is a great opportunity to learn more about yourself. You are there for a reason. There is something within you that you want to locate outside of yourself and rail against. If you work hard at it, you draw yourself back in and use this information to understand better your unconscious needs played out through these societal projections.

Complete this exercise by trying to identify themes of emotional qualities in your list of the qualities of the "others". These themes are waiting for you to be the stuff of your own emotional growth.

You don't have to give up on changing the world, but now you have the information to start to change it from within, where you might actually do some good.

Revision

Steps Four, Five and Six

These last three chapters and their conclusions introduce the fundamental dynamic of the projective mechanism and illustrate how it works to change our fate, our relationships and our society. Without resolution of the trauma that this is trying to stimulate, we remain stuck in a vicious cycle unable to move on from life's events in the simple linear way that the gazelle would.

The Vicious Circle of Projection, Fate, Relationships and Society

From birth onwards, we are faced with the internal reality of an undesirable accumulation of trauma. We respond to it in the only way that would be consistent with our unconscious spiritual ambition. We attempt to resolve it.

the Unconscious use of Projection and Fate

We use the mechanism of projection to become more highly functional and to achieve goals beyond the short-term priorities of the conscious mind. We influence our circumstances by making unconscious decisions and placing unconscious projections out onto our view of our world. We call these phenomena fate and other people. Much of the time we exist in this delusion uncorrected by the opinions of others, but inevitably we run into contradictions in close human interactions: in relationships.

the Unconscious use of Mutual Projections

When we live in close proximity with others such as in our families or in intimate relationships, we inevitably encounter feedback on our world view. We often disagree with it. This can create situations that are so disharmonious that our personal relationships break down and we are unable to use these situations to advantage our unconscious project of releasing our accumulated trauma. To maintain some possibility of safety within even this confrontational scenario, we place a lot of the threats that come from within us and from around us out onto other unspecified people: the bogeymen.

the Unconscious use of Tribal Projections

It is a great relief to place all that we fear and hate about ourselves and our nearest and dearest onto others whom we don't know. There's no chance of this version of reality being contradicted. Often we even go to war to attempt to reinforce our own projected world view and to stop others from threatening us in the one place where we really most fear aggression: against our own darkest and most threatening internal mental constructs, currently defended by the projections that we place onto the other societies of our planet.

the Unconscious use of Mutual Projections

Afraid of the world outside, we seek safety and solidarity in the companionship of likeminded people, tribes and races. At first we can easily find this as we bond with others who share our crude projections. But soon, the closer projections of individual relationships begin once again to be set up. We find that we are losing control over the security that we thought that we could establish by bonding with other equally scared and freaked out similar human beings.

the Unconscious use of Projection and Fate

We are alone, cursing the world and our luck. We blame other people for letting us down and life for dealing us a bad hand. We start again.

We've been unable to use all of these valuable experiences to learn about our unconscious projections, release trauma and move on automatically to a life of greater harmony, peace and understanding between ourselves, our close companions, our families and our society. Usually we fail to leave this circuitous trap.

Q&A

From the wwwyou?forum. You can see the original text and ask questions at whatswrongwithyou.com.

Power of negativity

Posted by: Trying Jun 28 2004, 10:13 PM

I have spent many years looking for a way out of my social anxiety (which I believe has led to my current state of depression). I am fed up reading self-help books, which I approach with the understanding that I have to read 650 pages of this "happiness manual" in order to do what, from my self-absorbed perspective, everybody else just does naturally. I am worried that anyone who has to turn to self-help books is, ironically, the kind of person these books will never be able to do anything for. I think a happy, confident person is one who does not even know that they are. I am starting to believe this because I have noticed that whilst the self-help guides, including the Cognitive Therapy ones, focus on the illogical thinking of the sufferer's brain, they never look at the state-of-mind of a non-sufferer which, after all, is the state-of-mind we want to achieve. These people, I am sure, NEVER spend their days repeating to themselves "I AM a happy person, I AM confident, I AM loving and appreciated..." Yes, I have learnt how to rationally think, say and believe I am all of these wonderful things – and it feels very good sometimes – but I cannot trick my fear-brain into believing it. NO magic quote or piece of advice on the planet seems to ever change my fear responses to social situations. This dominated my adolescence, made my "best years of your life" college years very unhappy and now, at 25, it continues to plague me. CBT operates under the assumption that some instant thought is taking place that makes me feel this fear, but I strongly dispute that. Putting this to the test and monitoring myself out and about, I have found NO thought, it is just fear. Science tells us that the brain is hardwired so that our fear emotions often react BEFORE our thoughts, because thoughts are too slow and would thus jeopardize our survival when threatened etc. Surely this doesn't support the CBT idea? I even read in one of these books that when you're about to hit a deer with your car, the following occurs inside you: 1.THOUGHT: "Hmmm, I don't want to hit this deer"; 2.BRAIN NEURON STUFF: fear/adrenalin; 3.RESPONSE: slamming down the brakes. I think this is nonsense. The deer would be dead.

Posted by: benjaminfry Jul 1 2004, 10:22 AM

If it doesn't work for you; forget it. There's a world of healing out there and pretty much all of it is intellectually incompatible with the rest. Somewhere inside each theory is a kernel of emotional truth but just as each person has accumulated their problems in a different way, each person responds to differently presented solutions in a different way.

I have some sympathy for your point of view. I have dealt with a lot of fear in my life and much of it comes from when my mother died when I was 11 month's old. I don't know if you spend much time with babies, but at that age they don't talk. If they don't talk, how do they think? The fear I experienced was "non-verbal". Just the raw, overwhelming emotions of a baby, coming out in an intellectually structured adult. That in itself was frightening enough, without the underlying fear.

As a self-help author myself, I'd like to hold out hope for the genre. Perhaps my ideas are less irritating that the ones you don't like. Perhaps this logical construction of the emotional world might interest you. Sometimes fear is just fear. After all, a one day old child knows great fear if it is hungry, cold and alone, but I'm not sure there's much thinking going on (at least not in the way that we'd recognise from our adult perspective).

Nonetheless, CBT is right in the way that it tries to expand the microcosm of our reactions. There is a condensed and unconscious thought process underlying much of how we react and behave. But it's not the whole story. For me, I see it more as an explanation of how some of the mechanics of the emotional drama work. It neither explains why it happens, or all of what happens.

You are right that happy people don't think about it. You need to unearth your emotional trauma which is being triggered by social situations. If you could fully excavate what at the moment is just a resonance, then you'd be free of this baggage, and in time, you'd never think about it either. In the meantime, there's one piece of social advice I can offer; other people are scared too. Don't let them fool you into thinking you're the only one.

It can be very stressful to carry your emotional conflicts in your thinking mind. I'd suggest that you could benefit from some more visceral experiences and some mind "quietening". Creativity (even if you are no good at it) is a great way to connect with emotions. Writing a journal can really help, especially since it seems that you are very literate. Meditation and/ or physical activities such as tai-chi and yoga would give you a welcome break from your mental conundrums. I'd strongly recommend them as a route to finding some balance.

Posted by: Trying Jul 1 2004, 04:56 PM

Thank you for your response. I kind of thought, as many other users perhaps do, that I would be the one not to get a reply. I was very touched to have you respond so thoughtfully to my woes!

I'm sorry if I sounded disillusioned with self-help books in general. I suppose what I really mean is my personal experiences have been frustrating because they simply haven't offered the way out for me. Others will undoubtedly respond more positively to the comforting guidance offered by many such books. I think in my case, part of the problem is not only the problem itself, but being obsessed with the problem! Almost like an addiction. I think you could put things like anxiety and depression in the same camp as addictions, because they are extremely hard to break. Even though one tries to satisfy an addiction for pleasure, and something like depression is anything but pleasurable, we "satisfy" it anyway, with brooding etc.

I think with my inclination to question just about everything that happens in my head, be it good or bad, I think self-help advice stimulates that part of me that I simply want to turn off! Irrespective of whether I am thinking negatively or positively, it's continually stressful because I am getting so worked up by it all, and it is the stress, ultimately, that is the upsetting part. I think the way out is an emotional and physiological one (do I mean that?) – not a thinking one, although I guess a little bit more positive thinking never hurt anyone. Have you any opinions about EMDR or hypnotherapy?

Posted by: Trying Jul 3 2004, 04:20 PM

Me again, but I will try not to get too dependant on this comforting little website. Oh, look – another problem in the making.

I was just wondering. I had an operation as a baby, and was very ill for a considerable amount of time, and almost died. Now I know plenty of people's lives start with hiccups like that, and like many of them I am absolutely fine now. The problem was put right and it has not come back to haunt me or anything, and has never affected my life. Or has it...?

In your reply to my first post you mentioned the trauma babies can pick up on way before their ability to "think" in the sense we look at it. Did the hospital, the doctors, the lights, the examinations, not to mention the anxiety of my parents – which was very great because I was so near to not making it – affect me permanently? I have a family that doesn't really like to talk about things like this. My mother just gets defensive whenever I talk about my up-bringing in terms of my current on-going anxieties because she thinks analysis, therapy etc just makes us all turn on our parents who have, after all, tried their best. I spoke to my grandfather – a big mistake – who simply says it's all rubbish because babies have no memory. Is there evidence that this is not true? He has always taken the point of view that human common-sense knows more than science. But before Columbus, common-sense told us that the world was flat! Common-sense is often ignorance, and it is an argument to avoid issues. He bases his memory assumption on the fact that most of us can't RECALL our baby memories, but that doesn't mean they're not there. Does it? T

Posted by: benjaminfry Jul 6 2004, 03:07 PM

You have all the classic hallmarks of a poor psychological health. You suffered tremendous trauma as an infant and your family won't talk about it. The first sets up the conditions for emotional dysfunction and the second preserves it, and teaches you to do so also.

There is a world of difference between the architecture of

the psychological mind-body system and your memory. They just are two different things. Just because you don't remember something with your conscious mind doesn't make it irrelevant. We don't remember the Jurassic Age, but we see evidence of it in geology. The same is true of your infancy. We don't pretend mountains aren't there just because we have no record of them forming. You should give your emotional system the same respect.

The fact is that you currently experience emotional difficulties, particularly associated with fear in a group situation. As a baby, I speculate that you would have been surrounded by strangers during this medical emergency and generally terrified. There's an easy link to make here.

Trauma in infancy can be some of the most difficult to heal. Partly this is because it was non-verbal, so if you can actually access it, there's no thoughts to go with it; just fear. You should try to find a trained professional who can help with these issues. Perhaps look into Post Traumatic Stress Disorder (PTSD) for some information on how this process is accepted to work in adults. (They don't "remember" what happened either most of the time).

Ignore everyone who doesn't want to believe that traumatic events in babies influence their emotional health as adults. There is a mountain of scientific evidence to prove them wrong (from psychiatry and psychology). People who wish to ignore this usually simply want to avoid looking into their own traumas. Join them up to the flat-earth society and get on with your own more inquiring life.

The past in itself is not the issue, it is the echo of the past that remains in the present. What you are dealing with is the after-effects of something that was too much for you to bear as a child. Those feelings are present, frozen, in your current mind-body system. You can work on evacuating them in any way you like, but a popular one seems to be to get the mind located in the events of the past. This often acts as a bridge to these lost feelings. Then they can be let out (e-motion) in the present. This in turn releases you to a new future.

Posted by: Trying Jul 27 2004, 05:41 PM

This sounds a bit melodramatic, but I almost found myself crying as I read your response to my post about baby trauma. Of course, I didn't cry because that seems to be another luxury I'm denied. Interesting in itself perhaps? I feel terribly alone all the time but I never cry about it, so there's "not really anything wrong with me." I always envied the girls back at school for being able to cry so much! They're the lucky ones. I remember the last day of secondary school, when everyone around me was weeping and hugging (I'm sure we all remember these scenes), telling each other how much they were going to miss them. Inside I was kind of screaming, because I hadn't really enjoyed myself at school. But they were the ones in tears, I had no emotion. Believe me I'm sure I was in more pain than them. Someone even said "don't you feel at all sad?"

Anyway, what you said affected me deeply. If only because the possibility that there really is something inside me that can be let free, as it were, momentarily landed me on cloud nine. The suggestion is as much of a treatment in itself. But there is a pattern emerging here...

Every time I discover some new approach, I try it, it works, I feel good – I feel great – I'm being cured – I'm escaping!!! And then, the down comes again because something in my life knocks me back. I'm the same as I always was. When I look back the actual life circumstances never changed. I'm not more confident or successful at anything. The high moments are simply the ones where I'm convinced I'm really changing. The low is the reality kicking back in again. I've definitely got a pattern going here. The 'ups' seem to get stronger, but always as a consequence so do the 'downs'. The downs get VERY down. I think I know the reason for this. I put my faith in the latest technique I've read about to help ME, but in doing so switch off my own will power. I expect the therapy to do the work. Any therapy is only effective if the patient makes it so, and I don't and can't make it so. All therapies therefore, are simply rendered powerless in the face of the impenetrable negative power of my mind. Do they teach THAT at therapist school? Because it's one hell of an obstacle. I'm spouting negative nonsense right now, so there's an example of it. Ever tried talking positive sense to a negative person? You are out-negatived every time! I know all the science, I know what I'm doing to myself. It doesn't change anything.

But I WANT to succeed and be happy. I eventually made myself phone some clinic about it, but I have never been a car crash victim, I've never been abused, or even bullied, so I felt a bit silly. They then quoted some ridiculous prices and I felt what I feel now – treatment is practised by the rich for the rich, and the rest of us can go hang. But, der! Surely those of us wanting the help, probably have no money because the problem has, among other things, prevented us from making any! The only thing I can do to help me is exercise. I took your advice about finding more visceral experiences and have started jogging regularly, if that counts – it's the only answer that's free! I now love it, and feel much better as a result. Great. But it doesn't make me any more happy with who I am around people. Even all the exclamation marks !!! I'm using are a disguise!!!!!! I find it difficult to express myself. I am just alone and scared, and don't have anyone to turn to. You'd have to be very brave to come in here with me.

Posted by: benjaminfry Jul 29 2004, 10:10 PM

You give a very eloquent description of what it is like to be emotionally locked up inside. Being unable to cry is just one of the results of having to keep your emotions frozen during your childhood. There will be others and you may be familiar with them across the emotional spectrum.

Interestingly the problem is mainly just one of lack of practice. The more emotional you are, the more often and the more open you are with the more people about it, the easier it gets. This begs the question how do you start when your feelings are like a block of ice? Well, it's not easy. It is slow and painful and every inch must be fought for because you want more than anything to clam up again. You have been able to start an exercise routine which is excellent. Keep going with that and follow your nose to whatever else you might find. If anything upsets you, do it again.

The cycle of elation and despair that you describe is also very interesting. There's a school of thought that this is bi-polar or manic depression: highs followed by lows. I actually take a fairly eccentric view of this syndrome which is that it is nothing more than variously exaggerated states of what you describe. (Many very well respected, knowledgeable and experienced professionals would disagree with me). I'm generally of the opinion that all mental issues are the same animal in different disguises. At the core of it all is a desire to release ourselves from our prison of frozen trauma. It is so depressing in there that any route out will result in a period of elation. But inevitably, as some trauma is lifted (or just avoided) there will be more to follow. If we continue to shut down when confronted from within by these difficult feelings, then we will continue to be depressed: until the next fancy idea gets us going again.

I'd suggest that you reconcile yourself to a long but worthwhile process. Resist the temptation to believe in any miracle cure. The ideas that you have read here may indeed give you the key to understanding yourself, but the work that must be done now that you have this understanding remains. I wrote my book to try to give people a better chance of cosying up to their difficult emotions. I try to repeat the same ideas here. But no-one but you can actually do the hard graft of going through those feelings.

Unfortunately you are right that therapy is there for the rich (or well insured) and very difficult to access without such funds. But like all people who can't afford the obvious solution to what they need, you can still be resourceful. 12-step meetings are free and function a lot like group therapy. Many yoga or meditation classes can be found quite cheaply. Exercise, as you have noticed, is easy to find. Journal writing, creative play and even movie watching are all stimulants of the emotions. Try role playing with an empty chair; put an imaginary person in the chair and say (and feel) everything that you couldn't if there were actually there. Anything that gets you going is worth doing, and anything that keeps you going in the company of other human beings is priceless.

The negativity is just the resistance of the conscious mind to the pain of these emotions that wish to emerge. You will find that if you connect emotionally with yourself, the negativity just evaporates since, like a valve on a kettle, you are no longer under pressure from within and therefore need nothing to keep you down. Don't discount your suffering. Don't discount your emotions. Once you can bear to reveal them to both yourself and others, you will be well on your way.

It's not a question of others needing to be brave to get in there with you; it is you that needs to be brave to get out.

Posted by: Trying Aug 2 2004, 06:14 PM

Not a problem, but a thank you...

Your replies are as much of a treatment in themselves. The one thing people who write into a sight like this need, more than drugs, more than a cure, more than an answer, is someone who listens without judgement and doesn't charge them an arm and a leg for it! Our nearest and dearest can't really provide this non-judgemental approach because of the nature of our relationships with them. I have a definition of unhappiness: patterns. We're all stuck in the pattern of our own experience, often created by the ways we relate to our respective families. We just don't ever stop to challenge it. But that's all it is, isn't it? Re-occurring patterns.

I may be safe behind the anonimnitytytity(??!!!) of my computer, but this an important step. I'm expressing my emotions I guess. I just had acupuncture for the first time. And guess what? I was told fear and anxiety is directly linked to the kidneys, and the operation I had as a baby was on my kidneys. How about that?

SEVEN

God

*The ultimate projection. The labelling of the source of
the power and the wisdom of the unconscious mind.*

Theory: Meaning of God

People often ask the question, "do you believe in God?" We
may answer "no", but by now at least we should be believing in
our unconscious mind. This can give us a clue to understanding
the incontestable phenomena of a belief in religion and God
among our species. Those who answer "yes" need no explanation of this, but nonetheless might still benefit from examining
how they personalise it (while accepting the validity of any
existing belief system). We have seen how we have used projections to alter our perception of reality in favour of the circumstances and experiences that we need to trigger a thaw of our
impacted trauma. Projections are applied to individuals in
relationships. Projections are applied to societies in politics. It
is reasonable to presume that projections may also be applied
beyond this scope into the realm of the somewhat unknown.

The existence of God is not something we can prove or
disprove to any universal satisfaction. Those who believe that
God's existence has been individually proved to them usually
can not find an infallible way to demonstrate this to others.
Therefore, speculation on the reality of the existence of God is

not very useful. "He" either does or does not exist. It is what is known as an ontological problem: a factual question that has a determined answer regardless of our perception or interference in it. The Buddha famously refused to answer the question of whether or not God existed, perhaps because the verification of an ontological fact doesn't really matter to how we live our lives. What matters is our experience of what we perceive as real or not: in this case, how the quality of our lives is affected by our experience of the meaning of the concept of God.

Many people experience nothing. (This blankness should not be dismissed as the absence of a reaction. A lack of response is also a quality that can be noted.) Many other people (and apparently something like more than ninety percent of our world's population today) have a distinct notion of what the word God means to them. However, it is clear that it is almost impossible to get a consensus of this meaning. There is often serious dispute even among followers of the same religions over the detail and applications of their creeds. These disagreements have been some of the most passionate in history and the cause of countless wars, atrocities and suffering. Clearly something quite profound is going on, and clearly it is something that matters a great deal to many people.

The fact that there are so many disagreements about what the word God might mean, and that these disagreements are so passionately fought (the same baffling phenomenon that we see in our own closest, personal relationships) is a clue that the unconscious mind is at work yet again. It is almost inconceivable that so many people could be responding so differently to one ontological truth (or lack of truth) without the explanation of the interference of a pattern of unconscious projections. Thus the meaning of the word God becomes in a sense our ultimate projection. It is the receptacle for all of our other unconscious gifts and baggage. Hence the great wisdom and compassion that it contains, but also the drive to wage war and inflict terrible violence on our fellow human beings. It has always been one of the great contradictions of the religious movements of the world that they all seem to stem from an evolved sense of human compassion and understanding, and yet so quickly descend into violence on an epic scale. This problem remains very much with us today.

Our truest wisdom and power (the kind of qualities that we associate with the great prophets of the world's religions, like Moses, Jesus, Mohammad and the Buddha) lie dormant in our unconscious mind. Usually the active tasks of most religions contain instructions on how to raise the consciousness to access these qualities. Each and every one of us has the potential to manifest these powers. Each and every one of us does so already in our lives through the actions of our unconscious mind, directing us to experiences and circumstances that help us to resolve our trauma. Each and every one of us also has the potential to align these unconscious gifts with our conscious mind's agenda. Then some measure of choice, control and will can be exerted over these unconscious skills. That is the holy grail of mindfulness and the path to a life rich with the automatic right to happiness.

In this sense, each of us manifests the qualities that we traditionally hear associated with the meaning of the word God. We just don't yet know it. We are not aware of it in our conscious mind. Our unconscious mind is fully aware of its own qualities, its wisdom and power, and it finds its expression of this in its projection onto the meaning of the word God. We are usually passionate and committed in how we "believe in God" (even if that means not believing in God). This is because we are, in this very important sense, really just believing in ourselves.

We are of course convinced by the reality of the projection that we place onto the meaning of the word God, because it comes from our own deepest, most sacred sense of ourselves.

That's why interpretations of the meaning of the word God vary so much, and yet are so passionately and violently defended. We are defending ourselves, and when we reach a point beyond which we refuse to go, that is where we will stop and stand our ground. There is no power on this earth quite as strong as the tussle between the unconscious mind and the conscious mind over the reality of our projections. When these projections become so fundamental, this power is at its most volatile. That is why religion is so often the fault line for man's most violent and destructive conflicts.

The less of our mind that our trauma has left us conscious of, the less that we are able to connect to any real experience of what the idea of God actually means. Therefore, in this literal sense, we might say that if we don't already have a conscious idea of what the word God means, then the meaning remains hidden from us, obscured in our unconscious. That's another reason why our views on the subject differ so widely. Our awareness and understanding of it vary with the awareness and understanding of our own minds, or in other words, with the narrowness or breadth of the scope of our conscious mind. If we equate the idea of God with the existence of the unconscious mind and ask ourselves again, "do I believe in God?", we get a more interesting result.

To properly answer the question, "do I believe in God?", we also have to ask what it means to believe in something. People talk about believing in something when what they really mean is that they are trying to form a judgement about whether or not something is real, based on their own intuition and an extrapolation from their past experiences. For example, someone might believe that the moon landings were a conspiracy and never happened. They might believe that aliens made the crop circles. They might believe that their cousin stole from their piggy bank. They might believe that their problems will soon be over. If we break this down, what is really being said is that the person doesn't have any first hand knowledge, but is prepared to guess that something is true. That guess may be informed by some factual evidence. But it is quite often simply based on a hunch, or a desire, for something to be true. What is real or not is not the issue. The guess is about what you think might be real, or hope is real, based on the limited information available to you from your experiences. So when someone asks us, "do you believe in God?", what they are really asking us is, "what is your best guess about the factual existence of God?"

The best answer to that question is to say, "tell me what you mean and I'll give you an answer". The question itself becomes impossible to define without specifying exactly what is meant by the word God. The person asking the question might have some specific ideas on what he is trying to ask, but these ideas may vary from the ideas about God held by the person who is trying to answer the question. And thus starts the God debate. It is often disguised as a question about whether or not we believe in God, but really it is a question about what the word God means to us. Let it be what dwells out of sight in our unconscious mind, and we can begin to see the whole phenomenon of God in a different light.

We must try to understand what is underlying this whole phenomenon of a belief in God. What does it really mean? How can understanding it can help us to better understand ourselves and our lives? What use can we now make of the word God? If we suspend our judgment about the ontological fact of "His" existence (which seems to be unprovable, if not unknowable), then we can use whatever meaning we may have already ascribed to the word of God as further clues about our unconscious mind. If we think of our interpretation of God as our ultimate projection (not the ontologically real or otherwise God, but our experience of it through our unconscious projections), then this God describes our most sacred selves, and is a window onto the power and the wisdom of our own unconscious mind. This holds just as true for followers of established religions as for atheists.

In this way, we can start to build a meaning for the three-letter word of "God" that we can use to see with greater clarity (and hopefully with the least possible controversy and discomfort) what constitutes our own divine nature. To complete the picture of what's wrong with us, we need to add to the organism described in Step One by augmenting our basic constituents with something that has a higher function than simply preserving our own lives. It is well known that some people will sacrifice their lives for the lives of others, and therefore there must be more to the story. Altruism is a reality. It happens. And it is more than just another successful adaptation mechanism. Compassion, empathy, kindness, love, honour and decency all exist to balance the greedy, selfish desires of our base, evolved organism. Where do they come from? At the very least, we can all recognise and accept the notion of good old-fashioned decency (which we could just call G.O.D. for short!).

If we are able to relate to the idea of common decency between human beings and have a basic understanding of the workings of the unconscious mind, then there begins to be a basis on which to define a pragmatic meaning for the word God. Almost all human beings on this planet have experienced some form of kindness, unselfishness, love or decency at some point. These aren't things which a person needs to "believe" in. They are experiences which are real, and can be remembered. Therefore, at its most base level, this is one way to answer the question, "do you believe in God?": "yes, I can remember real examples in my life of compassionate behaviour which I chose to define with the word God." This answer doesn't prove the existence of God, but it establishes a person's experience of G.O.D., and moves the understanding of the human condition on from the evolved piece of meat discussed in Step One.

Some people these days talk of alternatives to God such as spirituality, or a higher power, or something out there, or a greater purpose. These are all useful terms, and often used by people for whom the word God has too many negative connotations. Many people experienced uncomfortable coercion or situations in the name of what other people wanted to use the word God to justify. It is only natural that these people would seek a new language to define their understanding of experiences that go beyond the material frame of reference of their survivalist instincts. However, in the end it is really all just the same thing.

Whatever word we use, whatever we are trying to describe and however we chose to frame that description, we discover that it really isn't possible to articulate accurately a precise summary of the experiences that we are trying to communicate. That's about the only quality of God that everyone can agree on and is exactly why the word God is so devoid of a precise communicable meaning. It means something different to everyone, depending on their experience of it.

Case Study: The Desert

I didn't believe in God until he punched me in the knees in the desert of Arizona. But I couldn't come up with any other explanation for my experience. I was talking to a Baptist minister during a seminar at the therapy farm in Tucson, Arizona. The main thrust of this institution was to introduce its inmates to twelve-step meetings. The core of its business came from insurance-sponsored drying-out programs. A big part of twelve-stepping is a reference to our "higher power". This can get a bit confusing if you don't recognise one as I was reluctant to do. However, the desert has a fabled power. Jesus saw off the devil there in forty days and forty nights. I had less than three weeks but the results were still quite dramatic. Gradually, over the course of my stay, I began to experience a real sense of inner peace, calm and connection. As the outside influences of modern life receded into the background, the volume of white noise in my head seemed to lessen. This created an opportunity to perhaps tune into some of the quieter, more subtle background sounds of life. Slowly I began to recognise a different rhythm to myself, one that I suppose would be most accurately referred to as a more spiritual existence.

On the timetable for the day was a talk from a local minister about God. There really wasn't anything else to do but go to these meetings, so along I went. I found myself sitting in quite a sulk for no particularly good reason. Perhaps I felt marginalised. God was not a part of my life and I found the booming bass of the bible bashing southern Baptist minister too much of a cliché. I felt like I was in a bad TV show, far from home, surrounded by strangers. It was hard to relate.

I was minding my own business but at some point towards the end of the session, the minister turned to me and singled me out for conversation. He said that I looked like I was angry with the Lord. I was in a grumpy mood, however there was nothing unusual or necessarily specific about that. Such was the nature of the work being done there day in and day out that emotional overloads were quite common, understood and accepted. However, in order to respond to him, I had to consider if actually I was, as he had suggested, angry with the Lord.

I wasn't sure why I was angry. But if I was to admit to the existence of God (which I wasn't going to) then I would indeed have good reason to be angry with him. What kind of God takes a mother from a baby? Much of the work that I had been doing over the past two weeks had been related to grieving that loss and it did leave me angry, wanting someone to blame. If God was going to find his way into my world view, all that he was going to get would be a hot blast of my latent rage. What

would be the point of that? The minister was sympathetic but
pointed out that God did move in mysterious ways. I wasn't
too impressed by this argument, but I had been very struck by
the way that he had wheeled round during his talk and singled
me out with an instant summary of how I was feeling. It was
literally as if he had seen straight into the darkest parts of my
soul.

I'd never known a preacher who wasn't also a school master
and had certainly never taken seriously the idea that they had
any special qualities, spiritual or otherwise, but here in front of
me was the walking cliché of a black Baptist minister, and I had
to admit that he showed some sign of having a real talent for
his calling. Where at the outset of the seminar I had been
dismissive, now I was impressed, and even a little curious. I
wanted to understand a bit more about this man and how he
seemed to know in an instant what was going on within me as I
sat silent and anonymous in his audience.

At the end of the talk, I waited for the minister as he answered a few individuals' questions. Once I had him on my
own I continued with him a little my discussion about how
little appetite I had for God since for me God could equate to
nothing more than the source of the loss of my mother. Remember that she had died from a very rare reaction to a
common antibiotic. It was a one in a million chance. How do
you make sense of that, other than to put the instrument of
fate into another's hand? Who else could I blame other than
God? In fact, if I started to take seriously the idea of his existence, all I could feel was a profound sense of grievance that
just put me off the whole idea completely. I think it didn't help
either that my only experience of religion up to that point was
the compulsory routine of assembly at boarding school.

The minister began to answer my points. He gave a very
vibrant account of a kind of living God that I'd not been
introduced to at my dull school services. He spoke with pas-

sion of his real, important and emotional relationship with his God, and suggested that this was a relationship in which a great outpouring of anger or resentment was okay. He didn't sanitise his God or his approach to his worship. He was open to the full spectrum of the emotional rainbow in relation to our spiritual existence, development and understanding.

As he spoke to me a funny thing happened. I began to feel a week, dizzy sensation. My stomach became a little warm and wobbly; my head swam; his words started to blur in my recognition. Finally I began to feel like I might actually faint. Just before my reflex to avoid falling over kicked in, the last thought I had was that this man was filled with the power of God. Then I felt my knees buckle and grabbed onto a fortuitously positioned table. I made my excuses and left. I'd had quite enough of the minister and his God talk. The whole experience had quite freaked me out. I'd never before had a voluntary thought that might admit to the existence of God, at least not in that specific, present, working, vital and clearly labelled way. I was profoundly uncomfortable with it and wanted to retreat. However, as a keen collector and observer of life's experiences I had to admit to myself what had happened. I had been struck by something and the only explanation that came to mind was that God was indeed working through this rather gifted minister. It was an explanation that I would prefer to reject, but with the delicate sensibilities that my exile in the desert had begun to allow, I knew that that would be dishonest. Something had really happened.

Understanding Why?

It could be that the experience that I had with the Baptist minister was a genuine reaction to some external divine force surging through me, using the minister as its conduit. Or it could be a reaction to some internally generated projections that I had placed over him and the experience. The truth is that it is objectively quite hard to tell.

With practice and experience, perhaps the subtle differences in the quality of these two modes of experience would be distinguishable, but at this point it need not be of great concern. The distinction, and all the great debates that it throws up, can be neatly sidestepped (without loss of reality or respect) by using the word God to label the phenomenon either way. Obviously, if I was being tickled by the finger of God then it is correct to ascribe this incident to God. On the other hand, if I was projecting something into the situation that gave me an experience which I perceived as spiritually important, then there's no harm either in using that experience to define my understanding of the meaning of the word God. (The ontological truth is, I suspect, as usual, a confusing mixture of the two.) Then the word can start to have some real use to me, not based on hypothesis, conjecture, history, coercion or superstition, but based on real, remembered experiences.

Theory: a Role for God

Let's try to momentarily forget everything we've ever heard, or known, or read, or been preached to about God. We can do so as a temporary mental exercise without meaning any offence to the many established notions of God. Instead we'll make a space in our understanding for a simple acknowledgment of all the experiences that we've ever had that have been hard to understand or to explain; a space for all the feelings that have ever elevated us above and beyond our base desires and instincts; a space for all the interesting, weird or wonderful stuff that we have ever encountered, be it crop circles, telepathy, intuition, love, aliens, the presence of a dead loved one, or just a perfect sunset. We can remember it, acknowledge it, be comfortable with it, nurture it and accept it as a valid, remembered experience in our lives. In other words, we can make a space in our conscious mind, in our understanding of ourselves, for the simple acknowledgement of the many phenomena that we experience which are real but that we can't understand. These contain the unrevealed power of our unconscious mind, and if we deny ourselves this acknowledgment of these phenomena, we close ourselves off to all of our greatest potentials in life.

And if we chose to label this stuff God, then why not? After all, if the word God has become meaningless for us by now, then it is up for grabs to have something to mean. We can adopt it for our own meaning, and then use it to mean something to us and about us. That way, any reference to the word God is no longer some guess at a poorly defined and dubious idea, but instead becomes an affirmation of some of our real and remembered experiences; experiences that were valuable, pleasant or interesting to us. We don't have to believe in anything but ourselves to acknowledge our own divine potential, hidden away from us in our unconscious mind. We just have to remember and acknowledge our real experiences which (if we like) we can use the word God to help us to describe.

If we ever do fathom the depths of our unconscious mind, we will find our own understanding of the mysteries of the universe, including probably the real meaning of the word God. However, in the meantime, the more of a connection we have with whatever we come to understand as meant by the word God, the more comfortable our existence on this planet will become. The sense of security that comes from a good connection with our unconscious power is deeply comforting to our dissatisfied conscious mind. This connection lets us understand that we are already exactly who and where we need to be, right here right now, in order to get the most out of what we really need from our lives.

On this basis, everything we've ever heard about God (God

is good, God is everywhere, God is wise etc.) takes on a new light when related back to ourselves and our own unconscious wisdom and power. Expanding our awareness and definition of what this might actually mean is something that can get gradually, or suddenly, experienced over the course of a lifetime (or many, some say). It can be there in a series of tiny experiences or in a moment of blinding clarity. It can come out of the blue for no reason, or at a time of great significance: or not at all.

There's no consensus on experiences like these. They are personal, gradual, available but not compulsory. No life is devoid of them, but all lives find it difficult to absorb them, accept them and to understand them. Organised religions give one way to be guided in them, but equally they can become a negation of them. Modern trends emerging in the western world taken from other spiritual paths, such as yoga and meditation, often become another way for individuals to find some structure to these experiences that are outside of the mainstream of our cultural understanding.

Whatever the word God might be supposed mean, it doesn't actually really matter. What matters is that we give ourselves permission to notice the other stuff in life, the stuff that is not the by-product of our evolution. That's the stuff that lives in our unconscious mind. What matters is that we don't discount these experiences but add them up. What matters is that we value them, and use them to create a summary of our relationship with our unconscious selves; and therefore (if we like) create our own personal definition of the word God. We can then use this to become more aware of the great power that is already working and dormant within us.

The mysteries of the universe lie ready to be revealed within us, currently obscured from us only by the narrow focus of our conscious mind. Revealing it for ourselves is our opportunity to find automatic happiness. If we label as God whatever interesting but inexplicable experiences we have experienced manifested in ourselves and in our lives, then by definition God in that sense is experienced by us and therefore within us. We are ourselves experiencing God and manifesting God if we understand the word in this universally meaningful way.

Case Study: The Desert, continued

It was after my Baptist experience that I had been encouraged by a fellow inmate to ask God for a clue about how to react to my girlfriend's unexpected pregnancy. I had prayed for some help before going to bed and the next morning got the news that my grandmother had died in the night. In my grief over her death I saw with crystal clarity the preciousness of the life that I was now debating. This seemed like too much coincidence to lack design. But I had one more experience before I left the desert that led me further into a consideration of a realm just beyond our everyday understanding of life.

An important part of the process that this institution ran was the bringing people's families into the centre to share a communal family therapy session. It would happen in the third week of their four-week program for recovering addicts. I was only there for two and a half weeks and my family would not be attending anything so far from home. However, I was assigned to a family group meeting and invited to participate as if my family were there. The preparation for these meetings followed a simple but challenging format. We were given a list to work on, which we would use in the meeting to facilitate communication with family members. It seemed like a short piece of homework, but when I came down to doing it, it was surprisingly difficult and emotionally challenging.

I had to chose a family member, usually parents plus any other significant relative, and I had to come up with seven ways to appreciate them and seven ways to confront them. Even within this framework there was a very strict formula for the language of the work. Each statement would take the form of, "I do/don't like it when you do/say something like the time when you example of some real event. The feelings I have when you do this are list of feelings." And that's it. You do that seven times both for positive and negative issues for each person.

I chose to do my list work on my father, step-mother and mother. None of them were going to be there, which of course would have been the case anyway for my mother even if we'd been a local family. This was not unusual. Many people have issues with family members who are either dead or unavailable through design or circumstance. Our group had about six participants and all the others had two or three family members present. The sessions took all day. I spent the morning witnessing some incredibly powerful conversations and significant family resolutions. I grew a little uncomfortable during the day because I was aware that I had no-one to do my sessions with and therefore could not imagine that they could be anything like as meaningful as what I'd been witnessing. Really I just wanted to get it out of the way and let these people get on with their important work together. I volunteered myself shortly after the lunch break.

I started with my father and read out some of my lists. I was reading it to an empty chair. I'd been told by some therapists that doing list work to an empty chair could be just as powerful if not more so that with the relative present. However, I failed to see how this could really be so. The experience of the morning had been so effective because of the electric chemistry of the confrontations and the emotions pouring out from both sides. I was just sitting there talking to an empty chair. The stage was set so that the two chairs were in the middle of the room. The rest of the group sat in a circle all around the edge of the room. I felt a little lonely in there all on my own.

My lists followed a familiar theme. My father is a very kind

man and has been a benign, hard-working provider for us as
long as I can remember. It was not hard to find ways to appreciate him. However, my complaints were relatively specific. It
was hard for me to bear that he'd never spoken to me about
my mother. We were after all, for some brief months, a nuclear
family (my family) and for both him and me that was our first
experience of family life. That family had been lost with my
mother's death. Sadly, also lost with her death was our remembrance of her. My father had not carried her memory away
from her death and I was too young to do so on my own.
There was no shared grieving process, really no sharing at all. I
didn't blame him or judge him for it, because I don't think
people should be judged in their grief, but I was perhaps bitter
that I'd never known my missing parent through the eyes of
my surviving one and that the love that they had shared, that
had brought me into this world, was never woven into the
background fabric of my existence.

I wanted to tell him how I felt about my mother's death and
his avoidance of it in connection with me. I didn't want to
argue with him that he'd done something wrong, but merely
explain to him the emotions that this reality stirred up in me so
that we could understand each other better and perhaps be
closer despite this shared wound that seemed to force us to
always keep a certain distance. However, it just didn't work for
me with an empty chair. The core of the problem was that we'd
never talked about it. How could that be addressed by pretending to talk about it?

And so I moved on to my step-mother. Since our relationship had been set at a distance as long as I could remember, the
positives that I could find were limited to all the home comforts, like her excellent cooking. But there was not much
emotional nourishment. On the other hand, at that time I
found plenty to complain about. I was angry about being the
object of her aggression as a child. More than that, I was so

very hurt that I perceived her as the one who had stolen my mother's memory from me by jealously stepping into her place.

Again I felt that doing this list work to an empty chair lacked meaning. These taboo subjects would have been very powerful to air in front of her and I would have welcomed being able to do so in this safe environment where her emotional reaction could have been contained, but simply rehearsing subjects that had already spent far too long stuck in the solitude of my own head didn't do much for me.

I could tell that the therapists were a bit disappointed. They encouraged me to try to invest in the process with a bit more emotion and meaning. I was doing my best, but really so far I'd got little out of it. Now we started with my mother. Obviously I couldn't hide from the fact that she wasn't there. She'd never been there. Despite this, there was something very unfamiliar about the scene. I was addressing her. I'd never really done that before. I'd not grown up with visits to her grave or photographs to talk to. Instead I'd grown up with the fear associated with the taboo of mentioning her name. I'd positively avoided her and kept her a dark and distant secret from all but my closest and most recent friends. Now I was being sat in the middle of a room of strangers and being invited to talk to her.

It was hard to come up with much to complain about, except for the obvious that she'd failed me very badly by dying on me. That was something that I was very upset with her for. I had to come up with seven grievances. Her dying was six of them. For example, "I don't like it when you left me alone when I was eleven months old like the time when you died. The feelings I have when you do this are pain, anger, grief, rage, despair, fear, panic and devastating loneliness." The seventh was that she'd left me in the hands of people who were unable to help me to cope with her death. She'd abandoned me and left me with a gang of emotional Muppets. I wasn't going to let her off lightly for that. Even so, and despite the emotional weight of the subject matter, I still wasn't really getting much out of this process. As I sat there complaining about her absence in my life to an empty chair, I felt very little emotional progress within me. Somehow I just couldn't see it working without someone else actually being there.

It seemed like I was out of the woods. I'd gone for the hard stuff first with my mother and she was the last subject of my lists. Now all I had to do was get through seven appreciations of her. I started with the obvious, like the fact that she'd given birth to me. Clearly there was nothing that she'd done that I could actually remember and therefore there was nothing that I could respond to with a real remembered emotion. I got through the first six items with little difficulty. None of them were too earth shattering. I was now down to the very last item of my last list, having been though seven good and bad for each of my father, mother and step-mother. The process hadn't worked. The therapists were resigned to the fact that perhaps I wasn't ready or this just wasn't my thing. Then I delivered my last lines.

I'd long felt that there had at times been a light touch on my shoulder guiding me in life. There had been many simple incidents were it seemed a small matter of fate whether my life would go in a good or bad direction. Generally the good had prevailed. In a real sense, I'd always had the subtle impression of being watched over. However, I'd never dwelt on this, possibly because I just didn't understand it, but probably because it inevitably related in my mind to my mother and that was a subject I was reluctant to engage with. For my final vote of appreciation I had come up with this as my thank you: "I do like it when you guide me in life like the time when you brought me to this place. The feelings I have when you do this are peace, warmth, emotional security and unconditional love." The moment I'd said the words I realised that these were the qualities that I had so missed from her and had so desperately craved for so long. Then I cracked. There was no need for the therapists to prompt me any more. I felt a huge well of sadness open up within me and I was truly devastated.

I sobbed uncontrollably for a long time, alone, facing my empty chair in the middle of this room of spectating strangers, crying desperately for my lost mother. The therapist comforted me by acknowledging my loss but no-one tried to get me to stop or to dry my tears. I was allowed for the first time ever to grieve my mother publicly. It was pretty frightening. As I sat there exposed both physically and emotionally, I felt terribly alone. I was emotionally out of control, wracked by grief, on display and thousands of miles from home and my usual coping mechanisms. I couldn't see through the tears or the hands that held my head and I didn't know how to cope. I just felt a desperate need for help. At that moment, at my most emotionally open and venerable point I felt something magical. I felt a warm embrace.

I felt my mother there in the room and I felt her put her arms around me, but it wasn't the embrace of a human hug. As my heart was breaking, something touched it. It was a light feathery sensation. It was as if two wings were curled around my body and their tips met up curled inwards on my heart, stroking it lovingly, restoratively. I had the impression of being held in large angel's wings and knew, as surely as I knew that the chair before me sat empty, that my mother was there comforting her long-lost son. How ironic it seemed to me that the parents that I'd always relied on for their presence had not been there that day, but the one that had always been absent, actually was.

Understanding Why?

What sensible analysis can be brought to bear on my experience of the presence of my mother from the perspective of a non-desert dweller? This could have been my fantasy, or it could have been her visit. Obviously I know what it felt like at the time, and my perception of it was that it was very real. However, I can never be one hundred percent sure where reality stops and my projections begin. These projections though are part of the reality of myself that I am attempting to address and to define. Using the word God to do so helps me to understand these phenomena regardless of where the line is actually drawn. Since I can't know where to make this distinction myself in relation to unknowable matters such as God, it profits me little to attempt to. It is more useful to accept that there is a possible combination (in any ratio that pleases you) of a real, external theistic influence and projected, internal spiritual essence that combines to provide these experiences. It is the sum of these experiences that then becomes a useful definition of the word God; and conversely gives the word God something useful to mean to those for whom it currently means nothing.

Then I can answer the question, "Do I believe in God?" with some sensible certainty. I can clearly remember experiences which seemed to me to be unusual and perhaps related to some other plane of existence or understanding. If I chose to use these real events to define my understanding of God, then I not only "believe in God", but I have experienced God in the one way that I can usefully define and understand him.

Cure: an Understanding of God

A key step in understanding what is wrong with us, and therefore being able to do something about it, is to recognise how limited our experiences are of anything other than our basic evolved instincts; and how these other, different ways of experiencing our existence currently have little impact in our daily lives. There is a very good reason for our current state of limited awareness. The conscious mind doesn't want to deal with what it can't yet understand. It resists whatever does not make sense. It sabotages the unconscious mind's efforts to release our trauma. It narrows our field of view over our own mind, and we lose sight of ourselves, losing with that our ability to see our connection with our divine selves: and with that our automatic right to lasting happiness.

We may have experienced very little of this sphere of perception, but its potential is as vast and powerful as we can imagine. After all, every great religious history carries with it stories of miracles and superhuman feats. These are all, allegedly, performed by ordinary human beings, who have woken up to their divine potential. We are no different from that. We too can start to experience more and more of our own potential. In this sense, we can think of the word God as having nothing to do with its traditional notion of religion (if we want to). It can simply be the label that we give to the potential that we feel within us but that has not yet been realised.

There's a prayer widely used in twelve-step programs that goes as follows:

God, grant me the serenity to accept what I can not change,
The strength to change what I can,
And the wisdom to know the difference!

It is rather lovely and calming, regardless of life's situations. But really how different is that from our conscious mind beseeching from our unconscious mind thus:

Unconscious Mind, let me believe in my projections when I need to,
See through them when I feel strong enough to face reality,
And have the awareness to notice the difference.

An understanding of God, as we can see, may be just a matter of definition.

Step 7: Completing the Circle

The Conscious Mind meets the Unconscious Mind

Your inability to access your own infinitely deep personal reservoirs of understanding leaves you running around your life like a headless chicken. It might be convenient to label these untapped resources "God", since it helps to bring together in one short word all the plethora of theories of the unknown from the X-files to the creation, but really it doesn't matter what you call it. The point is that there is a great deal more to you than just the successful evolved package that brought you into this world.

If you can begin to ascribe some meaning to the word God (however trivial or limited), then you can begin to understand the power and knowledge that you have within you in your unconscious mind, waiting unobserved and unused by your conscious mind. If you can begin to understand the effects of the mechanism of trauma, and its cumulative diminution of the scope of your conscious mind, then you can begin to understand why you are currently only able to access so little of this infinite power and knowledge.

It would make your life a whole lot easier if you could reach further into it, and the first step towards being able to do so is to begin to understand why those experiences that you might want to label with the word God (for convenience's sake or from a deeper spiritual connection) are presently so rare and kept so far receded into the background of your life. Once your awareness of the reality of these phenomena grows, you will be able to absorb them into your present understanding of your universe. Then you will truly be beginning to understand, be beginning to work with and therefore be beginning to change the most fundamental part of all of what's wrong with you.

Exercise 7

Do you really know yourself?

Be really honest. Has stuff happened to you in your life that you can't really explain? Make a list of it. Like this:

In the desert   *Felt angel like quality of "spiritual" hug while crying for my mother.*

Be comprehensive. Don't leave anything out because it seems weird to even think about it. That is the whole point of this exercise.

Now take a long hard look at what you have in front of you. These episodes are just as much a part of your life and who you are as are your daily routines of chores that you understand.

You had these experiences. You are the person who noticed these things. That matters. Sometimes it is hard to let yourself go into a full acceptance of these event. But why? Write down what these events might need to imply for your logical, conscious mind. Like this:

In the desert   *That there is a spirit world and my mother visits me from it sometimes.*

Look at what you have concluded. Are these statements that you feel you might be judged for making? Are they at odds with the society that you think you live in? If so, then that would explain why you put some much effort into resisting noticing the original phenomena.

Instead of fighting against what you perhaps don't know or understand, try this for an exercise; call it "God" and dismiss it as unknowable and inexplicable. Use that word as a receptacle for everything on your list, just for the sake of it.

Now, does it get any easier to live with what actually happened?

It should do because all you are really being asked to live with is yourself. You were the witness of these experiences and you have the mind that fears their interpretation. Complete this exercise by writing down a list of qualities that you associate with these difficult conclusions.

These qualities are what you are projecting from your unconscious mind. You have experienced them and therefore perhaps should start to "believe" in them. Then you might start to believe in yourself and all the magic that lies therein.

Q&A

From the wwwyou?forum. You can see the original text and ask questions at whatswrongwithyou.com.

Apathy

Posted by: Anon Jul 23 2004, 10:12 PM

I don't know where to start. In many ways there seems to be nothing to say. I think I have, at stages in my life, been depressed but I am not sure that is how I would describe my situation at the moment. I just feel extremely tired of living. It is not that I am suicidal. I am just struggling to get excited about anything. Even when I am 'happy' I think if I could somehow disappear now that would be okay. I feel so hopeless at the thought of being alive and of a future. It makes me feel selfish to say that. Some people aren't lucky enough to have this choice but the guilt I feel about my thoughts doesn't get rid of them.

I've been having counselling and I find that it makes the existing easier but I don't really care about 'getting better'. And I know that I should care. Everyone around me gets on with life and doesn't seem to question it. They despair at my lack of interest in living. But this state feels so natural to me, I struggle to see what it is they are getting excited about and I get frustrated that they can't see my point of view and, even more so, that I can't see theirs. My life is not 'empty'. I am studying a subject that theoretically I know I enjoy and I have good friends. I guess I just have a sense that I shouldn't be here. Is life meant to feel like this? I feel that people are trying to tell me this is 'normal', that I should just 'get on with things' but I can't help feeling that there should be something more. Where am I going wrong?

Posted by: benjaminfry Jul 25 2004, 09:29 AM

You are experiencing "ennui", which is French for a kind of boredom that runs very deep into your very soul. It is recognised as a kind of depressive state. It is usually characterised by the simple question, "what's the point?"

As you will have noticed, lots of people don't care what the point is. They just get on with life and navigate its ups and downs without questioning their motives. Other people find this harder to engage with unless there is a good reason. That's no bad thing, but you need help finding you way to an answer. So I'll just give you one.

The point of life isn't actually to get on in the western materialist sense that we internalise from the year dot. It is to progress spiritually. For many people this very phrase is meaningless, so you will need somewhere to start. Spiritual growth follows on from personal and emotional growth. It is an inevitable consequence. We were born with a strong spiritual connection. This connection was usually lost as life's experiences overwhelmed us. A lack of love and an accumulation of traumatised feelings through infancy and childhood will shut down this spiritual connection. Processing these feelings as an adult will begin to open up that connection once again.

A life lived with a spiritual connection has a lot of point. It is informed by love and understanding. There is a real feeling of being part of something larger than the sum of the parts. You fulfil a tiny role in a gigantic inexplicable maze. When you feel that you are in the right place at the right time doing the right things, then it all makes sense.

Getting to there from where you are now can be a hard journey. You will need to find your first window into a wider world. I'm not sure what works for you but a meditation class could be a good start. Creative writing, journal keeping, yoga, psychotherapy and voluntary work for the less fortunate are all other possibilities.

You have reached a dead end on your current path. See it as a great opportunity to find a better way and start going through some new doors. If you do I promise you won't be bored for long.

Posted by: Anon Jul 26 2004, 10:52 AM

Thank you all for taking the time to reply – you have given me a lot of food for thought. There is a lot of truth in the idea that I am fearful of my feelings I think – often I waste time trying to persuade my counsellor to help me find a way of feeling nothing (he obviously doesn't go on along with my plan!)

Crystal you also made a valid point about there being no emotional risk if I already feel bored and disappointed. I think I can even pinpoint when exactly I decided that would be a good coping strategy. It seems perhaps it wasn't so good after all!

Benjamin, thank you for your response. It made a lot of sense and I was relieved that you acknowledged this might be a hard journey. Part of the thing that was dragging me down so much was the feeling I should just be able to 'fix' this. I am beginning to realise now that it may not be that simple and I should perhaps allow myself the time I need rather than trying desperately to find a quick-fix in order to satisfy anybody else.

Perhaps that way, as you said in another post, I can begin to appreciate the journey rather than worrying about how fast (or slowly) I am getting to the other end. I imagine it is quite time consuming to read and respond to all the posts so thank you very much. It is very much appreciated.

Best wishes.

Conclusion

Don't change your feelings to suit your life. Don't change your life to suit your feelings.

In Summary

So, what's the answer? It's one thing to know what's wrong with you, and quite another to know what to do about it.

Let's take it as a given that you have recognised in your life some of the symptoms of what's wrong with you as described in this book. Identifying with where my argument has led may have persuaded you to agree with some of my ideas. If so, then you may even be prepared to accept the hypotheses put forward in the early chapters of this book. Thus you will have learned the basis of what is wrong with you.

You may have learned from the later chapters why these factors contribute to keeping your life in a state of constantly unfulfilled potential and deny you your right to automatic happiness. What may not have been so clear is how to use this information to help you to move forward, away from this state, and to move on to a more rewarding existence.

The first thing to recognise is that you are already doing it. Just by reading this book and internalising its logical connections from one argument to another, you are building a causal understanding in your conscious mind of how trauma creates

unhappiness. Since your conscious mind is motivated to promote happiness (using the logical connections that it discovers
between cause and effect) you are, by reading and understanding this book, giving your conscious mind the ammunition that
it needs to start to allow you to modify your behaviour so that
you can begin to move towards a genuine authentic state of
contentment.

You are educating your conscious mind about the logical
cause and effect of trauma. You are helping it to understand
where emotions come from. You are giving it the information
it needs to correlate an experience in the present (like a sudden
surge of anger or fear) with an unknown experience in the past.
You are informing it that in fact this effect is not without a
cause.

Your conscious mind needs to be educated as it has yearned
to be all its life about what causes what in this universe and in
yourself. Once it begins to understand and to accept that there
is a predictable and explicable connection between today's
emotions and the past's events, then it will begin to become
more comfortable with today's emotions. The hard part is that
the events of the past are often hidden from the conscious
mind. That is precisely what defines trauma and what trauma
does. It drives the unbearable into the unconscious mind-body
system, and holds it there unresolved until the conscious mind
is and ready to let it go again.

Ordinarily the chain of cause and effect is learned by observing a cause and then an effect. However, the predictable
notion that an effect has to have a cause also allows scientists
to discover causes. That is how some planets were discovered.
Astronomers noticed that there were tiny variations in the
orbits of other planets, and deduced that these effects were
consistent with the cause of the gravitational pull of a planet we
could not yet see.

It is the same with your emotions.

You should use your emotions in the present as information to help you to deduce experiences and feelings from your past. These are the planets you can not yet see. You can only feel their effects.

This is the correct deduction to make.

This is the logical connection between cause and effect.

The connection that you usually make is to ascribe the cause of your emotions to the present: to the present stimulus of someone else's behaviour or your circumstances. The present however is just a catalyst. It is the spark that ignites the flame of your unresolved trauma. Remember that different people react differently to the same stimulus. The spark is not the cause of the flame. It is what lights the fuel that lies dormant within you, waiting to explode. That is what your trauma stores in your mind-body system: the fuel of your feelings, waiting to be ignited by today's trivial events.

Your conscious mind does not understand your experience of an emotional flare-up. This experience often becomes in itself threatening and sometimes even traumatising. It is this reaction, caused by your failure to understand yourself, that you have to educate the conscious mind away from. It is not too hard to do in theory since the conscious mind is a learning machine, but like all new skills it takes a lot of practice.

You can learn to accept that emotions are your friends and not your enemies, and that emotions do not have to be blamed on those people and circumstances closest to you. Your conscious mind can become less threatened by them.

The trouble is that a lifetime of habit is hard to overcome. It takes work and seriousness of purpose.

You start by understanding the theory and absorbing every step of the argument into your conscious mind. This will help you to stop being afraid of your feelings and to re-educate yourself to welcome strong emotions as the agents of change in your life: not to blame them; discard them; judge them; throw them back on to others; bury them; hide them; drink them under the table; avoid them through drugs, addictions, compulsive spending, eating, gambling, sexual excesses; abandon them or fear them. Your initial steps on the long road to recovering your true self and your automatic happiness are to welcome back into your life, through developing your conscious understanding, all of the forgotten and buried emotions that lie frozen in your unconscious, which were lost to the occluding mechanism of trauma.

Your first challenge therefore is to learn not to change your feelings to suit your life.

Your feelings are being prompted by your projections, created for you by the infinite wisdom of your unconscious mind. So accept them. Accept the product of your own wisdom, even though you are unaware of both your capacity to bring about such circumstances and your own wisdom in doing so.

Accept the gift of these feelings. Don't block them with judgements and fear. Defeat these conscious mechanisms that you have developed by reminding yourself of the argument in this book.

Remind your conscious mind, constantly, that it is a good idea to let these emotions flow out of you, to allow the e-motion.

Remind the conscious mind why these emotions arise.

Remind the conscious mind what purpose it serves to allow them to flow.

Remind the conscious mind of its own desire to help you to achieve a state of contentment in life.

If you do that every day, you should begin to find yourself developing a new reaction to your emotions. You should begin to feel safer with them, and to experience less conflict when they arise. You will begin to trust that although they may be uncomfortable at the time they will pass, and then you will be better off than before. You will begin to have faith in the higher functioning of your own mind-body system. You will begin to integrate the conscious and unconscious mind: to let them pull slightly less in opposing directions.

And then you will begin to move.

The second challenge is to learn not to change your life to suit your feelings.

Your circumstances are also the product of your own unconscious wisdom. You have arranged your circumstances yourself to suit the higher wisdom of your own unconscious mind. You are where you are today, not necessarily to get what you want, but definitely to get what you need. And what you need is help to resolve your accumulated trauma.

So welcome these circumstances. Don't fight them.

Don't look at your life and be constantly focusing on how to change it in order to get away from the negative feelings that it is bringing up for you. Instead accept your life and allow these feelings to flow through you, unfettered by fantasies of the future. Pay more attention to your present and to the way that it affects you than to the future and the hopes you have of a different emotional reaction to different circumstances. Because it won't happen.

The only way that your circumstances will change is if you let your unconscious mind do its work, and you release accumulated trauma. Then the agenda of the unconscious mind will shift and your life's circumstances will change. That is why most people's lives change at such a slow and predictable rate. That is the typical, highly retarded rate of change allowed by the conscious mind.

However, if you are prepared to accept your circumstances and to work with them to discover the lessons to be learned by them, then your circumstances will naturally alter to suit your changing needs for new and different emotional resolutions.

Pushing your own circumstances to change with the brute

force of your will is exhausting and constantly opposed by the powerful forces within your own unconscious mind.

Better to be willing to accept your life as it currently is, and to allow the emotions that this evokes to flow, be experienced, thaw and to resolve. Then change will be effortless.

Don't change your feelings to suit your life.

Don't change your life to suit your feelings.

You are unlikely to agree with this. You are likely to think that bursting into tears before a big presentation in the office will get you fired, which will make you unhappy. You are likely to think that if your partner is a pain you should leave him or her, and get a better one.

However, what you are missing is that if you don't burst into tears and keep your job, you'll be wanting to burst into tears every day for the rest of your employment, and if you leave your partner for a better one, soon enough you'll be sitting looking at this new person thinking what a pain he or she is. The one thing in common in all of this is you.

The sadness, the fear, the rage, the disappointment; it all stems from you. It is so tempting to think that it doesn't, but the first step to changing your life for the better is realising that it is, actually, your life.

If you are experiencing a problem, it is because you are the problem.

If something needs changing, it is you that needs changing.

The great news is that once you swallow this terrible lump of responsibility, you will realise that you only have to change you, not the rest of the world, to find happiness. And you can change you. You have the power and the opportunity to change you. You are unlikely to have the power and the opportunity to change the rest of the world.

You may spend most of your waking moments strategising

about how you are going to acquire more power and opportunity to change the rest of the world, but chances are you won't make it, and even if you do, you'll discover something even worse: that you still aren't happy.

It's time to move on from the delusion that your discontent is related to the world outside of you. Quite the opposite, the world outside of you has been organised that way, by you, to help you to bring yourself to contentment.

All you have to do to achieve lasting, automatic happiness is to align the conscious mind with the unconscious mind, and then you will be swiftly pulled along into a new world of dazzling understanding and automatic happiness.

Don't change your feelings to suit your life.

Don't change your life to suit your feelings.

Once you have really understood what that means, why it makes sense, why it is logical, and why it is true; once you have absorbed that message into your daily existence, worked with it, noticed it and practised it; then you will have learned the truth of, and be beginning to change the fundamental reality of what's wrong with you.

Revision

Steps One to Seven

We've seen in the first three chapters of this book how the conscious mind can keep you locked into a cycle of unhappiness. We learned the Three Hypotheses:

We prioritise Survival over Happiness

Consciousness is the Tool of Survival

Trauma is the Enemy of Happiness

The next three chapters introduced us to what the unconscious mind was doing about it, trying to lead us into situations that could provoke a change in this stasis.

Unfortunately, the conscious mind usually slows down these efforts to such a degree that again it seems as if we are stuck in a cycle, going nowhere. We learned the Three Consequences:

the Unconscious use of Projection and Fate

the Unconscious use of Mutual Projections

the Unconscious use of Tribal Projections

Then we saw how mysterious forces are at work to attempt to help us by jolting or guiding us out of this mire. Perhaps these forces are external and really exist; perhaps they are internal and a function of our wise, powerful unconscious mind.

Whatever the ontological truth (which we acknowledge is unknown and perhaps unknowable), we call this God, and use this definition as a tool to give us the wisdom, faith and strength to follow these maxims:

Don't Change your Feelings to suit your Life

Don't Change your Life to suit your Feelings

It's not hard. It just takes a little understanding. And lots of practice!

Essential Practice

Teaching the Conscious Mind to Understand the Cause and Effect of Trauma

- Remember that the conscious mind only respects what makes sense to it. You have to teach it to believe in the logic of the argument contained in these pages, so that it begins to accept the experiences of projection and fate as normal, valid and above all non-threatening.
- Remember that you are an animal on a spiritual journey.
- Remember that your great survivalist tool is your conscious mind.
- Remember that the conscious mind allows you to understand your environment, by linking cause to effect.
- Remember that this need to understand effects in relation to their causes results in a great fear of the unexplained.
- Remember that when trauma thaws in your mind-body system, your conscious mind can't make sense of it, because the logical and temporal connections between cause and effect have been lost.
- Remember that this lack of explanation freaks you out, and the opportunity to resolve the trauma is lost.
- Remember that the unconscious mind is much wiser than the conscious mind.
- Remember that the unconscious mind is searching for ways

to help you to resolve your trauma so that you can move towards a fulfilling and automatically happy life.

- Remember that the unconscious mind has the power to affect everything that you think that you see, hear, and understand.
- Remember therefore that when you experience an emotion in response to a person or situation, it is a product of your unconscious mind, working to help you to release you from your trauma.
- Remember that the unconscious mind is using your real experience as a screen onto which to project another layer of experience.
- Remember that the unconscious mind is filtering reality back to your conscious mind though the projection from your unconscious mind.
- Remember that the unconscious mind is deceiving you into reacting in a way that begins to allow your trauma to be released.
- Remember that the unconscious mind is helping you to heal.
- So let it.
- Remind your conscious mind why this in happening.
- Remind your conscious mind that it does actually make sense.
- Remind your conscious mind that it doesn't object to this happening, because it now understands it.
- Remind your conscious mind that although the emotions might not make sense yet, they are real, valid and must now need resolving (e-moting).
- Remind your conscious mind that there is no effect without a cause.
- Remind your conscious mind that therefore there must have been a cause in the past to connect with the effect of these emotions in the present.

- Remind your conscious mind that letting go of these feelings is healthy, healing, and helping you.
- Remind your conscious mind that once you let these feelings out, the unconscious mind won't need to project this experience any more and you can get on with life and people more easily, more harmoniously, and more successfully.

About the Author

Benjamin Fry is married with three children and lives in London. He read physics and philosophy at Oxford University and is now a writer and entrepreneur. He began his professional life as a male model after leaving school and then started in business setting up a nightclub at the age of twenty. His partnership established there led to the nightclub and restaurant chain K-bar which included the eponymous Soho flagship nightclub. Subsequently he set up the Westbourne Hotel in Notting Hill, London.

He spent two years at film school in Los Angeles and encountered there many of the ideas associated with the American West-coast movement of "finding oneself". He has directed one film and written film scripts subsequently.

He developed an interest in psychotherapy during extensive and varied personal treatment. He completed a foundation course in psychotherapy from Regent's College, London in 1998.

He writes a column in the Times' Saturday Body and Soul supplement, titled "What's wrong with your… ?"